S0-AHD-020

The Survival of Civilization

The Survival of Civilization

depends upon our solving
three problems: carbon dioxide,
investment money and population.

Selected papers of
John D. Hamaker

Annotations by
Donald A. Weaver

Hamaker-Weaver Publishers
Michigan   California

© 1982 by Hamaker-Weaver Publishers. All rights reserved. Printed in the United States of America.

Third Printing

International Standard Book Number: 0-941550-00-1

For additional copies of *The Survival of Civilization,* or to obtain the *Perspectives* supplement, send check or money order to:
    Hamaker-Weaver Publishers
    Route 1, Box 158
    Seymour, MO 65746
or:
    Hamaker-Weaver Publishers
    P.O. Box 1961
    Burlingame, CA 94010

Book price, $12. Discounts start at three books to one address.
Supplement price, $2.50.
Prices subject to change without notice.

Solar Age or Ice Age? is a bulletin which continues the thesis of *The Survival of Civilization* and coordinates the efforts of all those involved in the effort. It is published at irregular intervals by Donald A. Weaver at Burlingame, California.

"Nature imitates herself. A grain thrown into good ground brings forth fruit; a principle thrown into a good mind brings forth fruit. Everything is created and conducted by the same Master—the root, the branch, the fruits— the principles, the consequences."

Pascal

To continue any longer as blind consumers of life, without learning to be visionary restorers of life, will likely insure an end to both opportunities—sooner than most of us would like to look at. Yet to fully look, in search of what is true, must surely be the first step.

Donald A. Weaver

Acknowledgments

The indispensable ingredient in the publishing of this book is a 115-pound miracle named Anita. For forty years she has supported my efforts in every conceivable way, not to mention keeping me alive.

The book's editor (and I think all the editor's friends and relations), the typesetters and the printer all pitched in to get the book out in creditable condition, under the pressure of time. Time is slipping away from all of us.

My friend, the artist, did the artwork on the cover and the portrayal of the tectonic system components on page 132. I don't have to have artistic talent to see that he has added some "class" to the book.

The difficulty in writing about a multi-disciplinary subject—a synthesis of many subjects—is that the reader almost never has the background education and experience in all of the subjects that would enable him to make a reasoned evaluation of the synthesis. For this reason, it seemed advisable to include a review of previous studies in the various disciplines in the form of a few lines distilling the essence of their findings.

Of course you know I don't like to brag; but when I asked Don Weaver to take on the monumental task, I committed a "sheer stroke of genius." The reader will get a wealth of information from Don's "Perspectives"—I did.

This book exists because a small group of people thought it was worth their best efforts. I think there are many millions of people across the land who will join this attempt to insure that human progress and human life shall continue into the future.

John D. Hamaker

Contents

Introduction

Since the late 1960's, John D. Hamaker has published articles directed to the theme that the health of an individual, a society and a planetary ecology can thrive only as an integrated interdependent whole.

He has applied a highly-gifted and disciplined mind to seeing and understanding the facts and principles of nature operating on this Earth, and in recognition of these life principles, has been developing and communicating practical and essential approaches to our many urgent, long-evolving problems. As most people are aware of to some degree, numerous problems, all interrelated, are reaching the crisis stage.

The Survival of Civilization presents the profound synthesis of thought and principle that has emerged from John Hamaker's studies, and is found to be supported by advanced research proceeding from all the scientific disciplines he draws upon—from soil microbiology to nutritional science, glacial geology to palynology, pedology (soil science) to paleoclimatology, etc.

A very good sense of the real and potential significance of John Hamaker's message for the world of the 1980's is given through the words of Hazel Henderson, internationally respected author of *Creating Alternative Futures* (1978), *The Politics of the Solar Age* (1981), and co-founder of both Environmentalists For Full Employment and the Princeton Center for Alternative Futures. She has helped begin a wide distribution of Hamaker's writings, and in a cover letter (4/21/80) to Gus Speth (Council on Environmental Quality), Douglas Costle (Environmental Protection Agency), Dennis Hayes (Solar Energy Research Institute), Ann Cheatham (Congressional Clearinghouse on the Future), Amory Lovins, Norman Myers, Marilyn Ferguson, Jacques Cousteau, the Club of Rome, *New Age,* and others, Ms. Henderson placed John Hamaker's message in this perceptive context:

> ...Hamaker's thesis, for which he presents much evidence here, is that another crucial contributor (to atmospheric CO_2 build-up) is the progressive soil demineralization that runs on a long cycle from glaciation to glaciation (glaciation being the natural remineralization process). If he is correct, this means we can expect a continuous *rate* of increase of CO_2 build-up, and that climatologists were in error in advising the Administration that we had 50 years to complete the solar/renewable resource transition, before weather and climate changes would interfere with crops, etc...I have heard, for example, that the committees of the National Academy of Sciences have been worried about the general issue of destruction of topsoils, but that they have not chosen to share their concern very widely. Thus, this material is potentially a very big story.
>
> However, I do not see it as one more apocalypse story, to add to those of genetic diversity loss in plant and animal species, adulterated food and water, nuclear proliferation and all the rest. It is obvious to me that if one uses a model of morphogenetic change to view all these simultaneous-sub-systems-going-critical, as well as the acceleration of all these processes, then the pattern is clear: a total system global transformation is already taking place—also pushing changes in social systems, e.g. the tables are turning all over the world, from the crack-up of the world monetary system, a new international economic order, and various other social upheavals now visible. The point is, is it good news or bad news? Order and chaos are two sides of the same coin—and imply an observer. If you are on the outside in one way or another, marginalized by the existing system: e.g. women, minorities, Third World country peoples (not their leaders), citizen and public interest movements, etc., you may see the new order emerging (birth is a painful process, as women know).
>
> Thus, the hopeful side of this CO_2 build-up story is that if Hamaker is right, i.e. that we have not 50 years, but only 10 years to make the solar transition, and that we can remineralize the soil

with our existing resources and technology (without waiting for nature's glaciation method) then it means that not only is the transition to the renewable-resource based societies of the Solar Age economical, politically advantageous as a potential de-centralizer, good technologically, etc., etc., but that it is also *absolutely necessary for our survival.* Thus this new threat to our atmosphere—which we *can* deal with, might provide a very credible "external threat" which social scientists and philosophers have always maintained would be needed for the human species to act co-operatively. This threat is external, not in space (as the old idea of invasion from another planet) but in *time* (i.e. it is outside of human time, being part of a 100,000 year climatic cycle, to which we have contributed, to be sure, with fossil fuel combustion and ecosystem destruction). Thus, in principle, leaders from Jimmy Carter to all others in industrial countries of East and West (equally worried about CO_2 build-up), *could* sound the alarm and start joint emergency programs that would supersede in importance all the sub-games of competition and conflict over ideology, the idiotic discussions about the "economy," the banality of the electoral political process, etc. I am only saying that this is possible, as a scenario and that the world will only get more dangerous if we don't shift our attention soon from the insane political discourse (amplified by mass media) over non-issues, to some *real* issues. This might be one—and what is there to lose?

John Hamaker gave a simple answer to that question, when he said in a letter to Vice President Mondale: "We have everything to gain by remineralizing the soil, and *everything* to lose by failing to do so."

* * *

The Survival of Civilization is organized into 7 chapters; the first 6 representing a series of Hamaker's papers written from January 1979 to May 1981, and the seventh, minus the newly added preface, written in 1972.

A brief introduction and/or preface accompanies each paper, and each paper save the last is followed by an in-depth perspective that is intended to provide additional insight and overview on the preceeding article. This is accomplished, in part, by calling upon some of the most relevant scientific contributions that have been made in many fields over the past century, i.e., bringing to *practical focus* key findings and information serving to verify or refute the main thesis of this book—which obviously demands verification or refutation.

For easy documentation and reference, we adopted the system of noting published sources by author's name and year of publication, or name of periodical and date of issue, with a single alphabetical reference listing to be found in the back of the book. Pictures, tables, graphs, etc., plus quotes from various governmental and other sources are included where appropriate in illustrating a point or an important principle. Also, where fitting, are included reviews of recent news reports and events of obvious importance to our subject—especially in identifying what is now actually taking place as our biosphere changes.

The Survival of Civilization is offered for careful consideration to every political representative, farmer and gardener, forester and scientist from all disciplines——plus people in all businesses and services. It is *not* by any means intended to be a book of sensationalism or some pointless literary "harbinger of doom." Any experienced ecologist, or other aware individual, is by now acutely aware that life and the balance of nature is very fragile, and that "doom" for any life form may result from destruction or over-exploitation of its environment. For humanity this principle applies to the socio-economic as well as the natural environment, as the last chapter indicates.

This book *is* intended to express only truth, to the best of our understanding and ability. It is released into our semi-chaotic world in the belief that it is essential to do so, that the great principles and wonderful re-creative potential discernible through its chapters may be grasped by everyone seriously concerned with *removing the causes* of malnutrition and disease, starvation, poverty and unemployment and the destruction of the natural world—which must inevitably include the human race.

*   *   *

As the final preparations for publishing this book were being made, I asked John Hamaker what might be told to readers about his background, as I assumed there would be some interest in it. "You don't need to say anything," he told me. "You and I don't matter in this book—getting out the facts to people is all that matters."

In essence, I fully agree with him on this point. Nevertheless, some readers may benefit from even a very limited preliminary sense of the intelligence and life perspective of the man behind this book's message. A separate book would be needed to do John Hamaker full biographical justice, with chapters on the generous heart and deeply penetrating mind which motivate him, on his very subtle yet warm, self-effacing sense of humor, and on his highly stubborn refusal to accept the unnecessary self-destruction of the human race.

Therefore, to provide a brief insight into his background, and conclude this introduction, it is fitting to excerpt part of a short autobiographical sketch written on request of Michigan Congressman Howard Wolpe's office in early 1980:

> I have observed the things of the world for almost 66 years. The luck of the genes equipped me to observe and learn. I had the highest mechanical aptitude test score in a class of 110 Bachelor of Science, Mechanical Engineering students majoring in Industrial Engineering at Purdue University (class of 1939). In a Motor Maintenance Battalion of 650 men and officers in WWII, I had the highest army test score. So I became a "90-day wonder" and was discharged with a superior officer rating. In every engineering office where I have worked, the jobs requiring the most synthesis generally wound up on my drawing table. On the four occasions when I could not work because of chemical contamination, I have either worked on the problems that afflict humanity or I have spent time on inventions. I have found that the solutions to the problems of the economy and the environment can be found by the same rigid attention to facts and established principle which yield solutions to problems of machine design.
>
> In my 66 years I have seen more history made than any generation has seen before. Now it appears that I will see one more thing—the end of civilization as we know it during this interglacial period. For 10 years I have known the soils of the world were running out of minerals and that glaciation was inevitable. For 10 years warnings and the solution have been ignored by people in government. Now hard evidence insures that by 1995 the temperate zone will become a subarctic zone and the world will have lost its food supply.
>
> I don't think I care to see the tragedy which is scheduled to unfold in this decade.

The following preface by the author continues this amazing "story."

Donald A. Weaver

Preface

On July 4, 1776, fifty-five representatives of the people of the thirteen colonies dedicated "our lives, our fortunes, and our sacred honor" to the purposes stated in the Declaration of Independence. The problem in 1776 was political freedom; the problem today is far greater — the very survival of civilization. Yet it is doubtful if there is one legislator in the entire Congress of the caliber of the men who led the revolution. Congressmen, in their compulsion to do what they have to do to get re-elected, continue to serve the interests of the proprietors of an economic system which has ruined the land, impoverished the people and bankrupted the government. Meanwhile, the underlying causes of these problems are ignored as we move from crisis to crisis.

The attitudes of the people of the nation toward Congress cover a broad spectrum. There are those who are angry for a variety of reasons. There are those who feel no hope of any improvement. There are even a few who out of ignorance of the facts still express confidence in the government. If these divergent attitudes can be quickly mobilized toward those neglected issues which directly affect the earth's capability to provide, and our subsequent ability to survive, there may still be time to prevent the impending starvation of almost all of the world's people. Therefore this book presents a basis in truth around which a consensus can be built to solve the problem of our very survival.

It is useless to state a problem without also stating the solution.

There are three problems which must be solved if civilization is to survive. The three problems are shown on the book cover. As indicated by the curves, they are all increasing at an accelerating rate towards immediate crises.

The increase of carbon dioxide in the atmosphere is man's most urgent problem. In order to save civilization, we will have to take immediate action on a worldwide scale of a magnitude never before undertaken by mankind. *The carbon dioxide curve must be reversed and started downward by about the middle of this decade.* It is so urgent because crop losses due to the carbon dioxide-induced severity of weather conditions are creating a world that has virtually no food surplus for customers who can pay, let alone for those who are hungry and those who are now starving to death. The daily reports of harsh and enduring weather extremes around the world assure us that it won't be just the Poles and the Russians who are short of food by 1985. The stress of general famine will produce chaos and anarchy before the decade is over. Under those conditions we cannot do the job which must be done. There is also a point of no return at which the natural process of glaciation cannot be stopped by human efforts.

Our second problem is the money crisis. We can't function to accomplish the solution to the first problem with a dollar that is rapidly becoming worthless. The trouble is that the wealth of this nation (and that of most of the other nations) has become concentrated in investment funds, the income from which is put back into the funds to "make" more money. The doubling rate for such funds is now somewhere in the 6- to 8-year range and the time is constantly getting shorter as interest rates go up. Financial crisis will occur in this decade. We cannot avoid the strong measures and the economic reform necessary to establish a sound economy and a social order which makes peace instead of war.

The third problem has become critical because world population has outstripped world resources. At the present rate of increase, population will double in about 30 years. It will not happen—in fact, population will decrease drastically by 1990 due to famine.

Decreasing food supply, increasing population, and the inevitable result, are about as simple a set of facts as one can imagine. All forms of voluntary birth control have demonstrated that it will not get the job done. There is no alternative to laws limiting offspring per individual upon penalty of sterilization. If humanity cannot face up to these simple facts, then there is no chance that civilization is capable of effecting its survival.

This collection of papers was not written to please anyone. It was written as a search for truths upon which a peaceful and successful world civilization can be based. The broad truth is that without radical and immediate reform (particularly in this nation), civilization will be wrecked by 1990 and extinct by 1995. I resent the fact that my two children and three grandchildren have no future. If there are enough people who feel the same way, then perhaps we can effect our survival and establish a far better future for civilization than it has yet known.

John D. Hamaker

1

Introduction

This chapter is a composite of two of Hamaker's writings from 1979; most of it was published in the *Lansing State Journal* (1/21/79) as "Americans Must Accept Food For Thought." The paper stands as a short and powerful summary of humanity's crisis of social-ecological well-being and survival—as perceived by one individual—yet potentially obvious to all who will look and understand.

As always, Hamaker writes with an awareness that our problems *can* be resolved, if we will flexibly apply *what is already known* of how to work with and accentuate the natural operational principles of the Earth's ecology.

Because we have not fully recognized and applied these principles in key areas of our daily lives, Hamaker points out, we have brought ourselves to the point where we must now courageously face the totality of our problems.

Vapor from the sea; rain, snow, and ice on the summits; glaciers and rivers—these form a wheel that grinds the mountains thin and sharp, sculptures deeply the flanks, and furrows them into ridge and canyon, and crushes the rocks into soils on which the forests and the meadows and gardens and fruitful vine and tree and grain are growing.

—John Muir
John of the Mountains: The Unpublished Journals of John Muir

There is a nutritional basis for modern physical, mental, and moral degeneration.

—Weston A. Price
Nutrition and Physical Degeneration, 1945

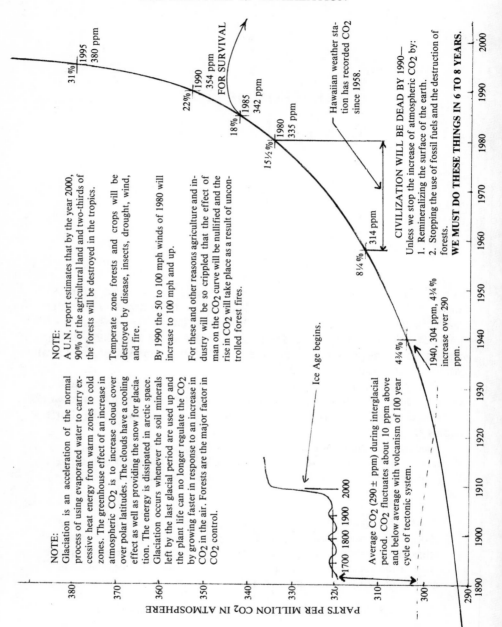

NOTE:
Glaciation is an acceleration of the normal process of using evaporated water to carry excessive heat energy from warm zones to cold zones. The greenhouse effect of an increase in atmospheric CO_2 is to increase cloud cover over polar latitudes. The clouds have a cooling effect as well as providing the snow for glaciation. The energy is dissipated in arctic space. Glaciation occurs whenever the soil minerals left by the last glacial period are used up and the plant life can no longer regulate the CO_2 by growing faster in response to an increase in CO_2 in the air. Forests are the major factor in CO_2 control.

NOTE:
A U.N. report estimates that by the year 2000, 90% of the agricultural land and two-thirds of the forests will be destroyed in the tropics.

Temperate zone forests and crops will be destroyed by disease, insects, drought, wind, and fire.

By 1990 the 50 to 100 mph winds of 1980 will increase to 100 mph and up.

For these and other reasons agriculture and industry will be so crippled that the effect of man on the CO_2 curve will be nullified and the rise in CO_2 will take place as a result of uncontrolled forest fires.

Ice Age begins.

Average CO_2 (290 ± ppm) during interglacial period. CO_2 fluctuates about 10 ppm above and below average with volcanism of 100 year cycle of tectonic system.

1940, 304 ppm, 4¾% increase over 290 ppm.

Hawaiian weather station has recorded CO_2 since 1958.

CIVILIZATION WILL BE DEAD BY 1990—
Unless we stop the increase of atmospheric CO_2 by:
1. Remineralizing the surface of the earth.
2. Stopping the use of fossil fuels and the destruction of forests.
WE MUST DO THESE THINGS IN 6 TO 8 YEARS.

31% 1995 380 ppm
22% 1990 354 ppm FOR SURVIVAL
18% 1985 342 ppm
15½% 1980 335 ppm
8¼% 314 ppm
4¾% 1700 1800 1900 2000

PARTS PER MILLION CO_2 IN ATMOSPHERE

380
370
360
350
340
330
320
310
300
290

1890 1900 1910 1920 1930 1940 1950 1960 1970 1980 1990 2000

Fig. 1

1

Our 100 Percent Junk Food Supply Is Destroying Us

The American people have so many disease problems that the costs of medical care have gone beyond the financial means of most citizens. It is not coincidence that livestock are also suffering from a variety of diseases. Clearly, the food supply as it is grown is unable to supply the nutrients needed to maintain a state of good health in man or animal.

Yet Gilbert A. Leveille, chairman of Michigan State University's Department of Food Science and Human Nutrition, misses no opportunity to defend the food supply, including the devitalizing methods of processing (*Lansing State Journal*, 1/7/79). Dr. Leveille seems to be too busy propagandizing for the food industry to have time for science, so I will review some recent findings.

In the last year numerous studies have been reported by behavioral researchers relating to the quantity and kinds of brain compounds to behavioral variations from normal. Whether or not those compounds are present in normal amounts depends on the proper function of numerous enzyme systems which are involved in the fabrication of all the body production, maintenance, and control systems. Whether or not there is an adequate supply of enzymes present depends on the food supply. In particular, it depends on an adequate soil mineral supply in the food, because it has been observed by microphysicists that the soil elements are required in the enzyme molecules. All of this has been established by direct laboratory methods.

So close is the relationship between human behavioral performance and the compounds in the brain that one science writer stated flatly, "You are what you eat." The laboratory proof is done. *Thus the many behavioral problems of epidemic proportions in this country are primarily caused by malnutrition.* Thirty percent functional illiteracy, crime, alcoholism, dope addiction, cultism, the killing of babies in the womb—all of these marks of a degenerate society are inflicted on us because we have permitted the food supply to become 100 percent junk food.

In the summer of 1977 a corn crop was grown on soil which was mineralized with glacial gravel crusher screenings. The corn was tested along with corn from the same seed grown with conventional chemical fertilizers. The mineralized corn had 57 percent more phosphorous, 90 percent more potassium, 47 percent more calcium, and 60 percent more magnesium than the chemical-grown corn. The mineral-grown corn had close to 9 percent protein, which is very good for a hybrid corn. All of the nitrogen in the mineral-grown corn (whose content in the food is the indicator for protein) came from the atmosphere by way of biological processes and was in the amino acids of the corn protoplasm. None of it was raw chemical nitrate, the precursor of the carcinogenic nitrosamines. No pesticides were used and there was no insect damage.

All of the elements are in glacial gravel. The large increase of the principal elements must be accompanied by a similar increase in the trace elements. This follows from the fact that the trace elements are required in order for the soil microorganisms to produce the enzymes needed to make all of their other protoplasm compounds. In order to show such a major increase in the principal elements and a corresponding increase in protein, the soil microorganisms must be able to reproduce abundantly, so as to furnish the large quantities of protoplasm required by the plant roots. Microorganisms can reproduce abundantly only when *all* minerals are present, along with plant residue to supply their carbon needs for energy and protoplasm compound building, plus nitrogen, oxygen and sea solids from the air, and of course water.

Everything is connected to everything else. We can have good social behavior in this country only if we have good health. We can have good health only if the soil microorganisms have good health. They supply the protoplasm compounds for every living organism above the ground. The basis of their health is the availability of the elements of the inanimate rock crust of the Earth which is the basic food supply of microorganisms and hence of all of us.

Virtually all of the subsoil and most of the topsoil of the world have been stripped of all but a small quantity of elements. So it is not surprising that the chemical-grown corn had substantially less mineral content than the 1963 corn described in the USDA Handbook of the Nutritional Contents of Food. The mineralized corn was substantially higher in mineral content than the 1963 corn. Hence, as the elements have been used up in the soil, a poor food supply in 1963 has turned into a 100 percent junk food supply in 1978. There has been a corresponding increase in disease and medical costs. Essentially, disease means that enzyme systems are malfunctioning for lack of the elements required to make the enzymes.

Hunza is a small country in a high Himalayan mountain valley. The health and strength and longevity of the Hunzacuts is legendary. The key factor is that they irrigate the valley's soils with a milky-colored stream from the meltwater of the Ultar glacier. The color comes from the mixed rock ground beneath the glacier. The people are virtually never sick. They do not develop cancer. Many are active workers at 90; some live to be 140. These facts are well documented, yet the world's "health professionals" ignore them while continuing the hopeless search for man-made "cures."

Ten thousand years ago the Mississippi Valley was fed and built up by runoff from the glaciers. The deep deposit of organically-enriched alluvial soil in Illinois attests to a long period of luxuriant plant growth. Yet, when the settlers plowed the valley, they did not find topsoil that would give the health record of the Hunzacuts. Ten thousand years of leaching by a 30-inch annual rainfall is the difference. Man can stay on this Earth only if the glacial periods come every 100,000 years to replenish the mineral supply—or man gets bright enough to grind the rock himself. There are several other places in the world similar to Hunza, such as the Caucasus Mountains in Russia where 10 percent of the people are centenarians. There are glaciers in the mountains. Regardless of where it is that people attain excellent health and maximum life, it can be traced to a continual supply of fresh-ground mixed rocks flowing to the soil where their crops are grown. Thus the secret of good health and long life lies not in the fountain of youth or in a chemical company's laboratory, but in the acceleration of the natural biological processes.

Failure to remineralize the soil will not just cause a continued mental and physical degeneration of humanity but will quickly bring famine, death, and glaciation in that order.

Glaciation is nature's way of remineralizing the soil. It occurs automatically because as the plant life dies out for lack of protoplasm, large amounts of its carbon move, as carbon dioxide (CO_2), into the atmosphere (See Fig. 1). Then we see what is occuring now. CO_2's "greenhouse" heating effect is causing large amounts of evaporation from the tropical oceans. Cold polar air moving over the cold land areas displaces this lighter, warm, wet air from the tropics, forcing the warm air to flow over the warm oceans toward the northern latitudes to replace the cold air, be cooled, lose its moisture to snow, and descend over the land mass.

The result is massive cloud cover under which huge amounts of cold air are generated and from which ever-increasing amounts of precipitation occur. Every winter must be worse than the last. We can stand them for some time into the future. What we cannot stand is for the winters to carry over into the summers to destroy crops and trees with frosts and freezes. Numerous temperatures from 32 degrees to 40 degrees were recorded in the summer of 1978 in the northern tier of states from Michigan to the Rockies. Cold waves, just a few degrees lower in temperature, can cause major crop losses in Canadian and Eurasian grain crops, most of which are at the latitude of Michigan or north of it. Famine could begin soon. At best it is only a few years away. The 1978-79 fruit and vegetable losses in California, Texas and Florida were indicative of what will also happen to summer crops in the years just ahead.

So now we are on the doorstep of a famine crisis and experiencing numerous crisis conditions as the result of malnutrition. I have been warning of both since 1970. The facts have not changed since then but the effects of those facts have changed drastically. It is too late now to prevent the deaths of hundreds of millions of people from famine. There may still be time to prevent the extermination of civilization for another 90,000 years of glaciation—or there may not be sufficient time.

If we are to survive we must remineralize all of the world's soils and double, triple, and quadruple the rate of growth of all plant life. We can then go on a solar energy cycle using food crops and tree crops for producing alcohol and methane and wood as fuels for our energy supply. Only in this way can we hope to reverse the flow of carbon dioxide into the atmosphere and ultimately eliminate the deadly effects of the onset of glaciation.

Technically remineralization is feasible. Our problem is lack of intelligent and courageous scholastic and political leadership. Perhaps the results of our lack of leadership—glaciation and famine—are the ultimate price to be paid by a people whose national philosophy has been the exploitation of man and nature.

1

Perspective

Most of what John Hamaker writes stands fully on its own as a unique synthesis and re-statement of facts and principles operational throughout nature, and recognized within the diversity of scientific disciplines he draws upon. This synthesis arises from a profound "common sense" and much practical experimentation. Yet a deeper understanding of the truth in Hamaker's words may be gained by a look at certain areas demanding further exploration. Initially, developing a measure of "geological perspective" may be most beneficial.

The Glacial-Interglacial Cycle

This cycle has been clearly revealed as of the 1970's by numerous workers in many fields of "Quaternary research." The Quaternary is the present geological period encompassing the Pleistocene epoch and the Holocene (recent) epoch—the present interglacial.

NAS Study
The National Academy of Sciences 1975 publication, *Understanding Climate Change*, explains it this way:

> The present interglacial interval—which has now lasted for about 10,000 years—represents a climatic regime that is relatively rare during the past million years, most of which has been occupied by colder, glacial regimes. Only during about 8 percent of the past 700,000 years has the earth experienced climates as warm or warmer than the present.
>
> The penultimate interglacial age began about 125,000 years ago and lasted for approximately 10,000 years. Similar interglacial ages—each lasting 10,000 plus or minus 2000 years and each followed by a glacial max-

imum—have occured on the average every 100,000 years during at least the past half million years. During this period fluctuations of the northern hemisphere ice sheets caused sea-level variations of the order of 100 meters." (p. 181)

Further on, the question arises:

When will the present interglacial end? Few paleoclimatologists would dispute that the prominent warm periods (or interglacials) that have followed each of the terminations of the major glaciations have had durations of 10,000 plus or minus 2,000 years. In each case, a period of considerably colder climate has followed immediately after the interglacial interval. Since about 10,000 years have passed since the onset of the present period of prominent warmth, the question naturally arises as to whether we are indeed on the brink of a period of colder climate. (p. 189)

And of obvious importance:

What is the nature of the climatic changes accompanying the end of a period of interglacial warmth? From studies of sediments and soils, Kukla finds that major changes in vegetation occurred at the end of the previous interglacial. The deciduous forests that covered areas during the major glaciations were replaced by sparse shrubs, and dust blew freely about. The climate was considerably more continental than at present, and the agricultural productivity would have been marginal at best. (p. 189)

At that point, in 1975, it is suggested that:

The question remains unsolved. If the end of the interglacial is episodic in character, we are moving toward a rather sudden climatic change of unknown timing... If on the other hand, these changes are more sinusoidal in character, then the climate should decline gradually over a period of thousands of years. (p. 189)

Report to the U.S. Congress

Weather Modification: Programs, Problems, Policy, and Potential is a document prepared for the 95th Congress. Chapter Four (Justus, 1978) confirms the NAS study in regard to our place in the cycle:

"In geological perspective, the case for cooling is strong...If this interglacial age lasts no longer than a dozen earlier ones in the past million years, as recorded in deep-sea sediments, we may reasonably suppose that the world is about due to begin a slide into the next Ice Age." (p. 153)

The Present Interglacial, How and When Will It End?

This was the title of a working conference of paleontologists, sedimentologists, stratigraphers, paleoclimatologists and others, held at Brown Univeristy in 1972. Over a dozen of the papers presented were published that same year in *Quaternary Research* (Vol. 2, p. 261-445). The papers strongly confirmed the 100,000 year average glacial-interglacial cycle, and *virtually every author stressed the fact that we should indeed be at or close to the end of the present interglacial.* Most presented solid evidence from their fields that this is the case; none could explain with certainty the precise "causative mechanism" of climate change.

The search for causes of "Ice Ages," beginning over a century ago and continuing up to this day, is one of the most fascinating stories imaginable —especially so in light of an imminent onslaught of a new one. Yet the answer literally lies beneath our feet, as finally revealed by John Hamaker in the fact of progressive soil demineralization of Earth's soil mantle, causing an eventual collapse of the global carbon cycle. Such a major breakthrough in understanding should logically lay a foundation for major shifts in how we look at and relate to life on Earth.

A closer look at interglacial soil demineralization, vegetational succession and collapse, the glacial process, and soil remineralization follows in the next chapters. In concluding here, another key contribution to our knowledge of the glacial-interglacial cycle should be noted:

In 1977, *Quaternary Research* published the latest work of George Kukla and Julius Fink entitled "Pleistocene Climates in Central Europe: At Least 17 Interglacials after the Olduvai Event." The study documented their work on the interlayered soils exposed in excavated brickyards of Czechoslavakia. *17 major cycles of glacial loess deposition and subsequent interglacial soil "decalcification" (and overall demineralization) over the last 1.7 million years are revealed.* The interglacial soils are shown to have supported the deciduous forests native to northwestern and central Europe until in some way they died off and gave way to the steppe vegetation of a chilled and wind-torn glacial desert where dust was blown freely about. Loess, which is simply mixed rock dust and silt ground by the glaciers and swept away by the winds, *always returns to cover the demineralized soils.* Then, again, over the centuries, the loess becomes "mostly consumed by the pedogenic process." (p. 369)

In the coming chapters, we must examine the forest die-off process—which is now quickly happening worldwide—and the interrelationships of the CO_2 crisis, our deteriorating weather and soil minerals and health. We will also look at the overviews of broad studies, such as the *Global 2000 Report* by the U.S. government.

2

Introduction

John Hamaker's "Food, Energy, and Survival" was first published in August 1979. The article received widest distribution when it appeared in the June and July 1980 issues of *Acres, U.S.A.*

Over 25 years of farming and gardening experience, extensive reading and experimentation, and observations of extraordinary depth concerning natural processes have preceeded this potentially "landmark" study of the principles of the natural agriculture process and the need—as an absolute survival necessity—for immediate worldwide support of this process.

May the reader "new to the soil" have patience with unfamiliar terms and perhaps difficult-to-visualize concepts (a second reading later may be most helpful), and may the experienced and "trained" agriculturist approach this work with a fresh mind and enthusiasm. The future of humanity and all life on Earth may well depend on this article *and* your approach to it.

It is not too much to say, that the publication of Professor Liebig's *Organic Chemistry of Agriculture* constitutes an era of great importance in the history of Agricultural Science. Its acceptance as a standard is unavoidable; for following in the straight path of inductive Philosophy, the conclusions which are drawn from its data are incontrovertible. We can truly say, that we have never risen from the perusal of a book with a more thorough conviction of the profound knowledge, extensive reading, and practical research of its author, and of the invincible power and importance of its reasoning and conclusions, than we have gained from the present volume.

—Silliman's Journal, in review of Justus von Liebig's *Organic Chemistry in its Application to Agriculture and Physiology*, 1840.

I had sinned against the wisdom of the Creator, and received my righteous punishment. I wished to improve his work, and in my blindness believed that, in the marvelous chain of laws binding life on earth's surface and keeping it always new, a link had been forgotten which I, weak and powerless worm, must supply.

—Justus von Liebig, late in life

Quoted from *Encyclopedia Brittanica*, 1899; removed from subsequent editions.

2

Food, Energy and Survival

At a time when there is a great need for food and fuel and an equally great need to withdraw the excessive amount of carbon dioxide from the atmosphere, it is imperative that the natural process for production of life in and from the soil be thoroughly understood. These critical needs can only be met in the time available by vastly increasing plant growth. Perhaps the best approach is by means of a brief comparison of the principles of chemical agriculture and those of the natural process, the most important of which is the availability of elements in the soil.

Chemical Agriculture

In 1840 the German chemistry professor, Justus von Liebig, wrote a book on agriculture. Among other things he said that humus did not supply plant food, that certain minerals should be supplied to compensate for deficiencies, and, most important, that acids would make the minerals more available to the plants.

That was the signal to the chemical companies to go into action. By 1850 they were prospering, and the professors of agriculture were reaching for the grant money passed out by the chemical companies.

Liebig later regretted that he had imposed his superficial knowledge on so complex a process as the soil life system. Those profiting from his error had no such misgivings. As a result, *civilization has been brought to the verge of extinction with virtually no knowledge of how to avoid it.*

Chemical agriculture holds that there is a "soil solution" which exchanges ions with plant roots and clay particles. It does not explain how such a water solution can stay in the soil while rain is percolating through the soil or flooding it and running off the top. The only soil solution which can be proven to exist is that which occurs when chemicals are applied to the soil and these solutions, plus the soil nutrients they liberate, are now fouling all our surface waters and the crops we grow.

Chemical agriculture says that the plants extract minerals from the soil clay and soil solution by ion exchange. This is unproven.

Chemical agriculture says that proteins are produced in the plant. This is unproven.

Chemical agriculture uses *soluble chemicals* which are either acidic or basic and which *have the final effect of acidifying the soil, destroying the soil life, using up the organic matter, and finally rendering the soil useless.* The primary reason these things occur is that whatever chemicals are used on the soil act selectively, readily dissolving some stones while leaving others unaffected. In particular the silicate stones are unaffected. They form the bulk of the soil and contain elements useful to the life processes imbedded in a matrix of silicon dioxide, which is glass. Glass is not affected by the agricultural chemicals. Therefore some elements are almost entirely removed from the soil and others are not made available.

Most of the elements in the soil are used by the microorganisms in making enzymes. A shortage of elements means a shortage of enzymes. A shortage of enzymes means a shortage of compounds catalyzed by the enzymes, and hence malfunction of enzyme systems in all the life forms dependent on the soil mineral supply. The fact that Johnnie can't read and that we have a $200 billion annual national medical bill both stem from the same cause—a poor delivery of elements from the soil in both quantity and balance.

Natural Agriculture and the Carbon Dioxide Cycle

This discussion takes place within a broad context of events. The natural system of soil remineralization calls for glaciation to start up every 100,000 years. The glaciers grind the rock in the top layers of the Earth's crust, and high-velocity winds carry the ground rock dust all over the world. We happen to be due for glaciation now.

Glaciation starts when the minerals in the soil are so depleted that they cannot support plant life. Forests, jungles, and other plant life become subject to destruction from disease, insects, drought, and fire. Ultimately most of the carbon in the plant life winds up as carbon dioxide in the atmosphere. *(See Fig. 1, pg. 18)*

Normally trees grow faster when there is an increased release of carbon dioxide into the air resulting from an increased activity in the earth's tectonic system. We are now in a hundred-year cold cycle which occurs when tectonic activity is high. The carbon dioxide released from volcanic and other tectonic system components is secreted in the earth by deposit of once-living organic debris. The faster growth of trees in response to an increase in carbon dioxide results in a volumetric increased storage of carbon in plant life, which subsequently increases the rate of deposit of plant life debris in the crust of the earth. *This keeps the carbon cycle in balance.* Unfortunately, the soil has run out of useful soil elements at the same time that exploitative man has compounded the problem by rapidly removing carbon from the crust of the earth where nature has wisely secreted it. Not just fossil fuels have been removed, but our agricultural soils have also been stripped of carbon.

At whatever latitude the sun is concentrating its energy, the greenhouse effect of carbon dioxide heats up the atmosphere, causing increased evaporation of water and huge cloud mass formation. The *increased temperature differential and hence pressure differential* between cold high-pressure polar air and hot, humid low-pressure equatorial air causes large masses of cold air to move southward, displacing the hot air. The displaced hot air is forced to flow toward the polar zones, creating cloud cover that can now be seen in August on the satellite weather pictures to cover all of Canada. Protected from the sun by the clouds, huge masses of cold air are generated to insure that every winter will be colder than the last, just as certainly as each year the percent of carbon dioxide in the atmosphere is increasing. The accelerating rate at which this is occurring is frightening.

If we are to avoid the consequences of having too much carbon dioxide in the atmosphere, we must understand the natural phenomena which support vegetative growth. Natural agriculture is the art and science of accelerating the natural processes from which the entire chain of life receives its nutritional support. The following should help clarify the urgency of applying its principles.

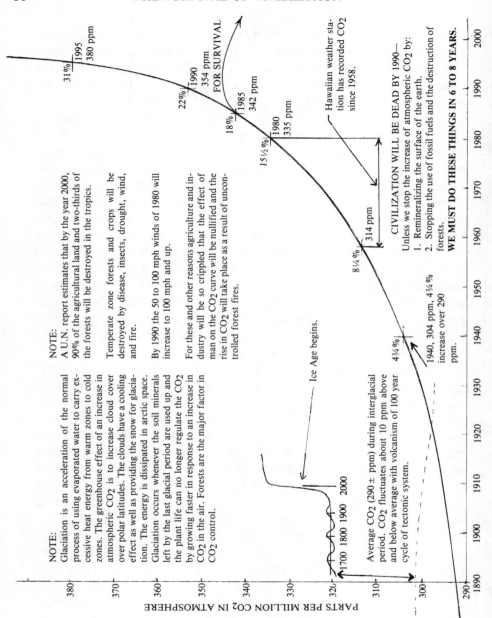

Fig. 1

This writer has ten acres of more-or-less typical, flat Michigan soil. Examination of rock content of the soil shows that there are about 2½ inches of unused rock left in the topsoil and none in the subsoil. In short, there are 2½ inches of sand and gravel which still have useful minerals and the rest is worn-out soil (subsoil)—nothing but clay (aluminum silicate) and tiny bits of glass (oxides of silicon) as deep (8 or 9 feet) as the backhoe would go. These subsoil elements and an occasional few others are in excess of the soil life needs.

Soil microorganisms were extracting the useful elements from the soil rock long before there were higher plants—and they are still doing the job.

Plants are predators like the rest of us. Their roots extract the protoplasm from the microorganisms. The plants, as well as all animals, alter some of the protoplasm compounds to provide enzymes, hormones, etc. specifically needed by them. *But the basic supply of protoplasm comes from the soil microorganisms. The quality (health, vigor, intelligence, longevity, etc.) of all living things depends on the quality of the protoplasm of the life in the soil and that depends on the availability of elements in the soil stone.*

Examine a stone, other than limestone, in the soil. Crack it open. Under a very drab demineralized exterior "skin," you will see the minerals. That skin represents the depth to which the microorganisms have been able to penetrate the crystal structure of the stone. At this point, the stone is passivated and will release its useful elements only as fast as the slow process of weathering (see footnote, Ch. 5, p. 101) removes bits of the demineralized stone skin, exposing a few more elements. Thus the 2½ inches of sand and gravel in the topsoil of the above-mentioned ten acres has such a slow rate of availability of minerals that the stunted corn plant it will grow produces only a nubbin with most of the grains of corn missing. There are very few microorganisms in the soil, and when cultivated it breaks up into hard clumps of clay.

The fact that the soil has been almost fully demineralized in the 10,000 to 11,000 years since the last glaciation has led to the popularity of chemical agriculture. The chemicals, unlike the microorganisms, will dissolve the carbonates and a few other rocks completely, liberating some of the remaining useful elements, thus stimulating enough of a growth of microorganisms to support a crop growth. Unfortunately, the crop therefore receives a short supply of an unbalanced protoplasm. *The result is that the crop is subject to disease and so are the people and livestock who eat it.*

The bits of useless demineralized skin weathered from the stone are ignored by the microorganisms as they build the granular, capillary soil system which provides aeration and water retention to the soil. Percolating water carries the bits of subsoil downward into cracks under large particles of unused stone. The cracks are caused by contraction (drying) of the soil. The percolating water washes used material off the top of the unused stone, leaving a space into which the stone can rise when expansion (wetting) of the soil forces the unused stone upward by the amount of material sifted under it.

Thus, in 10,000 years, eight or ten feet of glacial deposit has been cycled to the topsoil, demineralized by the soil life, and descended back into the subsoil to form a dense clay. There are only 2½ inches of the original deposit left in the topsoil, and there is no more on the way up.

From now on *we must provide* the minerals to the soil or glaciation will do it—and soon. There is only one-fortieth of the land mass on which life can continue through a glacial period. That will not suffice for 4½ billion people. We will mineralize the soil or almost all of us will die. Fortunately, it is technically possible to mineralize the soils.

For instance, a one-pound stone might have a surface area of 12 square inches. Ground to about 200 mesh, it would have a surface area of about 8 acres. One ton would therefore have a surface area of 16,000 acres. The significant thing about that 16,000 acres is that it is all freshly-broken stone with the useful elements exposed right on the surface. These elements are readily available for extraction by the microorganisms. Applied at the rate of three-fourths ton per acre to a test plot on the ten acres, edible ears of corn were produced with a full set of grains and excellent taste quality instead of grainless nubbins as on the control plot.

Availability of elements from a large surface area of stone is one requirement for large crop yield.

The stone should be a natural mixture which comes from the top strata of the earth's crust. All of the crust, except ore intrusions in the mountains, is sea floor deposit which has been raised up from the ocean in relatively small areas (like the Bering Sea floor) and welded together to form the land masses. A mixture of the strata is therefore much the same the world over.

There are extensive deposits of ground glacial gravel dust in the previously glaciated areas. These deposits are little changed in 10,000 years and can be used as found. A survey of well drillers and geologists would probably provide location information. Some of the deposits which contain very fine sand could benefit from a pass through a close-set roller mill. The following chart, adapted from the USDA system, gives a good idea of the relative feeding surface values for various small sizes of rock.

Characteristics of Soil Separates

Separate	Diameter (mm)	Number of Particles per Gram	Surface Area in 1 Gram (sq. cm)
Very coarse sand	2.00-1.00	90	11
Coarse sand	1.00-0.50	720	23
Medium sand	0.50-0.25	5,700	45
Fine sand	0.25-0.10	46,000	91
Very fine sand	0.10-0.05	722,000	227
Silt	0.05-0.002	5,776,000	454
Clay	Below 0.002	90,260,853,000	8,000,000

Note: The smallest three diameters listed will all pass a 200-mesh screen.

In addition, from experiments to date, it seems likely that most river gravels will give good results when ground to dust.

Any non-river deposit of mixed gravel is likely to be of glacial origin and highly active when ground.

All present gravel pits where crushing of gravel is done have large amounts of discarded fines which can be economically ground.

In all probability these sources of raw materials are adequate anywhere in the world for many years to come. Sometime in the future vertical cuts in gorges and mountainsides will be necessary.

An average spectrographic analysis of Michigan gravels can be used as a rough standard for gravels. The spectrograph will show between 25 and 35 of the elements, depending on the skill of the operator and the quality of the machine. If the principal elements are there in roughly the same quantities as in glacial gravel, and if the other elements are present, the gravel will be useful. An even simpler test is to grind a little gravel, mix it with an organic soil, and grow some radishes to compare with those grown on untreated soil. They should show a major difference in size, taste quality, and texture. *Any mixture that will give good growth and is found locally is what we must use.*

In 1893, a German named Julius Hensel published a small book called *Bread From Stones*. He had demonstrated that a mixture of ground stones representing a cross section of all the types of rocks would produce good yields of top-quality crops. The only reason he could not compete with the agricultural chemicals was the lack of a good grinder. Such a grinder has been patented and a small prototype built by the writer. It is far more efficient, far less expensive in initial cost and maintenance, than conventional rock grinders and it can be mass-produced in a size suitable for individual farmers or big enough for gravel pits. It was offered to the mining industry in the mid-1960's and refused unanimously. It would have cut the mining grinder business to a fraction of its then-and-present gross income. In this monopolistic economy, "the better mousetrap" concept is dead if the better machine will adversely affect a significant amount of invested capital and earnings. The grinder is not being built now because it would destroy the very non-competitive agricultural/chemicals industry.

If remineralization is to be effective in the short time left to us, some form of small, efficient grinder must be mass-produced. We need millions of units both here and abroad.

Improving soil fertility means feeding the microorganisms. Availability of the rock elements is one food factor. Another factor is sea solids. They come with the clouds whipped off ocean whitecaps. They are highly available near the coast and not sufficiently available far inland, where goiter problems indicate that iodine and many other elements, most of which are highly water soluble or water suspendable, are in short supply and should be added to the soil at 5 percent or 10 percent of the weight of gravel dust added.

The microorganisms in a rich soil build the soil to take in rain-water and hold it in storage. The proper proportion of water in protoplasm is 90 percent. It is important that protoplasm be maintained as a dilute solution. The sun evaporates water from the leaves of the plant, concentrating the protoplasm solution. It is characteristic of water solutions that the water of the more dilute solution will pass through a membrane into a more concentrated solution. This force of osmosis is very powerful. It is the force that moves the water to the top of a sequoia. Water is of course necessary to all cells in order for them to function. Cells have a way of opening up and engulfing the very large molecules of protoplasm. Since the cells are alive and expend energy, they probably pass the molecules or its components from one cell to another until it reaches the part of the plant where it is needed.

If dry weather depletes the water held by the soil and the microorganisms to the concentration of the water in the leaf cells, all protoplasm feeding stops and growth is arrested.

Irrigation is not the answer to water shortage problems. If all farmers irrigated, the underground water supplies would soon be depleted (as they are in the process of becoming now). The answer is to keep feeding the microorganisms until the aerated zone is 18 to 24 inches deep and capable of holding all of the rain that falls until the excess can seep into the subsoil and reach the underground aquifer, instead of running off the surface and taking the soil with it. It will take a decade or two for roots and earthworms to deepen the topsoil significantly below plow depth.

Nitrogen from the air is the ultimate source of most of the nitrogen in the protein compounds of the microorganism protoplasm, the solid matter of which is about two-thirds protein. It is not, however, the principal source of crop-growth nitrogen, as will be discussed later.

The same is true of carbon, which is the dominant element in all organic matter. The leaves take in carbon dioxide and give off oxygen, retaining the carbon for the necessary carbohydrate construction and for energy requirements. When the plant dies, it goes into the soil or on the soil where it is utilized as a part of the food supply of various soil organisms. Eventually it is all carried into the soil, principally by earthworms as they combine leaf mold with minerals ground in their gizzards to produce microorganisms. Their castings are almost all microorganisms, and a source of protoplasm not overlooked by the hair roots of plants. Since the rye plant has been estimated to have a root system seven miles long, it is apparent that plants can do a lot of searching for protoplasm. The root tips grow a lot faster than microorganisms can move, so the microorganisms are easy prey to roots. When in intimate proximity to the cell, the flow of protoplasm begins.

The root cannot take in the cell membrane of the organism. The membranes are held against the root by the pressure of other cells forced against the root by the diffusion pressure between the microorganism cells and the root cells. Soon the older root cells are all plugged with microorganism cell membranes, which subsequently turn the brown color of all mature roots. The root functions simply as a pipe, while the rapidly growing white root tips continue to devour cell protoplasm.

If the protoplasm of the root cells gets too dry, then the protoplasm intake must stop because osmosis requires that the more dilute solution in the microorganisms must flow toward a more concentrated solution in the plant cells. For this reason the root tips (which can take in soil water) constantly remove water from the zone where they are feeding, and the water is moved upward to the leaves, keeping the cells saturated and evaporating the excess.

The intestinal tracts of all animals work essentially the same way, except that the microorganisms and their food supply are inside intestines and the protoplasm compounds feed into the intestinal wall where they are picked up by a blood vessel system for sorting out in the liver. Excess water passes readily through the system and is ultimately evaporated from the sweat glands or extracted by the kidneys and excreted in the urine.

Nature has used just one basic design for all the living organisms with variations as required by each type of organism.

It should be noted that plant and animal digestive systems will readily pass water into the plant or animal. If toxic compounds are in solution in the water, they too will pass readily into the plant or animal. Therein lies the great danger of water-soluble chemicals used in the soil and in foods and beverages. Any toxic substance can enter the plant or animal with the protoplasm if it has been taken in by the microorganisms. Thus, anything other than the natural balance of elements and the natural organic compounds produced from them by the microorganisms is damaging to the entire chain of life. In particular, the continued buildup in the biosphere of non-biodegradable synthetic organic compounds is now in the process of destroying humanity by alteration of the genetic compounds.

We see, then, that the rate of production of microorganisms will be high if the soil contains: a large surface area of available elements; a large supply of plant residue for carbon and a little nitrogen; the nitrogen that many organisms can take from the air as the air breathes in and out of the soil with temperature changes; water and the other necessary factors from the air.

Since the life of a microorganism is only a few hours whether or not it is used by a plant root, a huge number of cell membranes (hereafter "skins") will be produced in a growing season. The skins are proteins, meaning that they constitute a ready supply of carbon and nitrogen and a few elements, which are highly available to grow microorganisms in the presence of available elements from the soil stone particles. Skins start accumulating as the soil warms up in the spring, and continue to build up until the crop root system starts removing carbon and nitrogen as protoplasm, thus depleting the soil of both live microorganisms and skins. As soon as the frost comes, the tide is again turned and the dead root system supplies carbon and small amounts of other elements to again build up the supply of skins.

It appears that the carbon and nitrogen of fresh skins are not available to microorganisms until the skins go through whatever changes are involved in turning black. Apparently, a colony of organisms working around a stone particle soon produce so many fresh skins that the colony is sealed off from the black skins and must therefore use nitrogen from the air. Thus the intake of atmospheric nitrogen goes on from the time the ground warms up in the spring until it gets too cold in the fall. When the plant roots start feeding in the spring, nitrogen and carbon are available in the black skins for rapid production of microorganisms. Earthworms can use both fresh and black skins to quickly produce microorganisms in their castings. In a natural soil, the earthworms contribute very heavily toward rapid plant growth. After a soil is mineralized in depth, tillage should be limited to weed control to avoid excessive worm destruction.

Obviously, from the preceeding discussion, soil needs a rest period if large yields are to be obtained. It would also be desirable to lightly disk crop residues into the soil to provide a winter mulch and to make the crop stalk easily available to the soil organisms for rapid breakdown.

It is also implied that a maximum amount of plant residue be returned to the soil if maximum yields of grains, vegetables, fruits and trees are to be produced. The reason is the proximity factor. If one ton of gravel dust per acre is added to the soil, the available elements are there only at one part per 1000 in the top seven or eight inches by weight, and even less by volume in a predominently clay (subsoil) soil. If there is not an abundance of skins present, the skins may not be close enough to the available minerals to be useful to the local colony of microorganisms. High yields depend on loading the soil with both a large surface area of available minerals and organic matter; the combination is turned into live microorganisms which then yield more skins. Note: others call the skins humus, not knowing what humus is.

If my ten acres were farmed chemically, the organic matter (skin supply) would be constantly depleted. The small overall surface area of unused stone in the soil provides an insignificant amount of available elements. The chemical fertilizer would release enough elements to grow sufficient microorganisms to feed a weak crop, but when the chemicals are used up (and on weak soil this often occurs before the crop has matured if the chemicals are inadequate in quantity or too fast in dissolving), the production of microorganisms would virtually stop. There would be no significant buildup of skins either in late fall or in the spring. Taking the stalk along with the grain, etc., as is often done, would limit the utilization of the very few available minerals in the dwindling supply of passivated stone particles still in the soil.

What I have been saying about how the soil really works to provide food (and fuel) can be easily proven. Mostly it can be done by simple experiments which, of course, can be verified by sophisticated microscopic equipment and other techniques.

Protoplasm can be extracted from soil either by centrifuge or simple mechanical working of the soil to burst the cell walls. If the soil is then flooded with water, stirred to put the protoplasm in the water, and soil particles allowed to settle, the solution of protoplasm water can be drawn off as a clear fluid.

The few microorganisms which live through the experience, plus those which are in the air, soon repopulate the solution. You can't see them because they are colorless, but if a plant's roots are placed in the solution, you can see the flocculated mass of skins which collect around the root. You can also see the color of the roots change as the skins seal off the cell walls of the root. Plants grow luxuriantly in protoplasm solution. Fortunately they don't know they are supposed to indulge in an ionic exchange with the rock particles of the soil. And they don't have any oddball ideas about following microorganisms around to consume any waste products they may discard. They just sidle up to an organism and take all the protoplasm it has.

Professor William Albrecht of the Univeristy of Missouri, some 50 years ago, decided to centrifuge soil to see if a single component of the soil was responsible for plant growth. The centrifuge inevitably broke all the organism cell walls and delivered the clear protoplasm off the top. It did give excellent growth to the plants. Unfortunately, he did not recognize that it was protoplasm, although he found carbon and nitrogen with repeated testing. He called it a soil colloid or soil solution.

As mentioned earlier, a water solution in the soil cannot stay there because it would diffuse into rain water and run off the surface or percolate into the subsoil. The only way it can stay there is inside a cell wall. This is clearly shown in the low spots in fields with a slow subsoil percolation rate. If water stands in such a spot for about two weeks, the cell wall of the aerobic organisms lyse, i.e. rupture, and spill the protoplasm into the water where it can diffuse into the pond. The sun dries the pond, leaving a hard protoplasm cake on the surface of the soil. The crop in the low spot will be badly stunted throughout the growing season and the soil will not be productive until the protoplasm cake is cultivated back into the soil.

Dr. Albrecht did a great deal of experimentation with various rock elements, relating them to plant growth and plant and animal health. Had he but realized that the elements were feeding the microorganisms which in turn fed the plant, the world might have been spared the crisis which is in the process of destroying us. On the other hand, the agricultural chemicals establishment has shown a remarkable ability to quash heretical statements of fact.

It is interesting to note that a highly organic soil can be turned to a sand color simply by adding a heavy application of gravel dust. What happens is that the availability of elements is so high that skins cannot exist in the soil without being consumed by live microorganisms. As soon as a microorganism dies, its protoplasm is consumed by live microorganisms. Since live microorganisms and fresh skins are colorless, only the color of the soil minerals is seen.

The fertility of such a soil is at a maximum until additional plant residue is added to the soil. Sufficient residue will permit the development of skins, and the soil will turn brown indicating a good balance between available elements and available carbon and nitrogen. A black soil indicates more carbon than can be used. Soils should show black in the spring, and brown in the fall. This color change phenomena, indicating the relation between available elements and the carbon-nitrogen supply, cannot occur if chemical agriculture is practiced because the skins would never build up in the soil to turn brown and then black.

Understanding how the factors in the soil work together makes it possible to tailor farming practices to the feeding requirements of the microorganisms. However, the elemental requirements for high yields are simply to load the soil with as much plant residue and available elements as the increased rate of production (hence income) will support. The upper limit of soil fertility (crop yields) is not yet known. A few examples of the application of the natural principles will both verify the accuracy of the principles and give some idea of potential crop yields.

Organic Gardens

Old organic gardens are invariably loaded with skins. Garden produce is not high in protein and hence does not remove the quantities of protoplasm removed by grain crops. The gardens are kept bare of grass and often mulched with crop residue taken from outside the garden. The available minerals spend most of the growing season just turning plant residue into skins. Thus, when ground gravel is added, the availability of carbon and nitrogen to the organisms working a dust particle is excellent. Given a good water supply, the microorganisms multiply prolifically.

One such garden was treated with about 1¼ tons of ground glacial gravel per acre; a squash plant crawled all over a nearby tree, making it look like a squash tree. The next year an additional 1¼ tons per acre of gravel dust was added, but owner George Haynes sold his house, and the garden grew up in weeds. It was rather awesome when one considered how to go about getting that mass of organic matter worked back into the soil so a garden could be planted the next year. The plants were 6 to 12 inches apart and grew to 11 feet in height. (See Fig. 2) In that massive woody growth, one could see the potential for wood plantations producing eight-inch diameter cordwood in about four years with fast-growing tree varieties (such as poplars, cottonwoods, eucalyptus, willow, locust, southern beech, etc.) One can also see how foolish it is to spend research money on photosynthesis. If the protoplasm is in the leaf, photosynthesis booms.

The same kind of weeds growing outside the Haynes garden on land which had not been farmed for at least 30 years were about four feet tall and widely spaced. On my farmed-out ten acres the same plants were growing two to three feet tall. Three different soils with three different levels of organism-feeding capacity. *It makes a clear picture of why all the living things on Earth have been slowly starving to death—needlessly.*

Another organic garden gained its necessary proximity factor in a different way. It was on a natural deposit of ground glacial gravel dust. The reason such deposits can remain almost as deposited is that they are so dense that plant roots and earthworms cannot penetrate them. The zone of aeration therefore remains very thin and the aerobic organisms cannot penetrate. A grass turf had a root zone of about two inches. Undaunted, the gardener dug it up and mixed all his leaves and grass clippings with the dust, and soon had it booming. In a garden only about 30 by 40 feet, he supplied the vegetables to raise a family. After a frost there were more tomatoes and melons on the ground than a lot of gardeners grow in a whole season. Carrots, still growing, were a foot long and 1½ inches in diameter.

Fig. 2.   "George Haynes grows the best crop of weeds in Michigan."

Another organic gardener grew potatoes up to three pounds. I saw his plants recently. They were three or four times as big as my garden plants and I grow respectable potatoes. This gardener happened to be the owner of a gravel pit, so when he added crusher screenings, he did not stint on the amount. About one-sixth of the screenings are 200-mesh dust. Screenings have considerably less surface area than ground gravel on a weight basis, and there is certain to be more demineralized stone skin in the crusher fines. Screenings are nevertheless quite active when used in sufficient quantity.

Finally, I have in my garden 11.2 tons per acre of dust on one end and 8 tons per acre on the other end. I also have peat where there is the most dust. When there was adequte ground moisture (which has not occurred too often between 1976 and 1979), flowering and yield have been excellent. With a long "Indian summer" in 1978, carrots grew to three inches in diameter and 1¼ pounds; cabbage heads to nine inches in diameter.

The garden was started on the worn-out ten acres. It has been mineralized to some degree since 1974. There has been a huge improvement in the soil. At both ends the soil continues to darken, indicating a buildup of skins. Yields have increased accordingly. The garden is 55' by 135'. In spite of the dry summers (and no irrigation), it provides the two of us with all of our winter vegetables as well as a surplus for our two daughters.

A more important experiment is the four and one-third acres of my ten acres which were mineralized with 46 tons per acre of crusher screenings in late 1976. The cost was $820. *Not a cent has been spent since nor will be for the next 10 or 15 years.* A farmer works the field on shares. After spreading the screenings on the weedy growth, it was plowed to get available elements in deep. Those elements at the bottom of the furrow probably did not become very useful until this year's crop because the zone of aeration had to be developed from the top down in the heavy clay soil.

In this third crop year, the soil seems to be well mixed and much darker in color. In 1977 a corn crop was grown. At 65 bushels per acre it was a good crop in an area of sparse rainfall. In 1978 a soybean crop of 25 bushels per acre was obtained. Local crops just dried up and quit in late August of that year, leaving most of the beans in an immature state. In spite of this the protein was up to 32½ percent — all protein, no false nitrate fertilizer reading. High yields cannot be obtained when precipitation is 5½ and 6 inches short of normal by the first week of September.

The weather pattern in 1979 changed from the previous three dry years. That year a cold dry spring carried to the 25th of June when frost damaged some crops. At one local point in lower Michigan, the temperature dropped to 28 degrees F. and killed all crops. Shortly thereafter we had a slow 3-inch rain which saved a lot of crops. Then it was dry again. But by mid-August 1979 we had adequate rain and were running only 2½ inches below normal. We were 450 temperature degree-days below normal, which ought to make all Michigan legislators do a lot of thinking about what it will mean when all of Michigan's farmers are faced with frozen crops some crisp summer day in the next few years.

The 1979 crop on the four and one-third acres was scheduled to be oats, but the ground did not warm up soon enough, so it turned out to be corn. A substantial part of the corn was 8 feet tall and a good proportion of the stalks made two ears. In spite of the two dry periods in the growing season, it was a good crop.

The mineralized organic gardens clearly show that there is a potential for increasing present yields by a factor of four. When this is accomplished across the land, we will have about twice the capacity we need to provide the present amount of food and all of our energy supplies. *The problem is the time scale in which we must work in order to survive.*

A small area of the ten acres was mineralized but not plowed. In the third growing season (1979), there was evidence of penetration of the available elements into the soil. Young trees which had seeded themselves were healthier-looking and growing faster than those on the rest of the ten acres. Crimson clover multiplied. From this meager information on a soil which had been too dry for perceptible growth during half the growing season, it appears that grazing lands and forests which have decaying plant litter on the ground will begin to show the remineralization health factors within two years, and the growth rate will increase year by year.

In the case of cropland which has been worn out and compacted like the four and one-third acres of now-mineralized soil, a heavy application of available elements has produced crops equal to or better than similar crops in the same rainfall area. For instance, the 65 bushels per acre corn in the first year compares very well with yields of under 25 bushels per acre experienced by a number of local farmers. In 1975, the last year of good soil moisture, 60-day golden bantam corn in the garden gave an excellent yield having 2, 3, and 4 ears per stalk. With a full growing season of good soil moisture, the present four and one-third acres of field corn would have done as well, for a probable yield of around 200 bushels per acre. The onset of glaciation has sent too many summer-time cold waves over Michigan and precipitated the clouds over areas to the south and west, leaving most of Michigan too dry. However, from Iowa east and south, corn has never had it so good. The same treatment I have used, if given to those areas, would now be producing super yields of over 200 bushels per acre of high-quality corn. Every year of adding back the stalk will produce a substantial jump in yield as shown by the organic gardens' performance and numerous single-plant experiments.

The yield limit is uncertain but the factor of 4 appears to be minimal. *It is this great potential which gives us a chance to get enough plant growth and convert far enough toward biomass solar energy to arrest and begin to reverse the flow of carbon dioxide into the atmosphere in the six or eight years in which it must be done.* The 1979 June and mid-August frosts lacked only a few degrees of temperature drop to have caused major crop losses in the top tier of states and Canada. We can expect much damage to these areas, and to almost all of Eurasian grain areas, before the rise in atmospheric carbon dioxide is arrested and reversed. It is therefore imperative that those areas where crops can still be counted on, be made to produce at a maximum.

Needless to say, no pesticides nor herbicides should be used, because they all kill microorganisms as well as the target insects and weeds. Only biological controls and quickly-biodegradable natural insecticides such as pyrethrins, rotenone and thuringiensis should be used. Money spent for chemical fertilizer will give more yield if spent instead for more gravel dust.

When widespread production of ground gravel dust is set up, the ground product will be substantially lower cost than crusher screenings. I estimate that the 46 tons per acre of screenings is just about as active as 10 to 12 tons per acre of gravel dust. Any transportation of stone is expensive, but transportation cost for dust is only one-fourth that for screenings. Distribution costs for screenings are also higher. However, either one is a far better buy for the farmer than agricultural chemicals. If the dust is applied heavily, it does not need to be applied again for a period of years; each ton per acre applied will last somewhat more than one year, unless it is desired to raise the production level. After 5 years my garden is still increasing in yield. The rate of yield will vary the requirement for minerals, of course, and with a given amount of available minerals the rate of yield depends on the amount of plant residue added.

Soil Minerals and Health

The 1977 corn crop was tested against the same corn grown with chemical fertilizers (see postscript after Chapter 7. Tests were made by the Detroit Testing Laboratory, Inc.—Report No. 712163-A). The mineralized corn had 57 percent more phosphorous, 90 percent more potassium, 47 percent more calcium, and 60 percent more magnesium than the chemically-grown corn. This major quality improvement was reflected in the 9 percent protein content, which is good for hybrid corn. Nationally, corn protein runs in the 6 to 8 percent range. What is true of the major elements must necessarily be true of the trace elements. The trace elements are required to provide the differential function of about 5,000 or more enzymes. The enzymes are catalysts which are themselves proteins.

If the enzymes are not present, the proteins cannot be produced and the total protein analysis falls off. That has been happening to our crops over a number of decades. It is therefore not surprising that all of our livestock and one-fourth of our people are too fat. Neither is it surprising that so many handicapped babies are being born to mothers suffering from malnutrition. *As the various elements required by enzymes disappear from the soil, various body functions must inevitably fail, so that the diseases of malnutrition become the norm rather than the exception.*

The USDA is still using food analysis figures compiled in 1963. They have lost their validity. In 1963, the food supply was poor in the elements and an honest appraisal now would show by comparison a drastic decline in soil element availability. The difference in element content of vegetables grown on different soils can be 1,000 to 1, yet both plants will look much the same.

Normally we could expect to get a balanced diet by eating fruits and vegetables plus meats, poultry, dairy products and/or nuts, seeds, grains, etc.—but it is no longer possible.

The purpose of food is the same as the purpose in establishing soil fertility: to feed a healthy crop of microorganisms. The human intestine does essentially the same job that the plant root does. It takes the protoplasm of the microorganisms and moves it into the bloodstream in the outer wall of the intestine. The intestine, however, does not plug up as the root does because it is lined with velvety projections called cilia which keep sweeping the cell walls of the organisms downward along the intestinal tract.

The food taken in must contain enough elements so that all of the solid food except the cellulose can be consumed by the microorganisms, the size of whose population is controlled by the element content of the food. Fruits and vegetables are supposed to have lots of elements and very little protein. The protein foods are just the opposite. With both in the diet, the microorganisms should obtain balanced rations. Unfortunately, if you ate enough of today's fruits and vegetables to get the required elements, you would get an overdose of toxic pesticides and of absorbed raw nitrate fertilizer. Millions of Americans suffer from constipation, which is the precursor of many problems, and the multi-billion dollar blasting-compound business is booming.

For four years now I have been taking about ¼ to ½ teaspoon per day of ground gravel dust. At first I did it to check out my conclusion that it would fill the intestine with live microorganisms and thereby end constipation, which it did. Now I take it because it turns low-element content foods into high-quality protoplasm which has many beneficial effects in the body. It is a sad commentary on the food supply when one must eat ground gravel dust in order to digest the food.

Animals know when their food supply is lacking in minerals. I know of a dairy herd which consumed more than a ton of dust one summer. They filled their rumens with hay and stuck their heads through a hole in the barn to get at the dust stored there. Those cows were making their own sad commentary on the quality of their forage. And it's also a very sad commentary when beef cattle can grow 25 percent faster when given cement kiln dust, which is simply very fine ground gravel dust that has not been heated enough to convert it to cement clinker. It is not coincidence that the meat of cattle fed kiln dust grades high, and they are free of disease.

Recently, investigators have found anti-cancer factors in various foods. Dr. Max Gerson knew they were there when in the early 1940's he testified before the Delaney Committee that he had removed, and put in remission, cancers in 30 percent of terminal patients other doctors had rejected. Essentially what he did was to cut off the intake of carcinogens by switching patients off contaminated commercial foods and onto organic foods, while at the same time vastly increasing their consumption of fruit and vegetable juices. What he was doing was getting enough elements in his patients to insure conversion of food to top-quality protoplasm which contained the anti-cancer factors. In all probability glacial gravel dust will do the same thing. Needless to say, applying it to the soil must hold highest priority. The people of Hunza, who do just that at least twice yearly, are 100 percent free of cancer according to authors McCarrison (1936), Wrench (1945), Rodale (1948), Tobe (1965), Banik (1960), and Taylor (1969).

Experimenting with ascorbic acid (vitamin C) and ground gravel shows that the abundant carbon in this organic acid is very readily available to microorganisms. When the acid is neutralized by the dust in a shallow dish, and the material is innoculated with the organisms in a pinch of dirt, and kept damp for 6 or 8 hours, a prolific population of microorganisms is produced. Nitrogen is readily supplied from the air which surrounds the thin layer of material. The high availability of the carbon in vitamin C has very important health implications.

Almost all of the animals make their own vitamin C. Man and the guinea pig and possibly a few other vegetable-eating animals seem to have lost the ability to synthesize their own vitamin C. When ascorbic acid or any other solution (toxic or non-toxic) is swallowed, it passes readily through the intestinal wall into the blood system just as such solutions pass through a plant root surface into the plant.

The blood has billions of microorganisms living in it. There are single-celled organisms like the red and white blood cells as well as numerous other organisms comprising a part of the body's maintenance and defense systems. For instance, a virus-like organism has been photomicrographed entering a harmful bacteria cell and totally consuming it while vastly multiplying its own population. If these beneficial processes are to go on, there must be an expenditure of energy derived from carbon. The very simple compound, ascorbic acid, $C_6H_8O_6$, must certainly be easier for any organism to use than the more complicated blood sugar glucose consisting of two sugars, dextrose ($C_6 H_{12} O_6$) and maltose ($C_{12} H_{22} O_{11} H_2O$), and dextrins (hydrolyzed starches), $(C_6H_{10}O_5)n$, plus H_2O. Glucose does, however, supply carbon for many useful purposes to the body cells.

The necessity for a quickly-available form of carbon in the blood is seen in the fact that all of the blood circulates through the body and back to the heart in 15 minutes. The live organisms in the blood stream have to "eat on the run," so to speak.

It should be obvious at this point that the anti-cancer factors in protoplasm cannot function without a carbon supply to energize the blood's maintenance and defense system organisms. Dr. Linus Pauling is right about the value of vitamin C with respect to cancer. Vitamin C does far more than prevent scurvy. In addition to energizing the blood maintenance and defense system organisms, it can tie up inanimate toxic products in the blood stream, rendering them harmless for removal by the kidneys.

Good vegetables and fruits are not commercially available to anybody. The poor cannot afford even the vegetables and fruits available. Therefore it would be the lowest cost "preventative medicine" possible to assure that ascorbic acid is made available to the poor at little or no cost. The program would pay for itself many times over in unneeded medical care.

The feeding of microorganisms both inside the body and in the soil must be carefully attended to. Good health starts with high availability of all the minerals in the top strata of the earth's crust. The price of that availability is less than half the annual cost of agricultural chemicals.

The Role of Government in This Crisis of Survival

We have an unprecedented crisis situation. The present level of percentage increase in carbon dioxide over normal levels will increase 50 percent in the next decade. The world grain supplies are now threatened by frost and freeze damage, as well as increasingly frequent and severe droughts, floods, hail, and high winds. Forests too are being assaulted by climatic extremes, plus four billion people demanding lumber and fuel.

We can expect serious crop losses in the first few years of the decade, and calamitous losses in the last half of the decade. The chaos of widespread famine and the violence of the weather will by then render soil remineralization ineffectual. *If soil remineralization is to be done, it must be done in the next six or eight years.* Our forests and jungles are fast disappearing while our use of fossil fuels is increasing. This is a sure prescription for mass suicide.

The first thing that the Congress should do is to go on record, perhaps with a resolution, declaring its intent to do everything it can to enable the remineralization of the world's land mass.

The Congress should set up an expediting agency with authority to expedite all things useful in removing carbon dioxide from the atmosphere and to eliminate as quickly as possible all things which introduce carbon dioxide into the atmosphere with no provision for removing it. I would suggest putting a hold on most space exploration until we find out if we are going to survive, and give the expediting job to the Space Agency. They have demonstrated an ability to get the job done.

The Congress should set up a loan guarantee program for the biomass capital goods required.

The Congress should establish an international coordinating team to work throughout the world to do the jobs which must be done if any of us are to survive. For instance, the jungles are being cut down by hungry peoples to get fuel or a few more crops off the demineralized jungle soils. *It is imperative that jungles be saved.* Many of the jungles are now living off the minerals in the decaying wood of dead trees. But they are usually in areas of high rainfall, and if minerals are added to the decaying organic matter, the trees will increase their growth rate and be immensely valuable in taking up and storing carbon from the atmosphere.

Again, the jungles must be saved or we will have no chance at survival. They obviously cannot be saved unless the croplands of starving people are remineralized. In all probability the air forces of stronger nations must do most of the forest work from the air. It would not be out of place to press all civilian air lines into service if the logistics of the job prove it necessary. The Armed Services have equipment and manpower plus the Air Force which can take on the job of forest remineralization.

And the Congress should stabilize the dollar. That can only be done by facing honestly the real cause of inflation. Most of the ownership in this country has become centralized in the hands of investors. The annual income from those funds is so large that the funds are doubling in less than ten years. That income must be invested to make the funds grow. And what do they invest it in? Multi-billion dollar nuclear plants whose total industrial leakage of radioactive materials must eventually destroy humanity. Billions of dollars are invested in chemical plants which produce non-biodegradable chemicals which are turning the biosphere into a vast "Love Canal" that will eventually destroy humanity. Billions are invested in fossil fuel mining and drilling equipment to take more carbon out of the earth and put it into the atmosphere. Our destruction from this practice will be certain and soon if continued.

As an emergency measure, the Congress must stop all investment in enterprises which threaten the existence of man, and Congress must control all transfer of funds into and out of the country. This will stop the inflationary pressure on capital goods, provide more than ample funds for the low-cost biomass capital goods, and leave plenty of funds to just sit in the financial institutions as a positive force to lower interest rates. At present the competitive bidding for capital goods raises the cost of all capital goods, which necessitates higher prices for goods sold. To buy the higher-cost goods, labor must have higher wages. But it is the centralization of wealth in pools whose only purpose is to increase in numerical quantity, uncontrolled by the needs and wants of people, which initiates inflation. For the duration of the emergency, investments must be controlled to serve useful purposes. Eventually the factors which permit centralization of wealth must be dealt with and eventually is not far away. The fact that we run an economy in which "the rich get richer and the poor get poorer" is why various forms of socialism governed by people are taking the place of societies governed by law. Our own nation will go the same way unless the laws are just laws.

Summary

Present day agriculture commercializes a microscopic bit of knowledge and imposes it on the vastly complicated life system as created. To understand the exact requirements of the soil, one must first understand the protoplasm of all the soil microorganisms. That may be possible with a thousand years of research. Meanwhile, the way nature works and the technique for accelerating her processes are available to vastly increase our supplies of natural organic materials.

The world's topsoils are fast running out of available elements. The rapid rise in percent increase of carbon dioxide in the atmosphere assures us of massive crop losses throughout the world due to frost and freeze damage. It will occur in the 1980's. The only way to remove carbon dioxide from the air is to get it into a massive growth of plant life and into carbon-depleted soils. This can only be done by mineralizing the world's land mass while eliminating the practice of using the carbon supplies secreted in the Earth.

If government acts in a way in which it has not performed since World War II, we may be able to effect our survival. If so, we will come out with a completely solar energy program. We will have a food program which will provide a very high level of health and longevity. And perhaps the world may come to realize that it is far better to use its brains instead of its armaments.

Fig. 3.

ONE PICTURE IS WORTH A THOUSAND WORDS. The actual difference between the nubbins and the ears of corn is soil remineralization. The picture might also be seen as the difference between nutrition in this country as it is and as it ought to be. It can also be viewed as the difference between death from starvation and glaciation and an abundance of the basic resources of life.

Recap 1981

The corn on the right side of the ruler (Fig. 3) was grown in 1977 after a fall application of 46 tons/acre of gravel crusher screenings. The corn on the left was grown in 1979 following soybeans in 1978. The yield increased by about 15 bushels/acre to 75 bushels/acre in 1979. This can be attributed to the better mixing of the screenings and the stalk residue of two crops.

Since 1975 the Lansing area of Michigan has been short of average precipitation at the end of the growing season by 5 or 6 inches for five years in a row. In 1981 it hit average rainfall by getting a 3 inch rain about the middle of May and another on the 26th of August. Between those dates the area went from + 2 inches to − 2 inches. The drought came within a week or 10 days of destroying all the crops in the area. Now in early October it is harvest time and a cloudburst has flooded the land with 3 inches to 9 inches of rainfall. Dry edible bean crops are expected to be a total loss to many farmers. Other crops may be worth harvesting if the land ever dries out enough to work the fields. Many farmers are expected to throw in the towel. A succession of low yields, low crop prices, this final crop loss, and prohibitive interest rates which preclude borrowing for next year's crops simply means that it is not possible to continue farming.

All over the country farmers are quitting for much the same reasons. The violence of nature is not the least of the reasons. When will our brilliant leadership make the connection between a rise in atmospheric CO_2 that is running wild and our weather which is also running wild?

The nubbins on the right side of the picture clearly show that there are not enough minerals left in the untreated soil to produce a crop. Most of the tillable land between the Rockies and the East Coast is in the same or worse condition. Much of the forest land is equally sterile. Yet it can all be made productive by the addition of ground glacial gravel.

2

Perspective

A further look at soil remineralization and its tremendous positive potentials will be of value here. Due to long-time general neglect of the need for balanced remineralization, these potentials are scarcely known, both by practitioners of the widespread "soil mining" chemical agriculture, and by the "organic," "bio-dynamic," and "eco-agriculture" practitioners. These last individuals have generally gone beyond the use of acidified chemical nutrients and toxic sprays, yet their means of producing food are often dependent on extracting fertility from one piece of land in order to enrich another, i.e. "robbing Peter to pay Paul." Meanwhile the overall fertility of the Earth continues to decline.

As may be obvious by now, it is helpful in the understanding of this book to see the earth as having a single soil (as it has a single atmosphere), nearly all of it 10,000 or more years "old," or in development, since the bulk of its surface "parent material" was laid down.

In addition to those cited by Hamaker, some other examples of results obtained with ground gravel (mixed rock) materials may help illustrate the great potential to restore youthfulness and productive fertility to any and all soil.

LePage in Vermont

Alan LePage is a young, intensive "truck crop" farmer, near Barre, Vermont, with an obvious love for the soil. Alan's father manages the local glacial gravel pit. Having missed John Hamaker's early *Acres, USA* articles, Alan was not fully aware of what he was doing when he spread about 6 inches of gravel screenings on an infertile, waterlogged section of his farm "to improve the drainage," and plowed it in. It did, of course, and also gave the soil microorganisms an abundance of all the minerals, something they never had while Alan used only the usual organic methods.

The first crop grown in that rejuvenated topsoil was clover. The organism development in that soil must have been awesome, because the plants showed no interest in terminating growth—*reaching 12 feet in length* when autumn's cold called a halt. Initial attempts to disk that clover back into the soil failed when the stalks proved too thick to cut. The writer is not exaggerating. The clover root systems were no doubt massive as well. Such outstanding biomass production reveals the natural way for farmers and gardeners to "get organic matter"—primarily by hauling it in, year after year, from the atmosphere via a thriving soil-plant life system.

Asked how his second-year crops, broccoli and carrots, had fared, Alan LePage informed me: "Great! Broccoli averaged around 2½ pounds per head, carrots 1½ feet in length." Alan needs no chemical fertilizer or pesticides, and states that his prime concern is to build soil fertility and produce good food.

Weaver in California

After visiting John Hamaker's Michigan 10 acres and garden in late 1978, observing the "miracle" of remineralized soil and eating the startlingly delicious produce therefrom, I returned to California. By adding river gravel screenings from the vast Kaiser and Lonestar Industry gravel pits east of San Francisco Bay to an average organic garden at rates of 40 to 80 tons per acre (2 to 4 lbs per sq. ft.), crop yields increased two to four times in quantity with unmistakable flavor enrichment. Pole beans, climbing out of prolific zucchini and tomato beds, went to 18 feet before being turned back under the weight of heavy beans at the top.

Now (1981) in this third year of soil improvement, with an additional application, at a 10-20 ton/acre rate, of a commercially-mixed rock dust from Utah, the very dark green bean leaves are already up to 14 feet in early July and producing heavily. Their flowers tell of another huge total crop—and the wonderfully sweet, rich (indescribable!) taste of these beans, the lettuce, carrots, zucchini, cucumbers, melons, etc. shouts the greater story of an end to malnutrition and disease.

One can not adequately describe the color and great vibrancy of plants grown in mineralized soil, yet perhaps an idea may be communicated of zucchini squash plants with up to 32 leaves each by July 9th (planted mid-May), with leaves up to 60 inches and more in circumference. No chemicals were used, and there is no insect or disease damage. There *are* friendly birds abounding.

Fig. 4. "Kentucky Wonder" pole beans in the 1981 Weaver garden grew luxuriantly, producing heavily from July to late October.

Fig.5. Picking tender 8-inch beans from a 20-foot, 4-inch long "stalk."

Apparently, there are at least 6 billion tons of the above-mentioned Utah deposit in reserve, and another 5 billion or more tons of a similar deposit in Nevada. Both are being *very gradually* quarried, ground and distributed to farmers and gardeners, and to doctors and dentists who use it in pill form as food "supplements." No doubt there are more than enough easily-accessible gravel materials in California already (California Division of Mines, 1957), but as an example, note that the Nevada deposit alone could provide the 100 million-acre land surface of California with 50 tons per acre of soil remineralization. Similar deposits, of glacial or other origin, are said to exist in Colorado, New Mexico, Imperial Valley of California, France, Germany, Africa, and perhaps many other parts of the world (Ambler Pennant, 1950).

There is not likely to be a shortage of accessible mixed rock anywhere in the world — even the Sahara desert and Brazil are underlaid with till from ancient glaciations (John, 1980)—only a shortage of *environmentally constructive* systems set up for quarrying, grinding, distributing and recycling the nutrients; and a lack of awareness of the need.

Soil Remineralization Past and Present

Concerned readers should be aware that at present there is virtually no "official" research being done on soil remineralization. An extensive computer search through the U.C. Berkeley agricultural data base in December 1980 showed *zero* published research on the following as soil additions: gravel dust, gravel screenings, gravel crusher screenings, rock dust, loess, volcanic ash, basalt. This search covered a huge amount of published work over approximately the past decade. There has been a huge amount of research done on *single* element effects on plant and soil processes, on chemical fertilizers, pesticides, and on measuring and intricately classifying the endless variations of demineralizing soil.

Apparently the last person prior to John Hamaker to publicly advocate remineralization was Julius Hensel in the late 1800's. A few words on Hensel's efforts may be enlightening here.

In the introduction to the re-published edition of Hensel's *Bread From Stones* (from Health Research, 1977), Dr. Raymond Bernard explains that Hensel and his writings were heavily scorned and attacked by the chemical interests of the day, who supported Justus von Liebig's doctrine of adding factory-acidulated nitrogen, phosphorous, and potassium in concentrated form to the soil (Liebig, 1852). The "Stone Meal," which a few companies in Europe had tried to produce, was forced off the market. *Bread From Stones*, which contained many testimonials to soil remineralization by the farmers who were actually using "Stone Meal" on their lands, was suppressed and even removed from libraries.

Hensel had this to say about the attacks on the message he offered the world:

> The men interested in artificial manures, who thought that they had attended to the funeral of Stone Meal as a fertilizer have learned nothing from history, or have at least forgotten that every new truth has first to be killed and buried before it can celebrate its resurrection. Besides I do not stand as isolated as these people suppose, for I have the light of truth and knowledge on my side—
> He who sights for truth and right
> E'en alone, has strength and might.

Hensel continued:

> What is lacking at present is that the manufacture of Stone Meal should be undertaken by men of scientific attainments who at the same time have sterling honesty, so as to make it certain that farmers will actually receive what is promised and what has proved itself to be so useful hitherto. I have received innumerable requests from farmers who asked for this mineral manure, but I had to answer them that with my advanced years I could not actively engage in this manufacture. The whole subject is of such immense importance for the common welfare that it is my wish to see this work placed into hands that are thoroughly reliable. I but point the way for the benefit of the human race. (Hensel, 1893, 1977)

Hensel also understood the important principle that Hamaker is now stressing, namely: "that the fineness of the stamping or grinding and the most complete intermixture of the constituent parts are of the greatest importance for securing the greatests benefit of stone-meal fertilizing." Much later, scientists M.L. Jackson and E. Truog demonstrated this principle well in their experiments and subsequent article, *Influence of Grinding Soil Minerals to Near Molecular Size on Their Solubility and Base Exchange Properties* (Jackson and Truog, 1939).

Note that Hamaker has no use for solubility and base exchange, since the microorganisms extract the elements, and the natural mixture of elements is neutral (pH 7).

It is perhaps a fascinating irony to note that Liebig, "father of chemical agriculture," recommended the use of (and himself sold) the simplistic N-P-K fertilizers, *based on* his analyses of plant tissue and ashes showing those three elements as "major constitutents." Had Liebig been able to utilize the advanced spectrographic or x-ray fluorescence analytical equipment of today, he would have discovered the *25* soil mineral elements *proven* to be essential for humans (Edell, 1979), plus virtually all the 90 + elements in his plants (Ermolenko, 1972). Then he too would likely have reached the obvious conclusion to add all the elements together as finely-ground rocks. This can also be inferred from his own words, from a later edition of his book: "By the deficiency or absence of *one* necessary constituent, all the others being present, the soil is rendered barren for all those crops to the life of which *that one* constituent is indispensible." (Quoted from Russell's *Soil Conditions and Plant Growth*, p. 13, emphasis Liebig's.) On the other hand, since he had himself become engaged in peddling his "Liebig's patent manure" (Russell, p. 12), perhaps he too would have ignored the evidence that multiple element deficiency and widespread malnutrition would be inevitable via chemical fertilizers. That he eventually did gain some realization of the ecological design of wholeness and balance we saw at the start of this chapter.

Since Hensel's time, two other well-known agriculturists, J.I. Rodale and Sir Albert Howard, gave voice to their perceptions of the need to remineralize soils—yet their words apparently had little positive influence at the time. In 1948, Rodale published his enlightening book, *The Healthy Hunzas*, which revealed how the world's healthiest people annually add to their soils the mixture of stones finely ground by the local Ultar glacier, together with the abundant organic matter produced by these highly-mineralized soils. (Little animal manure is added as the Hunzacuts keep few animals.) Rodale stressed the great value of adding the wide variety of rocks to soils in a "ground-up, flour-like form" by using the most efficient modern machinery (p. 100). He also pointed out the danger of adding imbalancing single-rock types, and concluded his chapter, "Rock Powders," by giving major credit for the Hunzacuts' outstanding health, longevity, and intelligence to the glacial rock powder, their provision for perpetual soil fertility and high-quality foods. Rodale was emphatic that we in the United States begin to utilize the billions of tons of rocks of all kinds, and apply them—the equivalent of the Hunza sediments—to our lands, in a powdered form.

Sir Albert Howard, often called the "father of organic agriculture," also described the Hunzacuts in his 1947 book, *The Soil and Health*. He too observed the Hunza Valley's glacial silt fertilizer, and the powerful evidence suggesting that—"to obtain the very best results we must replace simultaneously the organic and mineral portions of the soil." (p. 177)

Rejuvenation of Soil and Animal Life

In the published research work emerging from the universities and USDA laboratories there is, as noted, no *conscious* effort to learn how nature feeds the microorganisms who feed the plants (as documented by Krasilnikov, 1958; McLaren and Peterson, 1967; Jennings, 1963; Sanders et al, 1975; Marks and Kozlowski, 1973; Mori et al, 1977 and many others).

Yet in 1959, and again in 1963, the USDA fertilizer laboratory in Beltsville, Maryland released articles strongly corroborating the fact that nature's gravel dust methods do indeed work.

Cement kiln dust (noted in "Food, Energy, and Survival"), which is primarily derived from local gravels, was gathered for these studies from 20 cement manufacturers in Virginia, Maryland, New York, Iowa, Oregon, Missouri, Pennsylvania, Illinois, Florida, Tennessee, California, Wisconsin, Kentucky, Minnesota, Michigan, and Washington.

The authors of the articles, while they mention a number of the elements in the dust, think of it as a "liming" material rather than a broad-spectrum remineralization material. Significantly, they observe: "Use of cement kiln dusts for soil liming is not a new idea, but it seems to have received little attention and the relative merits of the dust and of conventional liming materials have not been well studied. The large amount of dust potentially available and the distribution of cement plants throughout much of the humid regions, where the dust could be applied to the soil without shipping great distances, makes this byproduct of special interest."

All the dusts were said to be about equal to each other as suppliers of calcium, and in comparisons with agricultural limestone (a single rock type) on yields of alfalfa, the cement kiln dusts "tended to be superior" to the limestone. Fortunately the researchers noted a few other elements in the rocks, concluding: "If applied at the rate of 4 tons the dusts would supply, on the average, 3 times the magnesium, 6 times the sulfur, 9 times the potassium (as soluble K) and, except for one dust that would supply only 9 times, 16 times the calcium removed in a typical 5-year rotation." (Whittaker et al, 1959, 1963) Note: The figures are based on the elements in chemically grown crops—not crops grown on mineralized soil.

Whether any farmers, foresters, doctors, or nutritionists were specifically informed of these studies is not known. Apparently no one at USDA's Beltsville headquarters became very excited over the value of the rock dust for soil-building and nutritional uplift, as another more recent article on cement dust in *Science* (Maugh, 1978) indicates.

"The Fatted Calf (II): The Concrete Truth About Beef" explains that some Georgia cattle ranchers "on impulse" dumped some of the cement kiln dust they were using on their soils into their cattle feed. When the "astonished" ranchers reported to Beltsville that the cattle grew unexpectedly fast, USDA researchers Wheeler and Oltjen were "skeptical." Still, they tried feeding 7 steers a control diet; 7 others the same with 3.5 percent cement kiln dust. They were quite surprised to discover, that after 112 days, that the dust-fed animals had *gained 28 percent more weight than those on the control diet*, while at the same time consuming *2l percent less feed*.

Analyses revealed that the extra weight was "all meat" of a higher quality than the controls, and these dust-fed animals were described as being "quite healthy." The article goes on to report how the dust, "a calcium-rich mixture of minerals," gave similar results with a second group of 32 steers, 60 lambs, and groups of laboratory rats. USDA's Mr. Wheeler speculates that "some element" may be responsible, or perhaps "the small size of the particles" is the key.

Perhaps one day the Beltsville Agricultural Research Center will stumble upon the dust's value for growing bigger and healthier soil organism populations, crops, forests—even a fading human race. Someone, perhaps the U.S. Congress, should probably inform them immediately, however. John Hamaker and this writer have tried at length to communicate with many USDA people, including the Secretary and Assistant Secretary of Agriculture, the Chief of the Forest Service, and the Director of the Science and Education Administration, Anson Bertrand. A scheduled meeting of this writer and Dr. Bertrand to discuss "Food, Energy, and Survival," in January 1980, was cancelled by Dr. Bertrand at the last minute for undisclosed reasons.

This is the same Anson Bertrand who, according to the USDA news release in June 1979, "has assembled a crew of experts he calls the 'Coordinating Team for Organic Farming.'" This news release concludes by saying:

> Many conventional farmers question whether organic farming can produce enough food to feed the millions of people who must be fed in modern times. Has new knowledge already boosted the productive power of organic farming?
>
> "We'll find out," said Bertrand. "When the facts are in, we'll use them to develop a program or policy recommendations for Assistant Agriculture Secretary Rupert Cutler and Secretary Bob Bergland. If it appears reasonable to do so, we may suggest additional redirection of research, education, and funding."

The fact is, the "Team for Organic Farming" crew of experts were specifically informed at least four times of the basic facts and potentials of soil remineralization; that there was indeed "new" knowledge that has greatly boosted the productive power of organic or any kind of farming. Invitations to visit Hamaker's soil and crops were ignored. A representative "brush-off" response to John Hamaker's many letters to USDA people said, in part: "Although we very much appreciate your interest and concern, we cannot agree that the measures you propose are practical ones for improving soil fertility...The fertilizer value of many kinds of rocks is nil. For all but a few kinds of rocks the fertilizer value is so low that it is impractical to grind them to improve soil fertility.'' (From Frank Carlisle, Jr., Administrator, Soil Conservation Service).

John Hamaker's perpective may well be brought in again at this point, by quoting from two of his letters to former Vice President Walter Mondale. One letter, regarding Rupert Cutler's idea to start more research on organic techniques, said this:

> Organic techniques have been researched up one side and down the other without results. The reason is that the name of the game is feeding microorganisms. It should surprise no one (but surprises everyone) to find that the best food for growing microorganisms consists of those things readily available all over the earth. The money spent on conservation has been wasted because no one can conserve the soil and water but the microorganisms. Mr. Cutler won't be worth his salary until he starts feeding the microorganisms. He could learn more from my four and one-third acre corn plot than he could from a thousand organic farms.

The other letter, also pertinent to this consideration, said this:

> Dear Sir:
> Enclosed is a copy of the response of my government to two papers. One paper proved that cancer, malnutrition, and the threat of starvation and glaciation can be eliminated. The other showed a demonstration of the process.
> Meanwhile, under the brilliant guidance of the USDA and its Soil Conservation Service, the Plains States are flying east on the wind.
> The arrogant ignorance of bureaucrats is going to come to an end. Either the Carter-Mondale Administration will end it or the laws of nature will do it. One way we live, the other way we die. And if you people don't act damned fast, there won't be an option.
> While Carlisle babbles about the impracticability of grinding the mixed rocks of the top layers of the earth's crust, a local gravel pit operator is investing in grinding equipment because the President of the Organic Growers of Michigan asked him to supply dust. Such small efforts across the land by very practical people are going on, but without the help of government in mobilizing and hugely accelerating these efforts, we will never be able to hold the dry western soils against wind erosion or the wet eastern soils against water erosion, nor can we get control of the destructive winds, tornadoes, droughts, blizzards, and floods. This country must mobilize and lead the whole world in an effort to save it. And it must be done now.
>
> Sincerely,
> John D. Hamaker

A final note. The above-mentioned *Science* article on cement kiln rock dust provided another bit of immediately valuable information. It said that *30 million kilograms* (66 million pounds or 33,000 tons) are readily available from cement kilns, in the U.S. alone, *each day*. Therefore at an application rate of 3 tons per acre, for example, 11,000 acres per day could be somewhat remineralized with this "waste material" alone. When we look at the ongoing process of forest die-off in the next chapters, it will be apparent how crucially important such immediately available materials may be, should we choose to try to save the forests.

3

Introduction

.

"Worldwide Starvaticn By 1990" was originally published in January of 1980, revised in the summer of 1980, and appeared in *Acres, USA* (October, 1980) and the *Price-Pottenger Nutrition Foundation Bulletin* (Vol. 5, No. 4, 1980). The paper has been widely distributed to people in many fields, including most of the 1980 U.S. Congress, the President's Council on Environmental Quality, the U.S. Department of Agriculture and Forest Service, and many others. Also it was given as part of a presentation of the same title at the "First Global Conference on the Future" held in Toronto in July, 1980.

"Worldwide Starvation By 1990" is a concise explanation, now documented by solid evidence, of the degenerative forest changes known to occur during the interglacial-to-glacial transition period. Sufficient evidence revealing the soil-based causes of this dying-out period, and of obvious signs that we are well into it, will be considered following this paper.

The U.S. government's *The Global 2000 Report to the President*, mentioned herein and purported to "serve as the foundation of our longer term planning" (Jimmy Carter), deserves some specific consideration. That may wait until the "Perspective" on Chapter 6, "The Glacial Process and the End of the Food Supply."

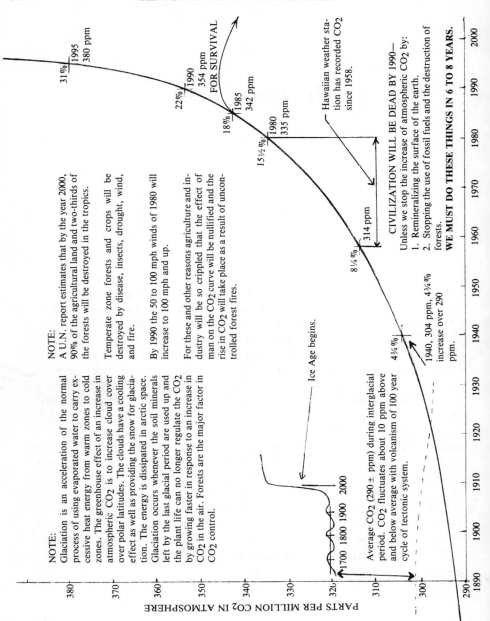

Fig. 1

3

Worldwide Starvation By 1990

For 10 years I have been warning that the world's soils are running out of minerals and that glaciation must inevitably follow. Now there is hard evidence that the temperate zone will become a part of the subarctic zone in approximately 15 years. Somewhere in that time period we will stop eating.

A report by G. Woillard in the English science magazine *Nature* (10/18/79) draws a grim picture from a study of pollen in the mud of a lake bottom in South Vosges, France. At the start of a number of past glacial periods, the vegetation changed from temperate zone trees to subarctic needle-bearing trees in a period of 150 years ±75 years. The change was one of gradual deterioration until the last 20 years. During the last 20 years the type of vegetation completely changed.

The 150-year death of the temperate zone vegetation recorded in the French lake mud corresponds exactly with a curve showing the annual percent increase of carbon dioxide over the interglacial level. The gradual increase in the rate of destruction of the forests corresponds to the rate of increase of carbon dioxide. The curve was drawn simply by extending the actually-recorded Mauna Loa Curve backward to the middle of the last century and forward to the year 1995 in a smooth curve with an increasing rate of change with respect to time (Fig. 1). By 1995 the rate of increase is so great each year that it is pointless to extend the curve farther.

At what point on the curve does the 20-year collapse of temperate zone vegetation begin? Why does the collapse occur so quickly? We already have the answer to these questions.

The mechanism of change in the interglacial forests involves several factors.

The process of deterioration starts with malnutrition about 150 years ahead of the collapse. Malnutrition results from the depletion of the minerals deposited by the last glacial period. The available minerals decrease in quantity to the point where enzyme systems no longer function vigorously. Disease spreads through the forests and they begin to die out.

The problem starts with the soil microorganisms. As the quantity of available elements decreases, the soil's organism population must decrease. One hundred and fifty years ago a virgin soil may have had 25 tons per acre of organisms; today's soils generally have less than 5 tons per acre. The importance of the soil microorganisms is that their protoplasm compounds are the source of the cell protoplasm of every other living thing on Earth.

A simple key to awareness of the mineral shortage is the easily-measured property of acidity of soil, water, and precipitation. If acidity goes up, it is because the mineral supply has become too weak in acid-soluble basic elements for the microorganisms to maintain a neutral soil in which they can thrive. It is the needle-bearing trees which can best survive the increasing acidity and reduced availability of protoplasm, because the needles have smaller mineral requirements and far fewer cells to fill with protoplasm. Unlike the broadleaved trees, these conifers can live with only the top branches green while the resin prevents (for a time) rot from quickly penetrating the trunk from the dead lower branches.

Needle-bearing trees have taken over from much of our worn-out one-time crop (and deciduous forest) soils. Other such soils are kept in production by periodic applications of agricultural limestone. However, the large quantity of basic elements available from limestone is not matched by an availability of other elements from the silicate rocks, because neither the acids of chemical agriculture nor those from acidic rain can dissolve the silicate. The result is specific element shortage, resulting in malnutrition and death.

When the tropical forests are dead and gone, the very badly depleted mineral supply will support very little life until glacial gravel dust borne on very high winds has remineralized the soil to start the process of plant growth. Temperate zone forests are those which will grow in the cooler equatorial atmosphere of the glacial period. They will begin the process of removing the excess carbon dioxide from the atmosphere and bringing the carbon back to earth to renew life on earth.

There have been numerous reports of crop damage due to acidic rains. Many lakes in the Northeast have become so acidic that no life can exist in them. Lewis and Grant (*Science*, 1/11/80) report some frightening statistics. On the Colorado section of the Continental Divide where there is very little industrial pollution in the direction of the prevailing wind, the pH of all precipitation dropped from 5.43 to 4.63 in just three years. Neutral is pH 7.0. The precipitation was already acidic three years ago, and it increased in acidity by .8 of a point on the pH scale in just three years. Since the CO_2 curve is almost vertical at the year 1995, we can go back 20 years to 1975 for the start of the 20-year critical period and not be off by more than a couple of years. The pH then must have been about 6.

Temperate zone vegetation (including crops) can not grow on acidic soils. The large numbers of dead and dying trees in our forests is directly attributable to the increasing acidity of the soils and decreasing quantities of available elements. Dead forests burn easily with a hot fire which oxidizes large quantities of atmospheric nitrogen. Lewis and Grant found that the oxides of nitrogen were dominant in the acidic precipitation. The more trees die and burn, the more the soils become acidified and the more trees must die. There are also a number of mildly acidic gases released from burning wood. These, plus the acidic gases from volcanism, are nature's way of bringing on glaciation. Man's fossil fuel fires are a big factor in the destruction. Logically, the 20 years for the change in vegetation should be much less because of industrial pollution.

The burning of the temperate zone vegetation will carry huge quantities of carbon dioxide into the atmosphere. In the zones of latitude where the sunlight is most intense, the carbon dioxide holds the heat at the surface of the earth, providing the energy to increase the evaporation and to move the massive cloud cover to the polar regions. The cloud cover lowers the temperature and increases the quantity of cold air which flows south over the land masses. The temperate zone will become a part of the subarctic zone. We can't grow grain in the subarctic. Growing seasons have already been shortened and interrupted by freeze damage. Furthermore, the acidic rain will destroy growth all over the world. The local areas to survive will be the few near the equator that are blessed with a constantly renewed supply of basic minerals sufficient to maintain a neutral soil in spite of the acidic rains.

Humanity should have seen impending crisis in the slow rise in atmospheric carbon dioxide and the deterioration of forests and jungles. It would have been easy 50 years ago to remineralize the world's soils and bring the carbon dioxide back to normal. Now we must stop the rise in carbon dioxide level in 6 or 8 years or we must die shortly thereafter. I all but begged the Carter Administration three years ago to institute a massive soil remineralization program and to propagate it worldwide as the condition for survival of all of us. Had Carter done so, the Russians would not have been playing power games in the Middle East, and Iran would not have held 50 hostages. Nobody on this earth has either time to waste or resources to use on anything but soil remineralization, and the associated food and energy programs compatible with our survival. There must be a common struggle for survival or we won't stand a chance. And if it doesn't start right now, we still won't stand a chance.

Most of the politicians in both state and local government have campaign debts to pay off. The people who control the wealth hold the I.O.U.'s. So after all this time we do not have a permanent energy policy. All the hired mouths are saying coal and nuclear power is the way to go. *Yet nature has decreed that only by increasing biomass growth rate 2, 3, and 4 times can we hope to get the raw materials for food and energy and at the same time effect our survival by taking carbon from the air and storing it in soils and forests.* My research has shown how we can accelerate the life process to give us food, energy, and survival.

The evidence points to several things which government ought to do immediately:

A. Declare a survival emergency carrying with it all the authority of a war emergency. Publicize the situation throughout the world as well as the information required to save ourselves.

B. The increasing acidity of precipitation must be stopped. That requires two things:

1. The first thing we must do is remineralize the world's soils. Since the soils are acidic now and will be more acidic by the time we get the job done, it would probably be best to use

a mix of about 1 part agricultural limestone, to 3 parts of a mixture of all the rocks such as in glacial gravel or most river gravels. Both should be ground to about 200 mesh for maximum availability of elements. There are substantial glacial deposits which can be used without grinding. Ten tons of gravel dust per acre with minimal organic matter will insure at least as good a crop as last year and require no additional expense for about 10 years. For a more detailed explanation see Chapter Two, "Food, Energy and Survival."

The jungles and forests must be mineralized to stop the deadly cycle of dying, burning and increasing acidity of precipitation. To do it rapidly, every aircraft capable of modification to carry wet rock dust and spreading it on the forests should be utilized.

Agricultural soils must be mineralized as well as tree plantations. Present U.S. crop yields are relatively high, probably because of three factors: there is a high availability of carbon dioxide for photosynthesis; on most of the grain-growing areas there has been plentiful rainfall; acidification of the soil dissolves some kinds of rocks, releasing their elements. This is the basis of chemical agriculture, and now the acid rains are increasing the action. Unfortunately, the acid is working on the last of the topsoil minerals, and as the minerals decrease in quantity, the soil becomes more and more acid. At some point the soil microorganisms which supply the protoplasm for all other living things on Earth are killed by the acidity and the soil becomes sterile. We have lost many millions of acres of crop land. By adding the natural balance of rock elements in a form to make them highly available, we can take advantage of the carbon dioxide and the rainfall to produce yields capable of supplying our food and energy needs.

2. The second thing which must be done is to minimize acidity of precipitation by controlling man-made fires of all kinds to burn at temperatures which will produce a minimum of nitrogen oxides since that is the acidic gas which, if not now, soon will be the dominant acid in the destruction of plant life.

In particular, internal combustion engines must be replaced by engines using a constant flame, such as steam engines. An alcohol-burning steam engine would eliminate virtually all pollutants, including the acidic oxides of sulphur which come from gasoline.

C. Loan guarantees must be provided for the rapid construction and purchase of all mechanical equipment required. At the same time there must be an end to the construction of all coal and nuclear facilities, tall smokestacks, armaments and any other junk inimical to our survival or unneccessary to it, so the funds will be available to do the things which we must do.

D. The entire domestic program should be placed under one expediting agency. The space agency is probably better equipped to do the job than any other. It should therefore be transferred to survival duty for the duration of the emergency.

These and other spartan measures must be taken if we are to effect our survival. Everybody is going to have to sacrifice until we have control of the situation. We don't have time for legal hassles. It must be done under emergency measures which pre-empt the civil law.

The bottom line is simply this. The hard evidence shows that world food supplies will largely be destroyed by the end of this decade. Only a massive effort on the part of all governments can possibly prevent our destruction. Since politicians have done nothing about soil remineralization in the last 10 years, there is no reason to think they will do anything now unless forced to act by their constituents.

3

Perspective

The Interglacial Soil Demineralization and Retrogressive Vegetational Succession

In researching this most fascinating subject, it was rather startling to discover so much information from so many scientists (including geologists, botanists, ecologists, pedologists, palynologists, climatologists, and others) which clearly confirms the foundation of John Hamaker's arguments. A broad representative look at this work is obviously called for.

It may seem incredible that up to now this work could have escaped becoming common knowledge, at least to workers in agriculture, forestry, geology, climatology and other such immediately-related fields. Apparently the many diverse pieces of the glacial-interglacial climate cycle "puzzle" had to be gradually discovered through various disciplines over decades, before at last enough pieces were evident to be joined in a coherent picture by a trained "ecological thinker"—John Hamaker in this case. Yet now everyone may see for themselves the truth in his synthesis. The looming question of "when does an individual, society, and world see enough to act intelligently?" awaits many answers.

A look at some more pieces then, starting with the work of one Johannes Iversen, and eventually returning to Genevieve Woillard and "her" 20-year interglacial-to-glacial transition period.

Dr. Johannes Iversen, State Geologist, Geological Survey of Denmark. In the preface to his last book, *The Development of Denmark's Nature Since the Last Glacial,* Iversen is praised as a brilliant and devoted scientist who mastered the subjects of Late-Glacial vegetation and Post-Glacial forest history. Using pollen analysis as a highly-refined instrument of botanical investigation, the preface to Iversen (1973) says, "He created a picture which was revolutionary in many ways and will stand unrivaled."

In his 1964 paper, "Retrogressive Vegetational Succession in the Post-Glacial," Iversen introduces this picture:

> At the end of each glacial epoch raw mineral soil, basic or neutral, covered the land left behind by the receding ice. Also in the adjacent periglacial regions soils were unleached and devoid of humus because of the removal of the upper layers by strong solifluction in the preceding stage.
>
> The early Post-Glacial succession is thus linked with a gradual soil maturation. (Iverson, 1964, p. 59)

Iversen explained that:

> Only successions that are irreversible under the prevailing climatic conditions, and which lead to ecosystems with permanently-reduced organic productivity, are regarded as true retrogressive successions. It should also be stressed that the concept of forest in this paper actually means the whole ecosystem, including the humus layer, in which the breakdown of the plant debris from the forest takes place. (p. 59)

Two types of retrogressive vegetational succession are next distinguished: one caused by local rise of the ground water table, the other "is connected with the leaching of the soil." This type, of course, "occurs more widely." (p. 59)

Iversen says that although the chemical-physical-biological aspects of the soil changes have been studied intensively by soil scientists, the actual undisturbed course of the retrogression—*and what point in the interglacial it begins*—are less well known.

Yet Iversen is here able to define this point as being, "When the yearly disintegration of the plant debris no longer keeps pace with the fresh supply from the living plants, and, consequently, a layer of mor (raw humus) is accumulated on top of the mineral soil." (p. 59)

Soil Deterioration Begins

Then five years later, in a paper styled "Retrogressive Development of a Forest Ecosystem Demonstrated by Pollen Diagrams from Fossil Mor," Iversen presents his discovery that this change from the "mull" humus (characterized by richness of available minerals, including bases—Kubiena, 1953, 1970) to the mor (acidifying humus) state is, "Marked by the accumulation of pollen grains which, due to the disappearance of earthworms, were no longer mixed into the mineral soil. The date of this change varied depending on soil conditions, the greatest age found so far is 6,300 C-14 (carbon-14) years B.P." (Iversen, 1969). Earlier (Iversen, 1960) he noted that such pollen must be laid down "at a time when soil deterioration had already produced very low pH values, otherwise the pollen grains would have disappeared as a result of bacterial activity." (p. 13)

Therefore we can see that from the 10,000 to 10,800 years B.P. (before present) date commonly accepted as the opening of the present interglacial , it took about 3,700 to 4,500 years for the *first* of the glacially-deposited raw mineral soils of basic or alkaline pH, to "mature" and then go into a gradual "irreversible" degradation. This process Iversen shows to be characterized by soil organism reductions and complete die-outs (the earth-worms, e.g.), and by a vegetation retrogression necessarily accompanying the soil degradation.

Sixty-three Centuries Later

What has happened to the Earth's soil(s) and forests in the 6,312 years since Iversen's oldest pollen samples were deposited? The answer comes in part by his description of the Denmark forest ecosystems which he labored in.

The Draved forest area is described as an extremely nutrient-poor, strongly acidic and swampy "moorland" of raised bogs which have trans-gressed over wide areas of former pine forests, then eventually overtook dying-out oak (Iversen, 1964, p. 60) and once-rich elm-oak-alder-pine forests (p. 69). Though the area receives only 750 mm (30 inches) of precipitation annually, the demineralized acidic soils, no longer hospitable to earthworms and microorganisms, form drainage-inhibiting hardpans and thick acid-humus layers. Again, this easily leads to death and swamping of the forests; as in Sweden, Germany, the British Isles, and elsewhere (p. 69).

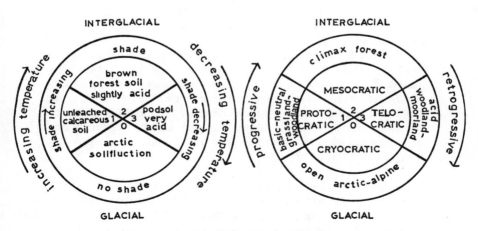

Fig. 1. Summary of the glacial/interglacial cycle (after IVERSEN 1958).

The soils *not yet swamped* have reached the "podzol" (or "podsol") stage of degeneration, podzolization being simply a form of demineralization. Vast areas of present or former forest lands in Eurasia (Vilenski, 1957), Western Europe (Kubiena, 1953, 1970), Canada (Legget, 1960), the United States (Marbut, 1935, 1928; USDA, 1975), etc., are considered podzolized.

This stage of extensively podzolized (demineralized) soils—the apparent pre-condition for a new glacial soil rejuvenation period—and the broad processes leading to it, are lucidly described by Iversen in *The Development of Denmark's Nature Since the Last Glacial.* Starting at the stage where temperate zone soils had developed the fertility to support vast deciduous and mixed forests, when the normal soil was mineral-rich mull, "the most favorable of all the soil types," Iversen depicts the changes:

> Mull changes in character as the millenia pass; the change is extremely slow in clay soil but faster in poor sandy soil. First the lime is leached out and the mull becomes acid. Moderately acid mull can also be very fertile, but if it becomes too acid the earthworms and the bacterial flora can no longer thrive; the soil begins to deteriorate. The rich mull changes to a poor mull. The larger earthworms, which constantly pull organic matter deep into the soil and deposit their casts on the surface, thus turning the earth over every few years, are the first to disappear. The smaller earthworms, which turn over a shallow layer, follow after them, and so only the smallest earthworms, which stay near the surface, are left. At about this stage, the bacteria which attack the pollen exines also seem to disappear, and pollen then accumulates together with humus on the soil surface. A critical threshold has thus been passed: mull has become mor...In pronounced mor the breakdown of organic matter is mainly carried out by fungi. (It may be noted here that soil scientists, botanists and foresters have found that most present-day forest trees and many other plants, in both temperate and tropical zones, receive their soil nutrients directly from the soil fungi, as in the well-known "mycorrhizal association," e.g. Marks and Kozlowski, 1973; Sanders et al, 1975).
>
> The mor layer causes the downwardly percolating water to become very acid, and thus the iron in the upper soil layers is dissolved and is re-precipitated lower down together with dissolved humus, forming a hardpan. This can be rock-hard and nearly impenetrable both for water and for plant roots, since the mineral particles are glued together by humus or by iron salts...The combination of mor, hardpan, and the intervening ash-colored leached sand, extremely poor in nutrients, makes up a podsol profile. (Iversen, 1973, p. 100-101)

An Important Consideration, and an Iversen Summary

The reader may now see that human land use practices over the past 10,000 years, and those of today, are characterized by the burning and cutting of forests; plowing, overgrazing, eroding, and continuously demineralizing crop and forest soils; and by the release of large quantities of toxic chemicals and fossil fuel carbon dioxide. The reader may then consider the likelihood of a sooner-or-later than average (10,000-12,000 years) end to the present interglacial. Yet we know now from Johannes Iversen (and others) that gradual soil de-vitalization is a *primary* ecological process of the interglacial periods, and in concluding his "Retrogressive Vegetational Succession in the Post-Glacial," he tells us, *and warns us,* that in former interglacial epochs: "The anthropogenic factor was negligible, and interglacial regional pollen diagrams demonstrate very clearly the increasing importance of soil degradation (Andersen 1963), until in the final stage the effect of the climatic factor becomes decisive." (Iversen, 1964, p. 69-70)

Svend Th. Andersen, Geological Survey of Denmark

Pollen deposit studies by Svend Th. Andersen of three past interglacial periods forcefully support the theses of John Hamaker and Johs. Iversen, as documented by three of Andersen's published papers. These papers are: "Interglacial Plant Successions in the Light of Environmental Changes," 1964; "Interglacial Vegetational Succession and Lake Development in Denmark," 1966; and "Interglacial Vegetation and Soil Development," 1969.

As did Iversen, Andersen clearly saw the broad picture, with interglacial stages representing, in his own words, "...stable intervals between the glacial stages of disturbance and chaos. The vegetation had a chance to develop until the new glacial released its destructive forces." (1969, p.90)

His studies demonstrate how "the interglacial successions of vegetation form uninterrupted sequences of forest stages," which he saw as "intriguing objects for reflections as to the causes of long-time vegetal changes." These vegetal changes, unlike the present interglacial, "are undisturbed by human influence." (1964, p. 359)

Andersen divided the interglacials into four broad phases (similar to Iversen's, Fig. 2) which he termed *protocratic, mesocratic, oligocratic,* and the final phase preceding the new glacial period—the *telocratic.*

At the start of the interglacials, open forest of *pioneer* species entered, which Andersen called the "quickly spreading trees and shrubs with unpretentious requirements to climate and soils." Birch, pine, poplar, juniper and willow were most important in Denmark.

In this most practical study, he notes: "This vegetation belonged to the fresh soil left by the glaciers, and as mentioned by Iversen (1958) this *protocratic* phase resembled the conditions in the early Postglacial strongly." (1969, p. 97) The rich mixed forest of mull vegetation had of course not yet developed, and the acid humus soils obviously had little role to play.

In the *mesocratic* phase, the soil had developed a high fertility, therefore, "the plants of rich soils reach maximum frequencies." This was a time when immense forests covered great portions of the Earth (Johnson, 1978; etc.), and the climate created by these typically immense trees (and the other factors) earned the name "Postglacial Climatic Optimum" (Lamb, 1977), which spanned the years from about 6,000 to 3,000 B.C. Lamb says these trees, such as oaks, were "reported to be often of remarkably large size, e.g. with trunks reaching a height of 27.5 meters before the first branch." (Lamb, 1977, p. 373) These are found preserved in now-degenerate treeless peat soils in England and elsewhere.

This phase is dominated by trees such as elm, oak, lime, hazel, ash, hornbeam, and alder, growing on stable mull soils which Iversen showed to eventually begin to retrogress. Andersen gives a description of the process similar to Iversen's, which in light of its immediate importance, is worthy of quoting here. In these mull soils, of roughly 6,000-3,000 B.C., "the leaching of the soil salts is to some extent counteracted by the mixing activity of the soil fauna and the ability of the prevailing trees and shrubs to extract bases from the deeper soil layers and contribute them to the upper layers during the decomposition of their litter. However, a slow removal of calcium carbonate will bring the soils into a less stable state, where the equilibrium may be more easily disturbed." (Andersen, 1966, p. 119)

This leaching of calcium carbonate (lime) is shown to be so significant to the topsoil ecology because, according to Andersen—"the leaching of soil minerals other than lime will be insignificant, until the calcium carbonate has been removed." (p. 121)

With this gradual leaching, "The mull forest could not maintain itself, and with the lapse of time, caused itself a depauperization and acidification of the upper soil layers, which extended so far that the dense forest receded and more open vegetation types expanded." (1969, p.99)

Andersen too (confirming Iversen), shows that the changeover from mineral-rich mull soils to acidifying mor soil conditions begins in the mesocratic, and with the gradual demineralization of formerly calcareous soils, growth of impenetrable hardpans and soil life die-outs follow. This creates shallow topsoils susceptible to drought or being easily swamped; and this infertile state leads to takeover by heathlands, peat bogs, and trees with ability to survive on acidic soils—spruce, pine, birch, poplar, etc. (p. 98) This condition becomes prevalent in Andersen's oligocratic phase, and is brought on, he says, "as a result of degeneration of the soils." (1966, p. 123) The increasing podsolization, characterized by increasing demineralization and acidity, continues up through the interglacial *telocratic* (end) phase.

Significantly, his pollen deposits reveal the conditions both in the oligocratic and the telocratic. The oligocratic shows clearly the "decrease of rich soil vegetation," indicating "a gradual expansion of leached and podsolized soils." *The final interglacial phase, the telocratic, is the time when the demineralized soils begin to be removed*: "The rigorous conditions at the end of the interglacial are reflected by an...increase in allochthonous mineral matter...no doubt due to increasing surficial erosion." (1966, p.121)

So, *where are we now*, after 10,000 plus years of this interglacial? Surprisingly, neither Iversen nor Andersen specifically raise the question. Andersen's articles, however, together with the information in virtually every textbook on soils, forestry, or ecology, leave no doubt that the present world civilization is (at least) deep into his *oligocratic* phase. His further strong evidence showing that the Scandinavian lakes and soils reflect a close parallel development from basic to acidic conditions (1966, p.117), and the fact that many thousands of lakes there and in the northeast U.S. and Canada are already acidified to lifelessness (with a final kick from acid rains), also confirms it. Rapidly accelerating worldwide erosion rates, exemplified by the U.S. where 1975 Soil Conservation Service (SCS) figures of 3 billion tons of topsoil lost per year (Brown, 1978) have jumped to 4 billion in 1978 (CEQ, 1978), and now, according to the Chief of the Soil Conservation Service, to *6.4 billion tons in 1981* (Berg, 1981). These facts, along with the increasingly "rigorous conditions" imposed by the weather since at least 1972, very strongly indicate that the *telocratic* end phase may indeed have begun.

Svend Th. Andersen just says: "Soil development was indeed an important factor in the Quaternary cycles."

The Picture Grows...More Obvious

The geological and ecological framework for the severely challenging picture presented by John D. Hamaker, and further clarified by the work of Iversen, Andersen, and earlier considerations, should now be intelligible to the reader. Over a dozen more books and articles, by as many researchers, have presented themselves as further proof of the regular cycles of the interglacial soil development-demineralization-glaciation (remineralization) sequence, suggesting an irrefutable status for the foundations of Hamaker's arguments.

In the interests of total readability for a wide and diverse audience, brief summaries of the above-mentioned books and articles have been omitted from this book. Included in the original manuscript, they are available as a supplement to those readers who require further documentation supporting Hamaker's thesis. Ask for "Supplementary Perspectives to The Survival of Civilization." Copies may be obtained from Hamaker-Weaver Publishers, P.O. Box 457, Potterville, Michigan, 48876, or from Hamaker-Weaver Publishers, P.O. Box 1961, Burlingame, California, 94010.

4
Introduction

"The Role of CO_2 in the Process of Glaciation," first published in April 1980, was written as a concise explanation of the glacial process which could be understood by the U.S. Congress, at a time when "the CO_2 problem" was just being recognized by some of its members, but not yet taken very seriously.

At one point, a member of Michigan Congressman Howard Wolpe's office (Keith Laughlin) informed John Hamaker that the paper would indeed be circulated to every member of Congress. Apparently it was never done. "Congressional Clearinghouse on the Future" Director Anne Cheatham stated in her letter of response, March, 1980—"Mr. Laughlin and I both agree that if Mr. Hamaker is right we had all better do something soon...We will be back in touch with you as the situation develops." No evidence of an effort to prove John Hamaker's thesis true or false has been forthcoming.

"The Role of CO_2 in the Process of Glaciation" appeared in *Acres, USA* in September, 1980. Its title refers to the relationship that has been virtually never considered by the hundreds of researchers of glaciation, starting with the first "Great Ice Age" theory of Louis Agassiz in 1837 (Imbrie and Imbrie, 1979).

Systematic measurements of atmospheric CO_2 began only as late as 1958 (Calder, 1975). Most climatologists, one may observe, seem fond of repeating the extremely dangerous oversimplification of CO_2's "greenhouse effect." "We are going to warm up" is the general message reaching the media and public from the climatologists.

The crux of this problem was perhaps stated best by John Hamaker in an earlier article ("Life or Death—Yours," 1976), in reference to two well-known, outspoken climatologists, when he said, "Of course, neither of these gentlemen know about the role of life in and on the soil in demineralizing it in a period of 10,000 to 15,000 years, depending on the amount of ground rock supplied by the last glacial advance. Nor do they know and understand the Earth's tectonic system and its role in determining the weather."

The first six chapters of this book offer that fundamental understanding.

4

The Role of CO2 in the Process of Glaciation

Facts:

Glaciation occurs whenever the supply of soil minerals ground from rocks by the last glaciation is used up. This exhaustion of soil minerals by the life in and on the soil initiates the whole chain of events which results in restocking the soil with minerals and a new proliferation of life.

It is a function of plant life to remove all excess CO_2 (carbon dioxide) from the atmosphere. It normally does this simply by growing faster in response to an increase in CO_2. *It can no longer do so.* Plant life gets its cell protoplasm from the soil microorganisms. The microorganisms produce the protoplasm by taking elements from the mixture of stone in the soil, and combining them with the carbon in some form of plant or soil organism residue to make the organic compounds. When the elements are no longer available in the soil (which is the case at present), the microorganisms die of famine, and the plant life also starves to death for lack of protoplasm.

The dead plant life is set on fire by lightning; the carbon in the plant life goes into the atmosphere as CO_2. The CO_2 traps the sun's heat radiating from the earth and radiates it back, thus increasing the surface temperature. The CO_2 has no heating effect at the poles in the winter when it is dark 24 hours a day. It has maximum effect in the equatorial region at the latitudes where the sun's rays are most intense.

When air gets hotter, its atmospheric pressure decreases. It is then easier for the cold air moving down over a cold land mass to displace the warm equatorial air and force it to move poleward over the warm ocean to replace the cold air moving toward the equator. This is the normal air circulation pattern impressed on the west winds. The temperature differential is minimal in summer and at a maximum in winter. During glaciation, when there is an extensive ice field, there is no summer because the refrigerated air from the ice field maintains the temperature differential required to carry the clouds to the northern latitude. Thus there can be unusually large masses of hot air in the equatorial latitudes and unusually large masses of cold air in the polar latitudes.

Glaciation, or for that matter anything else on this earth, can not take place without an expenditure of energy. By the time the ice sheet has built up between the temperate zones and the poles, the ocean level will have dropped some 100 feet or more, depending on how much CO_2 is in the atmosphere to provide the heat of vaporization. Ocean-level measurements of the water transferred to the land mass are not accurate, because land elevation varies with the ice load and with the hydraulic pressure under the land mass. Without a build-up in CO_2 and hence temperature, glaciation can not happen.

Glaciation is only a little more complicated than your refrigerator. Energy is put into the system to remove the heat from one batch of air and dump it into another. In the case of glaciation, the dump is the polar regions, which have an excess of cooling capacity. The refrigerated air flows toward the equator to gradually eliminate the tropical zones.

The average temperature at the start of a glacial period must be higher than the interglacial temperature, and must remain higher until the cooling effect of the ice sheet starts bringing it down. Unfortunately, that will not help agriculture, because the northern part of the temperate zone will experience summer freezes and frosts and the southern temperate zone will have excessive heat and drought. We can expect violent weather everywhere.

When an ice field builds up to about 50 feet thick, the pressure causes the ice on the bottom of a glacier to melt and in this condition the glaciers "flow." As they flow, they grind all the rocks they flow over. The ground rock moves with the melt water from high elevations to lower elevations. As the glacial debris clogs all the rivers, the water spreads out over the land filling the low areas with glacial till.

The water then moves on from one low area to another, thus leveling the entire land surface with fresh glacial till.

The temperature difference between the glaciated area and the equatorial zone induces violent winds which ultimately carry the finer particles of ground material all the way to the tropical zones. Luxuriant temperate-zone forests then begin the long task of withdrawing the carbon dioxide from the atmosphere. The build-up of ice stops as the CO_2 decreases in the atmosphere. The melting of the ice sheets reduces the excessive volcanism from the tectonic system. The temperate-zone vegetation follows the melting glaciers toward the poles, and tropical forests return to the tropical zones.

It is cloud cover which supplies the moisture for glaciation and protects the glaciated area from melting too much in the summer time. A necessary condition for glaciation is that snowfall shall exceed snow melt, plus pressure melt, by a sufficient amount to build up 100 feet or more of ocean water as ice on the land area during a total of 90,000 years of glacial advances that alternate with limited glacial retreats. The 1980 late winter floods in Hawaii and the unprecedented 11 inches of rain in a week in Southern California, the "worst in history" flood in Louisiana, the freeze in Florida, and the 120-mph winds at Anchorage, Alaska are a forecast of things to come. The waves of clouds now coming in off the Pacific on an almost daily schedule will give way to solid masses of clouds when all the forests have burned.

Glaciation usually occurs at a time when the earth's tectonic system has fired up volcanic activity by feeding ocean floor into the continental heaters, which are located primarily in the Pacific "ring of fire." Volcanic action releases large amounts of liquified gases trapped in the molten rock. CO_2 and sulphur dioxide (SO_2) are the principal gases released, and both cause the "greenhouse effect." The result is our present "hundred-year cold cycle." These cycles vary in their time interval, the intervals being determined by the pressure in the tectonic system. To the volcanic gases are added CO_2 from the decaying and burning mineral-starved vegetation. Together, they initiate the change from interglacial to glacial climate.

When the ice sheet is formed, the weight of ice forces the earth to sink lower in elevation. The more liquid part of the semi-solid, partially molten rock on which the crust of the earth moves is forced back into the tectonic circulatory system and is forced out from under the crust in volcanic actions. One of the actions is along the mid-ocean ridges where the increased weight of exuded rock increases the pressure in the entire system. Volcanism in a glacial period is several times that of an interglacial period. The dust exerts a cooling effect by radiating back into space some of the sun's rays. It provides dust particles for inducing precipitation. It assists in the job of remineralizing the earth's surface. The increased amount of CO_2 released by the increased volcanic action intensifies the glaciation. When the ice melts, the pressure drops rapidly in the tectonic system, volcanism decreases, and the glacial system collapses back into the interglacial climate conditions.

The acidic gases from volcanism and burning forests quench the life on earth by leaching the few remaining basic elements into the subsoil. Thus the change from interglacial to glacial conditions occurs in about 20 years as reported in *Nature* by G. Woillard in 1979. Man's contribution of CO_2 from fossil fuels, acidic gases from various sources, and forest destruction has probably moved the present glacial process forward in time by perhaps 500 years. It will probably shorten the 20-year change period.

That's essentially all there is to the glacial process—all but the consequences to mankind. *All of the requirements for glaciation are in place and accelerating in intensity at a very fast pace.* The percentage of CO_2 increase is rising rapidly, and the pH of precipitation is rapidly moving toward intolerable acidity. Within a very few years the 1979 crop losses in Russia will be intensified and spread throughout the temperate zone. Most of the world's population will be starving to death. Summer frosts and freezes, short growing seasons, drought and violent storms, plus rapidly diminishing soil minerals and increasing rain acidity will destroy the world's grain crops.

Fallacies:

It may be that the *average* temperature of the atmosphere is getting warmer. However, it is totally false to assume that the polar ice will melt and that temperate zone crops will have to be moved toward the poles. The time scale that has been allowed by the "experts" (on whom government is relying for reacting to the falsely-assumed weather change) is much longer than we actually have because the first stage of glaciation is now occurring—the killing of the plant life which includes our crops. We must react immediately or prepare to die.

The idea that we can keep on using fossil fuels is totally false. On the 25th of June, 1979, a cold wave came out of Canada and killed frost-sensitive vegetables from Minnesota to Michigan. In a small area of each state the temperature dropped low enough to destroy all crops. This is not supposed to happen in late June but it did. A few degrees colder and all crops would have been wiped out. The principal cause of the problem is CO$_2$ in the atmosphere. By June of 1979 the percent of increase of CO$_2$ over an assumed normal level of 290 ppm was about 15 percent. In 1985 it will be about 18 percent. It is a certainty that crop losses will be extensive by 1985. By 1990 the percent of increase in CO$_2$ in the atmosphere will be about 22 percent (50 percent more than it is now). The world's crops are already under heavy pressure from adverse weather conditions. Yet we go on bringing carbon out of the ground and putting it into the atmosphere.

It is a fallacy to think that conservation of anything will prevent nature from going ahead with a process which is well on its way. Conservation of forests is impossible when the trees are dying because the soil will no longer support the life process. You can not conserve crop soils which have been virtually stripped of some of the available elements. *It is too late for conserving; we must rebuild.*

It is a fallacy to think that any form of solar energy which does not result in withdrawing CO$_2$ from the atmosphere and storing it in biomass or in the soils will have any effect whatsoever on the need to save us from starvation.

Summary:

The Congress has been evaluating the CO$_2$ problem on the basis of a consensus reached by specialists. These people freely admit that they do not know what causes glaciation. Yet they say that the average temperature must drop several degrees C. before we can have glaciation simply because they have evidence that it does get much colder during glacial periods. They ignore the fact that historically glaciation has been alternating with interglacial periods on a roughly 100,000 year cycle and the fact that glaciation is due. Do they think that the fact that crop soils of the world are turning to deserts at the same time that the weather is throwing one natural catastrophe after another at us is just coincidence? Actually, they have not even thought about the soil and its relation to glaciation, nor do they understand the role of the tectonic system in the glacial process.

The people charged with the responsibility for the CO_2 problem are simply not trained to solve problems. They are trained to be observers and they have done a creditable job of that. But the job of making a rational synthesis of the facts as a basis for Congressional action ought to have been assigned to engineers and physicists, both of whom have been trained to work with the facts and laws of nature. The fault lies at the higher levels of education, which have neglected the necessity for interdisciplinary education and action in favor of specialization.

That mistake, if not corrected immediately, will become, and may already have become, a fatal mistake for all of us.

If an effort is made to save humanity, Congress is going to have to grant to some existing technical group, such as the National Aeronautics and Space Administration, the absolute authority to press into service all elements of the nation which are capable of contributing to the soil remineralization effort. The basic nature of soil fertility and how to obtain it quickly have been detailed in my paper, "Food, Energy, and Survival." These principles must be applied and applied quickly. For example, every plant generating electricity that burns fossil fuels should be required to establish, in the summer of 1980, wood plantations of sufficient size on remineralized soil to replace fossil fuels at a time not later than 1984. They should further be required to use any surplus waste heat in extensive greenhouses so that local requirements for vegetables can be met without expending the fuel to bring them from Florida, the Rio Grande Valley, Mexico, or California. Air travel should be cut to necessity use only. Ninety percent of the planes should be stripped of weight and refitted for forest remineralization.

All of the nations must make a similar effort.

Make no mistake. We must revolutionize what we do and the way we do it. And we will do it NOW or we will die. We can not do it while there is so much confusion about the CO_2 problem and its effect. The Congress must hammer out the facts and lead the whole world in what must be the greatest human effort ever undertaken. If we don't remineralize the soil, nature will and her first act will be to eliminate almost all of the life on Earth.

Footnote:

It is possible to very quickly release enough CO$_2$ into the atmosphere to turn the world into a steaming jungle planet with the tropical zone replacing the subarctic and that part of the temperate zone which is not under water. If sufficient amounts of water are evaporated and moved toward the poles fast enough so the clouds can retain enough heat to fall as rain at the poles, the polar ice sheet can be washed into the sea. The tropical condition would remain for a very long time because there is very little loss of either carbon or minerals when a jungle floor has built up a deep layer of decaying vegetation. Mineral loss can be largely made up by the sea solids in the rain. These conditions can occur only as a result of a catastrophic event in the tectonic system. The result is a submergence of a substantial part of the land mass (thus limiting vegetative growth) and minimal tectonic activity.

Such a condition probably occurred after a mid-ocean ridge (part of which is now California, Oregon, and Washington) was overrun by the westward moving continent. At the time, the Gulf of California was a mountain range and part of the Sierra Nevada mountains, with a continental heater under them. The high-pressure, high-temperature melt in the heater broke through into the ridge and the thin, newly formed crust could not stand the pressure. It blew out and molten rock met ocean water in a continuous explosion. It did not stop until the liquid melt had run out from under the plateau now called the Great Basin, creating such things as the crustal crack called the Grand Canyon on the southeast, and the sinkhole called Lake Tahoe under the sheared-off east wall of the Sierras.

The amount of CO$_2$ and other gases released from so much molten rock could turn the world much warmer and give rise to the huge leaf-eating mammoths and the large carnivores which were common in the Pliocene epoch. The rock dust from such an explosion would mineralize the whole earth.

In 1972 the Atomic Energy Commission tested a 5-megaton bomb a mile below sea level on the Aleutian island of Amchitka. The Aleutian chain is a continental heater and the Bering Sea floor is slowly being raised to plateau status. The underground bomb test had the ingredients for a total change in the world's weather. Fortunately a group of senators headed by Sen. Phillip Hart persuaded the AEC to stop the testing.

It is conceivable that if all the fossil fuel supplies in the crust of the earth could be burned (or some lesser amount), we could produce a warmer world. It can't happen, of course, because when there is sufficient CO_2 in the atmosphere, the temperate zone vegetation will be destroyed and the consumers of fossil fuels, too.

The talk about how long it will take to double the normal level of CO_2 and what the average temperature will then be is pure nonsense. We will be dead and gone before the increase in CO_2 reaches 30 percent—about 1995. Our ability to extract fossil fuels will be lost by 1990.

4

Perspective

In light of Hamaker's essentially positive message, "We must rebuild," let's examine some more key parts of this whole amazing picture as others have studied and reported on them.

At least four areas immediately present themselves for further overview: CO_2 build-up, weather changes, forest fires, and acid rain and snow. The first three will be looked at here, while the urgent threat and reality of acidic precipitation, as well as insect/disease destruction of the forests, will be considered in Chapter 5.

CO_2 Build-up

David P. Adam of the U.S. Geological Survey, a long-time student of glacial periods, has emphasized the point that to understand what causes them, one must solve the "energy problem" they present (Adam, 1976). In his *Quaternary Research* paper, "Ice Ages and the Thermal Equilibrium of the Earth (II)," Adam clearly shows that an essential requirement to begin and sustain a glacial period is an increased transfer of (excess) energy towards the glaciated regions, and that energy is in the form of moisture. This is, of course, precipitated largely as snow, thus forming the initial perennial snowfields and subsequent ice sheets. He states that some increased energy source must therefore be invoked to sustain these vast energy transfers, yet he does not consider in his paper the fact of excessive CO_2's solar heat-trapping effect as the possible "booster" for providing this increase of effective energy, which, as Adam points out, is "required to fuel a continental glaciation." (Adam, 1976)

In a personal communication to this writer (1981), David Adam agreed that Hamaker's CO_2 theory could indeed fulfill the requirements of providing the glacial energy fuel. Yet, surprisingly, he knew of no one in the history of modern Quaternary research who had postulated a CO_2-glaciation relationship, perhaps due to the relative state of infancy of modern CO_2/climate studies. David said there was one well-respected climatologist who *had* presented an explanation of the basic glacial process very similar to John Hamaker's—Sir George Simpson of Britain.

Simpson, as explained by Willett (in his chapter on "Atmospheric Circulation" in *Climatic Change*, 1953), was the first to point out the impossibility of accounting for the glacial pattern of circulation and climate by a general *decrease* of solar heating. This is because a decrease must lower the mean temperature of the Earth's surface, especially in the tropics, decrease the equator-to-pole temperature gradient, and distinctly lower the moisture content of the atmosphere. Simpson (1934, 1957) realized that it is obviously paradoxical to expect fulfillment of certain fundamental requirements for glaciation—*intensified* equator-to-pole temperature gradients, *stepped-up* atmospheric circulation, and *increase* of poleward heat and moisture transfer—with a model of declining surface temperature, especially in the tropical regions.

So Simpson postulated a hypothesis of a "variable sun" which must at times send more solar energy to the Earth to cause extra surface heating that would be greater at the equator than at the poles due to the shape of the Earth. This, Simpson said, would increase cloudiness, storminess, and precipitation in higher latitudes; while the cloud cover causes overcast skies and cool temperature in summer, snow and glacier build-up in other seasons, with strong winds and violent storms common the year round. The clouds and snow would greatly increase global albedo and generate huge amounts of cold air to plunge equatorward. The glacial period would be well underway.

Since no substantial evidence of a variable sun has come forth to lend support to Simpson's heat-increase model of glaciation, his entire well-reasoned hypothesis has never been fully accepted, and parts of it required rejection as the newer knowledge of the 100,000 year glacial cycle was made clear. The fundamental principles are still considered sound, however, and nearly every author on climatology recalls Simpson's major contributions to understanding the "mystery" of glaciation (e.g., Willett, 1953; Wexler, 1953; Ponte, 1976; Lamb, 1977).

John Hamaker, while unaware of Sir George Simpson's theory, was apparently the first to correlate the basic heating and circulation principles operating at glacial inititation with the soon-to-be-infamous *differential* "greenhouse effect" of CO_2.

Other recent warnings on this differential heating effect have come from Lester Machta, head of the National Oceanic and Atmospheric Administration (NOAA) Air Resources Labs, who said (in Green, 1977) that the CO_2 could indeed cause the massive cooling cloud coverage; and from Justus (1978) of the Congressional Research Service, who stated, "If the Earth's temperature rises, the water vapor content of the atmosphere is likely to rise. A rise in water vapor would quite likely increase the fraction of the globe covered by clouds. Such an increase could cause the amount of primary solar radiation absorbed by the Earth to fall." Justus goes on to conclude that "some combination" of increased temperature and cloud cover will "balance" the heat absorption effects of excessive CO_2.

If these climatological principles and relationships, along with the broad ecological picture painted by Hamaker (and confirmed by many studies mentioned earlier) can be proven to be fundamentally incorrect, some one should obviously do so right away.

Are we now experiencing excessive CO_2-induced differential heating that causes increased cloud production, precipitation, storminess, wind speeds, etc.? Probably any reader over 15 years of age can recognize not all is well "weatherwise." A representative look at the increasing weather violence and destruction will follow shortly. First, some additional notations of immediate relevance to the CO_2-glacial relationship, and how some people are responding, *and not responding,* to our "invisible crisis."

** In a 1977 paper, John Hamaker asked the question: "How rapidly is CO_2 increasing in our atmosphere? In 1977, a National Academy of Sciences panel on energy and climate provided a very frightening statistic arrived at by Charles Keeling (*Science* 9/2/77): Keeling said that there had been a 13 percent rise since the industrial revolution began. The alarming thing is that 5 percent of this 13 percent had occurred since 1962." (That same *Science* article discussed the oversimplified computer models of CO_2's "general warming" effect, and stated that there are some scientists who "privately suggest" that because of "complex feedback phenomena," global cooling could result.)

** James Peterson of NOAA says that between 1958 and 1968, the annual CO_2 increase amounted to .7 ppm (*Environment*, 1979). Between 1970 and 1975, the annual increase went to .8 ppm (*Weatherwise*, 10/77). Between 1977 and 1978, it was up to about 1.5 ppm (*Environment*, 1979). Now, John Gribbin (*New Scientist*, 4/9/81), noting the intensification of worldwide forest destruction and fossil fuel combustion, reports that the present annual increase has jumped to *2 to 4 ppm* , and "is increasing rapidly today." It is now clear that Hamaker's CO_2 curve projection may prove quite conservative.

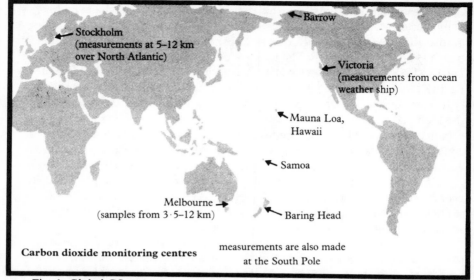

Fig. 1. Global CO$_2$ measurement stations [Commonwealth Scientific and Industrial Research Organization (CSIRO)1976]

**   A U.S. Department of Energy study released in April, 1979 stated: "It is the sense of the scientific community that carbon dioxide is potentially the most important environmental issue facing mankind." (*Baltimore Sun*, 1/13/80)

**   In July, 1979, four scientists submitted a report to the President's Council on Environmental Quality entitled "The Carbon Dioxide Problem: Implications for Policy in the Management of Energy and Other Resources." The scientists state conservatively that:

> The CO$_2$ problem is one of the most important contemporary environmental problems, is a direct product of industrialization, threatens the stability of climates worldwide and therefore the stability of all nations, and can be controlled. Steps toward control are necessary now.
>
> The potential disruptions are sufficiently great to warrant the incorporation of the CO$_2$ problem into all considerations of policy in the development of energy.

We may observe that as of July, 1981, no such incorporation has taken place. The scientists—Woodwell, Revelle, Keeling, MacDonald—go on to stress the great need for at least a minimum ecology restoration program, as stated thus:

It seems elementary that we have reached a point worldwide where the CO_2 problem alone dictates a need to balance the harvest and other transformations of forest with some other storage of carbon. The regrowth of forests is the obvious solution: total respiration, including fires, should be less than or equal to, but not more than, total photosynthesis on a regional and worldwide basis. There are many additional advantages in such a program, quite apart from the advantages gleaned from wise management of the CO_2 problem.

That no such minimum program has seriously begun, nor has even been recognized as "elementary" by the vast majority of the world's people, including political representatives, does not speak well for humanity's future. From many sources comes a similar message: to continue any longer as blind consumers of life, without learning to be visionary restorers of life, will likely insure an end to both opportunities—sooner than most of us would like to look at. Yet to fully look, in search of what is true, must surely be the first step.

Some additional notes on the "greenhouse effect" are of importance.

Recent investigations have established that other man-made pollutant trace gases may increase the "greenhouse effect" *by another 50 percent* (Flohn, 1979; Kellogg and Schware, 1981). These gases come primarily from burning vegetation (Crutzen et al., 1979), release of industrial halocarbons (freons) (Flohn, 1979), and the denitrification of nitrogen fertilizers in the soil (J. Williams, 1978).

Two books on CO_2 and climate have recently been published. *The Greenhouse Effect*, by meteorologist Harold Bernard, issues a strong warning that the heating effects alone will likely be devastating to humanity due to increasing climatic stress; agriculture in particular will suffer greatly. Bernard cites a coming agenda of increasing destructiveness characterized by tornadoes, hurricanes, floods, searing "dust bowl" type droughts, water depletion, and massive forest fires *if* we continue on the fossil fuel route. He presents a whole "bank" of arguments against doing so. He says that "solar energy" and "conservation" look like the ways to go. Yet, incredibly, in regard to the solar energy collectors (and CO_2 consumers) known as plants and trees (biomass), he suggests that the 1 percent of the energy coming from biomass today (U.S.) could maybe reach 6 percent by year 2000.

As for withdrawing CO_2 from the atmosphere and storing it in soils and trees, Bernard chooses to ignore ecological realities by implying that the natural process is "really nonsense" because, he says: "One can imagine the number of trees required."

Harold Bernard deserves thanks for his warnings on the likely destruction to come from increasing climatic stress, and for his chapter, "We Can't

Put Weather In A Test Tube," which says the scientists studying the CO_2 threat to date may be wrong because of incorrent assumptions, inaccurate modeling techniques, and of their *ignoring of important processes through lack of knowledge*. It is clear that the interglacial soil demineralization is one such process they have ignored. The knowledge is now freely available.

Climate Change and Society: Consequences of Increasing Atmospheric Carbon Dioxide was released in early 1981 "under the auspices of the Aspen Institute for Humanistic Studies, and supported by a contract with the U.S. Department of Energy," according to the first introductory page. Later, in the forward, it is explained that the DOE became the book's "principal sponsor" and that "additional support" has come from the Weyerhaeuser Foundation, Volkswagen Foundation, and Mitre Corporation, among others.

This book is mentioned here because it presents such a good example of the growing attitude of some who wield influential powers, that *whatever* the effects of CO_2 pollution and Earth destruction are, "we" will accept them and try to "mitigate them" (in the sense of "to make less severe.") This attitude seems little concerned to perceive causes, to restore ecological balance, or to build a future for today's children.

The book's 178 pages devote 2 pages to considering how the Earth's living plants might come into the picture, and one paragraph to "protecting" the soil because "entire civilizations" declined due to past soil abuse. The following *ideas* concerning biomass solar energy and reforestation are given in their discussion of how to control CO_2 buildup.

**   According to one scientist, an increase of only one percent of Earth's plant life could absorb an equivalent of the annual fossil fuel CO_2 release, but if we keep burning an extra 4 percent of the fossils for 17 more years (an implied necessity), we will then have to increase biomass by 2 percent, "probably an unreasonable level." (p. 112)

**   Once the biomass is grown, we'd need to find "disposal methods" in order to keep that carbon from going back to the air. [It seems the authors do not appreciate the natural system for wood and soil humus/biomass storage of carbon; forests contain about 1.5 times (Whittaker and Likens, 1975) and soil humus about 4 times (Stuiver, 1978) the total of atmospheric carbon. Nor do the authors appreciate the potential of ground rock dust to vastly increase old and new forest growth and humus storage.]

**   We might try spreading nitrogen and phosphorous on the ocean to grow algae to withdraw CO_2; the carbon would eventually reach the ocean floor for storage there. (Admittedly "unlikely" as an effective scheme).

**   Or we could try using the nitrogen and phosphorous for growing trees instead; however, "a great number of trees would be involved," *and* "significant environmental problems" could result from programs to plant all those trees. This is because part of the land that could grow trees is already being used for other things, and much more *is in the process of being deforested*—for lumber, grazing land, and agriculture [such as Volkswagen Foundation's former virgin forest land of about 300,000 acres in Brazil, now used for an expanding cattle export operation involving deforestation at an average 13,000 acres each year (Grainger, 1980); and Weyerhaeuser Corporation's 6,000 square kilometers of timber concession in the fragile rainforests of Indonesia (Myers, 1979)]. Yet if we *really* want to rely on biomass as a CO_2 sink, we'll need to find land *somewhere* of sufficient size which can be "successfully planted." (p. 112). However, that problem of *disposing* of so much carbon would still remain.

**   Biomass can, of course, be converted to various fuels, but this requires an energy investment; and since there would be *so much* biomass available for fuel conversion from massive reforestation programs, the energy used in the conversion would likely require "enormous resources" and thus might "exacerbate" the CO_2 problem (p.113). The new biomass would also require considerable expansion of transportation facilities to handle it as it comes in "complex and heavier forms" than the coal, oil, and gas now being extracted from the Earth's crust.

**   Finally, the "ecological implications" of reforesting the Earth must not be overlooked. "Additional climatic consequences" could result from "changed vegetation patterns," which could absorb more solar radiation (unlike deserts and snow which reflect it), thus warming the Earth rather than producing "the intended cooling effect."

Having not too subtly tried to write off biomass energy and the Earth's terrestrial carbon storage system as unworthy of serious consideration, the book moves on to the next section, "Mitigating the Effects." We may move on at this point.

Weather/Climate Changes

Hamaker estimates that the beginning of a likely 20-year changeover period from interglacial to glacial conditions was about 1975.

If this estimate is accurate, then tremendous weather changes should have begun by that time, signified by growing intensification of all storm effects, including unusually heavy rains and snows, record cold and heat, drought, hail, tornadoes, etc.—all *symptomatic* of increasing temperature and pressure differentials, greater evaporation of moisture, and an overall speeding up of global atmospheric circulation.

1972 is generally seen as the approximate year when the world's weather became obviously "abnormal." Even in 1970 the droughts which had brought starvation to perhaps 400,000 people in Africa's Sahel region were occuring (Ponte, 1976). Numerous books, such as Calder's *The Weather Machine* (1975), Ponte's *The Cooling* (1976), Gribbin's *Forecasts,*

Famines, and Freezes (1977), and Roberts and Landsford's *The Climate Mandate* (1979) and others summarize much of the increasing weather destructiveness during the 1970's.

These many extreme events of the early and mid-1970's are too well-known to need repeating here. This weather report will primarily focus on *what has actually been occurring* since the late 1970's up to now (July, 1981), and to note, where it is not obvious, how these weather *effects* and trends may directly relate to an understanding of where we actually are in terms of this interglacial-to-glacial cycle.

The main sources of the following reports are: the NOAA/USDA publication *Weekly Weather and Crop Bulletin*; NOAA's *Storm Data*; NOAA's weekly "Assessment of World Weather Events"; *Weatherwise* magazine and others; and assorted U.S. newspaper accounts via AP and UPI, primarily.

The "Weatherwise" Annual Summary, 1979 and 1980

"The Weather of 1979" issue (2/80) reveals the following seasonal events:

In the U.S., after the exceptionally severe winters of '76-'77 and '77-'78, a third consecutive year of severe winter weather struck, an unparalleled occurence in modern times. A great number of records were broken; nearly every state recorded below-normal temperatures. Winter was colder and stormier than usual over middle latitudes, causing heavier than normal precipitation to fall, mostly as snow. One of the coldest Decembers on record (in 1978) over much of the Northwest, Rocky Mountains, and northern Great Plains; and one of the snowiest on record from the northern Rockies to the Great Lakes, led into a record cold January for dozens of cities in the Northwest, Rockies, Great Plains, and Mississippi Valley. Parts of the Midwest had a third consecutive January of record or near-record cold. Average temperatures were 16-19 degrees F. below normal in areas of Kansas, Nebraska, Wyoming and Montana. Precipitation was heavier than normal over most of the U.S. and again fell largely as snow, with record rains elsewhere. Some cities reported the snowiest January ever.

February extended the cold air flow patterns, bringing record cold temperatures to cities all the way to the Atlantic coast, and the entire month was ranked as one of the coldest Februarys ever recorded. Again, heavy precipitation this month, and record snows in the Atlantic States.

The summer of 1979 saw greater than normal precipitation over most of the U.S., though with serious drought affecting the Northwest and northern Rockies where extensive forest fires were finally relieved by August rains. Extensive cloudiness and heavy rains covered much of the U.S. east of the Rockies. Higher than normal temperatures in the West contrasted with a cool East and South, which persisted into the first half of July. The colder than normal polar air masses brought the coldest June on record to parts of the Carolinas.

Fall, 1979 brought both record early season cold and snow, and record late season warmth to parts of the Northeast and Atlantic States. Hurricanes David and Frederick hit the U.S. mainland, while many areas in the upper Midwest and Great Lakes had their driest September on record. In October, abnormally rapid middle-latitude westerly air flows produced very mobile storm systems, and unexpectedly fast weather changes resulted. 103 degrees on October 1st and 99 degrees on the 12th in Texas were all time record highs, while a record early snowstorm hit New England and the Appalachians on October 10th, heavily damaging deciduous trees in full leaf.

1979 flood and flash flood destruction was second only to those of 1972 in monetary losses ($4 billion compared to $4.4 billion) as the worst in history, killing over 100 people. The worst of these included: Hawaii's "great rainstorm" of February which broke every rainfall record there; Illinois' March floods when every river in the state flooded at nearly the same time; Texas' 6 days of heavy rains causing half a billion dollar losses in April; continuing flooding in Illinois which finally ended on May 28th after 13 weeks; a fourth consecutive month of killer floods in Texas by June followed by the record flooding rains of early July which were commonly 20 inches, including 45 inches near Alvin, breaking the all-time U.S. mainland record. September brought Texas its seventh consecutive month of severe flooding as 21 inches fell in Brazoris County, and Hawaii had heavy property and crop losses when another 15 inches fell in November.

A crucial question stands prominent—how much cloud cover and excessive precipitation is now occurring in the high and middle-high latitudes where the ice sheets of the glacial period begin formation (John, 1980; Calder, 1975, et al.)? Specific data on this question has proven elusive, yet if the unusually deep and severe penetration of cold air and snow into the temperate zones over the past five winters is an indication of increased high latitude cloud cover, snowfall, and cold production, then this would be perhaps the strongest and best evidence available.

One article in this *The Weather of 1979* issue, "A Record Cold Month in North America", reviewed some of the numerous record cold temperatures in the winter of '78-'79, and noted that none were more significant than those recorded in the Northwest Territory of Canada. At Eureka (NWT), the February mean daily temperature was -47.9 degrees C. (-54 degrees F.), the lowest mean temperature ever recorded in North America for any month in history. For 17 straight days the mercury failed to exceed -45 degrees C. Several stations within the Arctic Circle also reported record February cold; at least four experienced all-time low mean temperatures, and at least nine stations north of 60 degrees N reported their coldest February ever.

It was further noted that the persistence of the cold day and night was an "astonishing feature" of it, and that the lowest reading of -55.3 degrees C. was the all-time extreme low, -1.4 degrees C. colder than the previous record set in 1972. Finally, the authors note with much interest that the five coldest months on record, during 33 years of observations, have occurred *since 1972*. That does indeed seem a highly significant year.

Tornado statistics for 1979 revealed an increase of 59 over 1978, continuing a consistently upward frequency trend of many years. And in 1980, tornadoes increased in the U.S. once again—up from 847 to 866, and 88 more than 1978. The "normal" is given as 673, an out-of-date figure based on past averages. The clashes of heat and cold which produce thunderstorms and tornadoes are clearly increasing in frequency.

Note: the remainder of this lengthy section on weather has been put in the "Supplemental Perspectives to Chapters Three, Four and Five" mentioned at the end of the Perspective to Chapter Three. For copies of the supplement, write to: Hamaker–Weaver Publishers, Route 1, Box 158, Seymour, Missouri 65746, or to Hamaker–Weaver Publishers, P.O. Box 1961, Burlingame, California, 94010

It was mentioned earlier that this section would conclude with some additional evidence throwing further light on John Hamaker's urgent thesis. In short, this supporting data strongly confirms the obvious—that there is no longer any shortage of evidence needed for the initiation of intelligent worldwide cooperative action.

**   The *Monthly Weather Review* of March, 1980, carried an article by W.S. Harley—"The Significance of Climatic Change in the Northern Hemisphere 1949-1978." The lengthy article is summarized in its abstract: "No evidence of climatic warming is found."

**   The National Geographic article of November, 1976 entitled, "What's Happening To Our Climate" quotes Dr. J. Murray Mitchell of NOAA as saying that a distinct drop in average global temperature has ocurred since 1940, about .5 degrees F., with a greater drop in high northern latitudes. This is precisely the opposite of what most climatologists, predicting "global warming" from the CO_2 build-up, have anticipated.

**   S.A. Bowling of the University of Alaska's Geophysical Institute contributed "Possible Significance of Recent Weather and Circulation Anomalies in Northeastern Canada for the Initiation of Continental Glaciaton" to the book *Climate of the Arctic* (Weller and Bowling, eds., 1973). Bowling notes the past tendencies for extremely rapid shifts to glacial conditions, and states that the first observable signs of continental ice sheets are widely agreed upon— primarily an increase in perennial snow cover in northeastern Canada and/or Scandinavia. Bowling suggests that the recent weather extremes in North America and elsewhere are analogous to those to be expected in the early stages of a glacial period.

**   Barry, Bradley, and Jacobs, in the same book mentioned above, contribute the article, "Synoptic Climatological Studies of the Baffin Island Area." Baffin Island is of course in northeast Canada and a site of past ice sheet coverage. The scientists reveal the fact that in the 1960's (just prior to the study), summer temperatures in the area distinctly declined, while winters grew snowier.

**   A third article in *Climate of the Arctic* is "Recent Climatic Changes in the Eastern North American Sub-Arctic." Scientists Schell, Corkum, and Sabbagh show that beginning in the early 1970's, the number of icebergs counted drifting southward past 48 degrees N latitude grew to about 2 to 4 times the 1921-1950 average, and about 4 to 8 times the 1950-1970 average. They interpret this as obviously indicative of climatic change but are not able to define it.

**   Lowell Ponte, in his 1976 book, *The Cooling*, states that in 1971 the Arctic areas with ice and snow cover suddenly increased by 12 percent (an area equal to France, Italy, and Great Britain combined), and has persisted to the time of his writing (1976). He also notes that parts of Baffin Island formerly bare in summer are now snow-covered year round, and that the Antarctic is expanding also.

**   "Recent Year-To-Year Variations in Seasonal Temperatures and Sea Ice Conditions in the Eastern Canadian Arctic," by Jacobs and Newell (*Arctic*, 12/79), states that the record cold temperatures experienced in the winter of 1978-79 in the Baffin Island area are part of a worsening weather trend in that region. The trend began in the 1960's and is characterized by growing coolness of summers and more severe sea ice conditions.

**   "New Data on Climatic Trends" (*Nature*, 12/15/77) is an article by nine scientists from three countries which states that the cooling of the northern hemisphere observed over the past 30 years has not yet reversed, and that spring snow totals in North America and Eurasia increased throughout the 1966-75 period. Thus, they say this means a general decrease in absorbed solar radiation at the Earth's surface.

**   The Encyclopedia Brittanica's 1980 Book of the Year (p. 179) states that scientists aboard the icebreaker "Glacier" discovered that the Mertz and Ninnis glaciers of Antarctica, receding between 1911 and 1958, have advanced 12 and 15 miles, respectively, during the past 21 years.

**   "Recent Climatic Trends and Local Glacier Margin Fluctuations in West Greenland" (*Nature*, 3/13/80) by J.E. Gordon, states that in northwest Greenland and throughout the Canadian Arctic Archipelago, a distinct summer cooling has occurred since 1963 along with a winter precipitation increase. He notes this as a climatic deterioration which has produced documented sea-ice cover increase, advance of glaciers up to at least 1978, and lowering of average July freezing elevation by up to 500 meters.

** "Ice-Sheet Initiation and Climatic Influences of Expanded Snow Cover in Arctic Canada" by L. Williams (*Quaternary Research* No. 10, 1978) says that a large increase in October 1st snow cover in the Canadian Arctic took place from 1967-70 to 1971-75. Williams suggests that similar effects would be expected at the onset of continental glaciation. No explanation is offered for the cause of the increasing snow cover.

** Finally, we note the article from *Weatherwise*, April 1980, "Snowiest Cities of the Decade"

Peter R. Chaston, its author, is Meteorologist-in-Charge of the National Weather Service office in Rochester, New York. Chaston has been tabulating snowfall statistics for the past decade. What he says is that much of the Northern Hemisphere experienced a "dramatic upsurge" in snowfall over the 1970's compared with the last several decades. It is an established fact, he says, that along with this dramatic snowfall increase, a small drop in the Earth's overall temperature occurred during the 1970's. Chaston also says that the greatest snow cover extent ever observed was revealed by weather satellites scanning North America in the late 1970's.

Meteorologist Chaston further says it is debatable whether or not what he calls the "Snowy Seventies" signifies a major cooling trend or is just a temporary irregularity, and that 50 *meteorologists* would likely give 50 different opinions on the matter. And he says this is why meteorology is so exciting—the fact that even with advanced computers and the ability to model the motions of the atmosphere, we remain far from comprehending the mechanics of Mother Nature.

Forests and Fires

The crucial role of epidemic forest fires, as indicative of an accelerating transition into glacial conditions, was strongly emphasized in John Hamaker's last 2 papers.

Are the forests of the world increasingly going up in smoke as they should be in a time of demineralized and thus "droughty" soils, increasing climatic stress (including record heat and drought), worsening acid rain effects, deforestation and spreading deserts, chronic insect/disease epidemics, etc?

They are. The trends of increasing and accelerating destruction seem unmistakably clear from the available evidence, presented here. Relatively little information on areas outside of North America have been found by this researcher, yet the story is more than likely the same or worse in other temperate forest areas. Tropical forest wildfire data is scarce, though it is reported (Grainger, 1980, see Chapter 2) that the nutrient-poor soils and highly carbonaceous (mineral-poor) vegetation there burns terrifically when moisture is withheld for a time. Wide-scale drought and acidic rains will provide the final pre-conditioning influence prior to the tropical forest conflagrations predicted by Hamaker's glacial onslaught scenario. Even at "only" the present rates of human deforestation and desertification, these forests are, according to most researchers, "scheduled" for virtual extinction in 15-30 years. A new awareness of the glacial process, or the process itself, should alter such a schedule dramatically.

Here is the summary of the key forest fire information gathered over the past few years.

The editorial page of the April, 1961 *American Forests* magazine was entitled "Fire Weather Ahead." The editor warned of the explosive fire situation building up in the U.S. forest lands, and exhorted his readers to "do something!" because so little was really known about how to control fires. We desperately need "more research" was his plea. He also warned of the great dangers of the forests' existing susceptibility to drought, and he called the recent fire record "pretty grim."

This record was summarized as 80,308 fires in 1958; 86,737 fires in 1959; and in 1960 preliminary figures said over 420,000 acres had burned, the greatest loss since 1942. Only four previous years, he said, had losses been so high. The worst losses of 1960 were 80,000 acres in southern California, 110,000 acres in Oregon-Washington-Idaho-Montana, and 17,560 acres in Wisconsin. So this is how things appeared in 1961.

Since 1961, according to the latest available data, from *USDA Agricultural Conservation and Forestry Statistics 1979*, there have been significant jumps in both the number of fires and number of acres consumed. The accelerating destruction of the temperate zone forests may be seen in the following summary of USDA's statistics.

	1964-75	1976-78	% Increase
Average # of fires per year	119,000	207,000	74 %
Average total acreage burned per year	2,720,000	3,612,000	33 %

A report in *Science* (4/14/78) by C.S. Wong entitled "Atmospheric Input of Carbon Dioxide From Burning Wood," gives the latest figures available to him for forest fire losses in Canada. These show that the average annual acreage burned from 1959 through 1968 was 1,083,000 acres. (A little more than this of non-wooded acreage burned.) The latest information report comes from a Canadian Press release published in the Toronto Globe (7/24/80). The article quotes Don Merrill of the Canadian

Forestry Service, who reports that already in July this was the worst forest fire season on record: *almost 8.2 million acres* had burned across the country.

UPI stories from May (5/24/80) and June (6/27/80) told of some of these fires, as many as 500 burning at one time through drought-parched Ontario and western Canada; the fires were unbelievable "infernos" of 35,000; 40,000; 50,000; 80,000; 110,000; 132,000; 215,000; and 275,000 acres!

These figures should help clarify the state of the forests in terms of their great (soil-based) vulnerability to drought, hence vulnerability to fire and quick return of their huge carbon stores to the atmosphere. They should also help to put the perspective and recommendations of John Hamaker in very sharp contrast to those of the *American Forests* editor, and countless others up to 1981, who tell the public that what we really need is... "more research!"

More research through recent media reports only turns up more destruction, more *effects* of a failing ecology produced by the *causes* of a failing ecology. The following serve to exemplify such effects:

**   The worst fires in drought-stricken southeast Australia since at least World War II sweep through over 100,000 acres of woodlands. (*Reuters*, 10/4/80)

**   Forest fires rage on Spain's Mediterranean coast from Barcelona to Alicante province. (AP and UPI, 10/16/80)

**   25,000 acres of Michigan's Huron National Forest are consumed at an "incredible pace." (*American Forests*, 7/81)

**   A record 16-square miles (over 10,000 acres) burns in a wilderness area of Colorado's White River National Forest, while 12,000 acres burn in the Sunflower Mountains of Arizona in 100 degree-plus temperatures. (*San Francisco Chronicle*, 6/30/80)

**   140,000 acres (220 square miles) burns in Idaho in August, 1979. (*American Forests*, 3/80)

**   In four months of "fire season" in 1979, officially one of the worst seasons ever, hundreds of thousands of acres burn in Western states, including 150,000 in Idaho, 200,000 in Arizona, 250,000 in California. "Drought" is implicated as the major factor. (*San Francisco Examiner*, 7/6/80).

**   50,000 acres burn in less than a week in 26 Kentucky counties in November, while 27 forest fires burn out of control in West Virginia where 26,400 acres have been consumed since summer's end. (*AP*, 11/13/80)

**   Millions of acres of pine and oak are tinder dry, "just like a bomb," during record Texas heat wave. Over 250,000 acres did burn. (*American Forests*, 11/80)

** California Department of Forestry official Robert Connelly, after the 23,000-acre Napa fire and the 61,000 acres lost in southern California fires, says that in the past decade 1977 was "the worst." 1981, though, "has every indication that it will surpass that." (*AP*, 6/29/81)

** Over 46,000 acres burn in Alabama and 41 of 67 counties are put under alert due to the "critical fire situation," as 227 new fires are reported on Sunday. (*San Francisco Examiner*, 3/16/81)

** In the first 2½ months of 1981, over 500,000 acres of timberlands have been destroyed in Florida, Mississippi and Alabama—already more than in the entire drought year of 1980. (*Coming Changes*, May-June 1981)

** Rainfall helps firefighters to "stall" Alaska fires, touched off by lightning strikes, which have burned over 400,000 acres of woodlands. At least four other western states report that dry weather has nourished hundreds of fires, including a 73,000-acre conflagration in Idaho. (*San Francisco Examiner*, 6/29/81)

** Over 4,000 army troops, aided by firefighting planes and helicopters, are attempting to stop fires raging across southern Greece. These fires, some burning for a week so far, have destroyed "hundreds of thousands" of woodland acres. Ancient Olympia, birthplace of the Olympics, is threatened, and another huge fire is out of control in Western Greece near the Ionian Sea. Emergency legislation to aid the damaged areas is being proposed as the fires travel on. (*San Francisco Examiner*, 8/7/81)

In conclusion, a note on two articles which have further bearing on fire, human responsibility and the state of the forests.

"War Technology Comes To The Forests," by J.A. Savage, appeared in Friends of the Earth's *Not Man Apart* in December, 1980. It describes how the U.S. Forest Service is adapting technologies used in Vietnam to "modern silviculture." In addition to the arboricide Agent Orange, flamethrowers and bombs of napalm-like jelly are used to achieve a "clean" burn of all the "debris" left after clearcutting. With these methods, no slash is left, only "charred dirt."

"Burning Desire" (*American Forests*, 1/81) quotes the Wood Energy Institute's figures that the number of wood-burning stoves (in the U.S.) has increased from 250,000 to 2,000,000 in five years, yet the supply of firewood hasn't begun to keep pace with this growing demand.

As Erik Eckholm made abundantly clear in *Planting for the Future: Forestry for Human Needs* (Worldwatch Institute Paper No. 26), the "gargantuan" demand for firewood, lumber, and undepleted agricultural land is making short work of the Earth's tree cover the world over. The assistance being provided via insects, disease, and acid rains must be summarized in the next chapter, but here some appropriate words of summation may be offered. They are the words of John Hamaker in sending a follow-up article and letter to Representative James Weaver of Oregon (3/3/80).

The article was "Worldwide Starvation By 1990," and the letter simply said, "If you want the forests to come back in Oregon you will have to bring them back throughout the world."

5

Introduction

John Hamaker completed this article in May of 1981. In it he further clarifies the present advanced (late-interglacial) state of soil demineralization. He explains the long-neglected and abused soil phenomena involved in the soil's natural drainage system, showing the relation between this basic system and our survival. Hamaker depicts, most convincingly, how close is the relation of soil quality and human health—and how deeply critical the degenerating quality of both has become

As always, the fundamental way to re-build and restore soil, as well as human health, is emphasized. Thus the perceptive reader will again see the immeasurably valuable, practical, *positive* messages Hamaker offers *which make it possible to deal, in a truly* "wholistic" way, with the apparently awesome negative realities at hand. With the whole life and future of humankind at stake, such a way must be recognized and, obviously, acted upon.

Fig. 1

Dirt removed
from ditch.
Old topsoil

Subsoil

Gravel layer.
Dense clay soil,
probably glacial
advance preceding
the last one

Stream bed

Fig. 2

5

The Subsoil Drainage System and Our Vanishing Food Supply

Preface

Since the early 1960's it has been clearly recognized that the population curve was going to outrun the food supply curve in the decades immediately ahead. What was not recognized is that the food supply curve was going to drop to very low production levels, forcing starvation on the world much sooner than anticipated.

Much of Africa is suffering from drought. In its remote areas there is anarchy. Armed bands roam the countryside taking the little food that farmers have and leaving them to starve to death. Those who saw TV newsman John Hart's pictured essay of the starving families may have thought, "Those could be my children and my grandchildren." By 1990 they well may be your children and mine.

Twenty years have passed and nothing of substance has been done to prevent the destruction of civilization. Part of the failure is due to the unholy alliance of government and the owners of this country whose only interest is profit. Part of the failure is due to the fragmentation of the efforts of innumerable groups of do-gooders who insist on "scratching at what itches." The result is that nothing of substance has been accomplished. We are on the threshold of starvation and the environment is deteriorating at an accelerating rate. Twenty years of failure.

The only possible way out of this morass is to recognize the basic problems and attack them head on. This paper is about the basic problems and the relationship between some of the "what itches" problems to the basic problems. If these things are known and understood, perhaps we may yet effect our survival.

Food production in the northern hemisphere in 1980 seems to have lost about 20 percent of potential because of adverse weather. On this continent it was drought and heat. On the Eurasian continent it was cold, wet weather. In the southern hemisphere, the growing season started with drought in Australia, Africa, and South America. The world food reserves are expected to be gone by the spring of 1981. We will probably have a worldwide food shortage by 1982. *There is no reason to expect the weather to improve, because the atmospheric carbon dioxide which is destroying the temperate-zone climate is increasing at an accelerating rate.*

Everyone who has ever studied the CO_2 problem has warned that the consequence of permitting the rise of CO_2 would be to alter the weather in ways which would be destructive to agriculture. More recently, some have warned that if anything is going to be done about the problem, it must be done now. With the world on the verge of famine, I would think that is the least that could be said. I was saying the same thing 10 years ago. Now my opinion is that, based on past human performance, it is unlikely that we have sufficient time to do what must be done if we are to prevent the destruction of almost all of the present world population by starvation.

Weather problems are not the only reason for the impending famine. Far more important is the fact that the soils are almost stripped of minerals. In fact, the weather problems are caused simply because the soil does not have enough minerals worldwide to support a sufficient growth of plant life (forests in particular) to remove the amount of CO_2 from the atmosphere which is going into it from all sources.

Farmers all over the world have known for centuries that it would be better to eat the seed than plant it in subsoil. Only in the few places where the glaciers left unusually heavy deposits of ground rock are there enough minerals left in the subsoil so it can be made productive. For a good many decades we have been completely dependent on a few inches of topsoil for our food supply. We have spent hundreds of millions of dollars on agricultural research; yet the problem was not even recognized. Incredible! Now we face the crisis —mass starvation.

The Drainage System

Many people have difficulty in comprehending the fact that the soils are running out of minerals. Perhaps the following discussion will help to explain our dilemma.

About 25 miles northwest of Lansing, Michigan (one mile west on Price Road from Francis Road), there is a portion of a drainage ditch called the Wandell Drain. (Fig. 1 and 2, p. 94)

The pictures show a streak of gravel, sand, and clay on both sides of the ditch. Gravel and boulders strewn on the bank and in the bottom of the ditch simply fell out of the backhoe bucket as it was drawn up the bank. I followed the ditch for about four miles and the gravel streak was continuous. The visible streak is a cross section of a layer of gravel which lies about 6 to 10 feet below all the land drained by the ditch.

The gravel layer averages about a foot thick, varying above and below this dimension. Below the gravel layer is a very dense clay with a very slow rate of water penetration. Above the gravel layer is typical worn-out subsoil. The ditch is in a natural stream bed. Consequently, there is much more organic matter in the subsoil than there is on the crop land in the drainage basin. When there is water in the subsoil, numerous small streams of water flow out of the gravel layer. The streams of water have, in a few weeks, cut many small ditches in the dense clay below the gravel layer.

The information in the ditch ties into something learned from a backhoe hole dug on my 10-acre plot in a vain effort to satisfy the asinine septic system requirements of the Michigan State Health Department. They require that a septic field be connected to an underlying bed of deep sand, presumably on the theory that sewage improves the nutritional quality of well water.

On the sidewall of the backhoe excavation close to the bottom, there was an oval area of sand about a foot wide, through which a stream of water was flowing. The sand was a rather large-grain size, making a porous vein through which the water could flow toward the ditch.

In retrospect, it is apparent that the depth of the gravel layer now exposed in the ditch is about the same as the stream of water close to the bottom of the backhoe hole, and that the water was flowing to the ditch through the gravel layer. What the backhoe brought up at that depth was mostly subsoil with a few pieces of large gravel and a little sand.

The above observations are very instructive. They permit our drawing two significant conclusions:

1.   The thin drainage layer of gravel is all that is left of the approximately 6 to 10 feet of glacial till which was deposited by the last glacial advance in this area.

2.   This bottom layer of that glacial till constitutes the natural drainage system which prevents the land from becoming saturated and turning into a vast swamp. It also supplies water for the deep roots of plants in dry weather.

The thickness of the layer of glacial till immediately following glaciation 10,000 years ago can only be guessed at. We know that erosion has removed some of the worn-out rock residue; we do not know how much, since we do not know if the present elevation of the gravel layer is at the original elevation. Furthermore, water filtering down from the topsoil and flowing horizontally in the drainage layer of gravel and sand keep this layer cleared of the fine particles of worn-out material. Above the drainage zone, the worn-out particles, carried by percolating rain water working in conjunction with the soil expansion and contraction, flow under the larger particles of unused material and gradually displace them upward to the topsoil. *One thing is certain. On my 10 acres, the only significant amount of unused glacial till is in the drainage layer and in the topsoil.* In the topsoil I found a total of 2½ inches of unused material, and it has been so badly leached by the acids of chemical agriculture that four of the trace elements (zinc, tin, strontium and lithium) found in glacial gravel by spectrographic analysis did not show up at all in a similar spectrographic analysis of my soil.

Virgin forests take in 100 percent of the rainfall. A couple of hundred years ago, Michigan was largely covered with virgin forests. At that time, the amount of water flowing in the drainage layer of till was undoubtedly enough to keep the entire layer flushed out and in place. The land was converted for farming and, as a result, the bank of fertility, instead of being recycled as in the virgin forest, has been converted to crops and shipped out. The remaining forested land has been harvested repeatedly, thus removing soil minerals.

The lack of soil moisture has become a major problem. Under natural conditions, a drainage basin stream tends to fill with sediment up to a foot or two above the gravelled drainage layer, thereby slowing the discharge of water from the drainage basin subsoil. This holding back of the water in the drainage layer causes streams and rivers to run at about the same level the year around instead of being dry or flooding.

Ten years ago, there was a shallow pond plus 4 or 5 acres of marshland behind my 10-acre plot. This water-saturated area exerted a constant pressure of about 10 feet of water on the slowly-permeable dense clay below the gravel layer. It must have been a prime source for the underground water supply. When the drainage layer under the drainage basin was full of water, it also greatly enhanced the penetration of water into the underground reservoirs.

Now there is a ditch about 15 feet deep through the marsh. The marsh and pond have been drained. In the pond area, there is about 10 feet of peat exposed above the drainage layer of gravel. The underground reservoirs are obviously being depleted.

Five acres of marshland have been made available for agriculture, but the underground water has been pulled out from hundreds of acres of cropland subsoil. No wonder the crops are in trouble after a couple of weeks of dry weather! The crops are almost entirely dependent on a thin topsoil that is low on organic matter and contains too few available minerals *to support a soil organism population adequate to prepare the soil for good water storage.*

There is another effect taking place. The base of the gravel drainage layer is a sharp line, but the topside of the layer is up-and-down, as seen in the picture (Fig. 2). When the trees were cut down, and the moldboard plow sealed the subsoil clay, the water started moving laterally on the hardpan into the low areas of the field. My four-and-a-third acres of soil mineralized with 46 tons/acre of gravel crusher screenings is still doing that after four years, although to a much lesser extent than when the first crop was planted. Throughout the world, soils similar to my ten acres have only enough water reaching the drainage layer to keep small streams flowing at intervals of 6 or 8 feet. The rest of the gravel layer has become infiltrated by clay, and the gravel has begun to rise toward the surface. We are in the process of losing the drainage layer on a worldwide scale.

The destruction of the drainage layer has been further intensified because some farmers have listened to the "geniuses" at the ag schools and have installed toxic plastic drain pipes a few feet below the surface in order to short-cut the percolating water and thereby further dry up the drainage layer.

About 25 years ago, in East Texas, I dug a pond. The cut ran about 250 feet along the base of a hillside. In all that length, there were only two or three sand channels where the water was still coming down the hill. All the rest had been sealed up by clay long ago. The water simply penetrated the 8" sandy loam to the dense clay beneath it and drifted downhill — an ideal set-up for sheet erosion if anyone tried to plow the land. Even the weedy growth on the hillside did not prevent some of the topsoil from eroding during heavy rains. *There is a penalty for failure to maintain the drainage layer.*

Michigan's County Drain Commissioners are trying to outdo the ag professors in destroying agriculture in Michigan. Does anyone know of anything sensible that the agricultural establishment has done for the soil?

If drain commissioners were to do what makes sense, they would fill the ditches to the bottom of the drainage layer, put in a foot of gravel to reestablish the drainage layer, and let the stream take over. In order to refill the drainage layer with water it is necessary to obtain nearly 100 percent penetration of rain. *A soil remineralization program must be maintained.* In about 50 years, there would develop a deep organic topsoil that would take in all the rain that falls and hold it until the excess water could sink into the subsoil to refill the drainage layer. With water in the drainage layer, the increased flow would eventually remove the clay, consolidating sand and gravel as it should. The water in the drainage layer would induce deep root growth to sustain the plants in times of drought.

If we assume that in this particular area there was a mixture of 10 feet of coarse gravel and sand 10,000 years ago, then 1 foot was consumed every 1,000 years, or .1 foot (1.2 inches) every 100 years. There is still left 2½ inches, or theoretically enough for 210 years. This is a rough figure, needing a lot of interpretation, but it does give some perspective about what has happened in the approximately 200 years in which the land has been farmed.

Two hundred years ago, we can estimate, there was about twice as much rock in the topsoil as at present. Since weathering affects the surface area of all the particles of rock equally, the loss of rock is partially due to reduction of particle size of the rock which is still there, and partially due to the change of smaller particles into demineralized subsoil. As the percentage of rock still containing useful elements decreased in the topsoil, the quantity of fine particles (produced by weathering of larger material) must decrease. *When the glacial mix was still feeding up from the subsoil, the balance of parti-*

cle sizes could be maintained by new material. That is no longer true, and probably has not been true for at least 400 years.

The significance of the loss of small particle-size rock is, of course, a huge percentage loss of rock surface area. The weathering*

---

*The term "weathering" is a poor description for the process of reducing rocks in the topsoil to minute particles stripped of minerals of value to the life process. "Weathering" over-emphasizes such factors as freezing and thawing.

If weathering were a significant factor, no gravel would ever reach the surface in the northern states where freezing of the ground extends to depths of 3 or 4 feet. The gravel would be reduced to the very fine particle sizes in worn-out subsoil before it ever got to the topsoil. It doesn't happen. Gravel does not break down until it reaches the aerated topsoil. Furthermore, if weather factors (freezing, thawing, moisture, and weak acids in the rain under natural conditions) were significant, then the more vulnerable rock would disappear from the total glacial mixture long before the mixture is exhausted in the 10,000 years after glaciation. This process does not happen. The balance of soil elements remains the same right down to the time of exhaustion.

The only explanation for this breakdown of rock is the expenditure of energy by microorganisms. The crystal structure of the silicate rocks (about 2/3 of all the rocks) is mostly useless to the organisms. However, the minerals between the crystals of silicon oxides or aluminum silicate are useful to the microorganisms. The organisms simply cut the crystals loose by working down the sides of the crystals and across the bottom. Only at this point can the weathering factor have any effect in removing the crystals from the rock particles.

The microorganisms can not break down some rocks and neglect others because if they did, the topsoil would be filled with undesirable rock that in time would result in starvation of the microorganisms. But nature in the infinite wisdom which constitutes "the balance of nature" has provided organisms which prefer the combinations of elements found in each type of rock so that all of the rock is consumed in accord with the needs of the total microorganism population. The microorganisms swap minerals (probably as organic compounds) so that all get the exact balance of elements they need. Then nature has provided plants which prefer the protoplasm of specific organisms, so that all the organism protoplasm is brought to the surface and the minerals therein ultimately go into the rivers, mostly as leaf mold, where they may go through many more life cycles before coming to rest as sedimentary deposits on the ocean floor.

"Weathering" is an obsolete word.

of the total surface area of rock determines the rate of exposure of elements useful to the microorganisms in the soil. The plant roots feed on the protoplasm of the microorganisms; thus, the amount of plant life growth is dependent on total rock surface area in the soil.

A ton of ground gravel will make something on the order of 16,000 acres of surface area available to the microorganisms. *The minerals exposed on the surfaces of the ground rock do not need weathering to make them available. This is what makes soil remineralization practical.*

The mathematical statement that there is enough rock left in the soil to last 210 years is just the sort of silly figure we often get from statisticians.

When lands begin to fall off in yield, they cease to have useful productivity in a few decades. That happened in East Texas in roughly the period from 1930 to 1950. Now it has about run its course in the glaciated area of Michigan in which my ten acres are located. The "thumb" area of Michigan saw its white bean yield drop from 2,000 pounds per acre to 1,300 pounds in the decade of the 1960's. No amount of agricultural chemicals can bring that production back or keep it from dropping to a lower yield.

What has happened, of course, is that the unused, fine rock material has stopped coming up from the subsoil because there isn't any more. During the few decades when the soil collapses in yield, the fine material is used up and the major part of the surface area of rock in the soil is gone. Or to put it another way, *the availability of the elements has all but ended.*

The discussion of the gravel and sand drainage layer in one area of central Michigan applies to all the land. All underground water eventually drains into a stream bed, or lake; it then comes up in springs at a lower elevation or runs directly into the ocean. The point is that the capacity of the subsoil drainage layer in any area has been geared to the annual rainfall and water penetration under natural conditions. When we alter the amount of water reaching and being maintained in the drainage layer, we are in trouble. If we decrease the amount of water by losing it to surface run-off, we will lose water and therefore sand and gravel from the drainage layer. This sand and gravel cannot be replaced. Arid soils have very little drainage layer left, simply because a drainage layer which is not kept full of slowly flowing water will clog up with fine, worn-out particles which will eventually displace the drainage sands and gravels and lift them to the topsoil. The sea salts carried in by the infrequent rains have generally accumulated in the soils for lack of sufficient water to establish drainage systems and thereby flush the salts back to the ocean. When dry lands are irrigated, they tend to become water-logged for lack of drainage. The salts dissolve and are left on the surface when surface moisture evaporates.

The best use of arid soils is to put them back into grass, the way most of them were when the land was settled. With remineralization more and better grass can be grown than was there originally and the land can be used for grazing animals. The water that is left in the underground reservoirs should be reserved for people and livestock. The refill rate of the reservoirs is much too slow to support irrigation, as shown by steadily falling water tables in most exploited areas.

In spite of the excellent mixing and selection of the types of rocks in a glacial mix by the tectonic and glacial systems, soils vary somewhat in their ability to supply the elements useful to the microorganisms. The sea solids are a back-up system for supplying minerals to the microorganisms. When the sea solids fall with rain, they are either in solution or of an extremely small particle size. On well-drained soils they pass through the soil with the water and go back into the ocean. All of the elements are in the sea solids. This makes it possible for the microorganisms to choose what they need as the elements pass through the topsoil. Where the supply of sea solids is adequate, the sea solids are an important factor in the quality and quantity of microorganisms and hence the crops which grow there.

The mineral requirements to support the growth of soil organisms (and hence plants) are a *natural* balance of the available (to the microorganisms) elements in the total mixture of the rocks on the top layers of the earth's crust, and the *natural* balance of elements dissolved and suspended in sea water brought with the clouds.

The mineral balance of salted soils must be restored by remineralization and by allowing large quantities of plant refuse to go back into the topsoil. The plant refuse would provide the carbon requirements of the microorganism; the gases in the air and water complete their food requirements .

The lands which have adequate rainfall and salvageable drainage systems must be used for food and fuel crops. The latter will have to be mostly wood plantations grown on mineralized soil. The wood, grown where people are, can provide firewood, alcohol, and methane gas. *With small local alcohol and methane power plants serving local needs, the very heavy cost and energy requirements for transportation of energy supplies can be minimized.*

The Decline of Soil Minerals and the Rise of Malnutrition

The true measure of the annual mineral supply coming from the soil is the state of health of plants, animals, and people living on the land. Now the record shows that everywhere one looks, there is malnutrition and death. It is a time for dying, and the reason is quite clear.

The following is quoted from *Hunza Health Secrets* by Renee Taylor:

> In December 1945 in the United States Soil Conservation publications the following statements were made:
> "The U.S. produces more food than any other nation in the world, yet, according to Dr. Thomas Parran, Jr., 40 percent of the population suffers from malnutrition. How can this be true? The majority of people get enough to eat. Evidently the food eaten does not have enough of the right minerals and vitamins in it to keep them healthy. What causes food to lack these necessary elements? Investigators have found that food is no richer in minerals than the soil from which it comes. Depleted soils will not produce healthy nutritious plants. Plants suffering from mineral deficiencies will not nourish healthy animals. Mineral-deficient plants and undernourished animals will not support our people in health. Poor soils perpetuate poor people physically, mentally, and financially."

Parran's observation was in 1945. In 1950, the USDA put out a handbook, *Composition of Foods*; revised it in 1963; then put a new cover on it in 1975 and called it *Handbook of the Nutritional Con-*

tents of Foods. To my knowledge, there has been no revision as of 1980. The agricultural chemicals industry, which has been running USDA for decades, probably wouldn't like to see an updated mineral comparison with the 1963 figures. However, the protein content is high or low in just about the same proportion as the minerals. This is so because just about all the minerals are used in the proteins called enzymes, which in turn are catalysts which assist in making all the other protein compounds. So with the protein in corn down from the poor protein content of about 9 percent in 1963 to 6 percent now, the mineral content must also have dropped about 33 percent. *Malnutrition of 40 percent in 1945 has risen to about 100 percent in 1980.*

The malnutrition which Parran observed in 1945 is a reflection of the fact that many American soils were collapsing in crop protein yields (soil microorganism protoplasm proteins). William Albrecht (*The Albrecht Papers*, page 276, published by *Acres, USA*) noted that Kansas wheat dropped from a range of 10 to 19 percent protein in 1940 to a range of 9 to 15 percent protein in 1949. In 1940, the western half of Kansas produced wheat ranging from 15 to 19 percent. In 1949, only 5 counties had wheat as high as 15 percent protein. Almost the entire state wheat crop had dropped below 13 percent, and most of it was below 12 percent protein. U.S. wheat averages 8 to 12 percent now—about half what it ought to be. The best land in the corn belt produces wheat around 15 percent. We are being robbed of our food supply by our profit-hungry financial rulers and the government they have bought and paid for. So Johnny can't read, crime is on a rampage, the cost of disease is staggering, absenteeism from the work place is 14 percent in the auto industry, the army can't use half its applicants because of physical or mental reasons, etc.

Year by year, as the last of the soil minerals disappear, our strength and vitality are being thrown away. What better example than the 35,000,000 of us who are handicappd by arthritis. Basically the problem is that one member of the body, such as bone or muscle, rubs against an adjacent member without sufficient lubricant between them. The body's mucus is supposed to do this job. However, if the intake of zinc is too little, the mucus will lose its lubricity and viscosity and turn to the consistency of water.

Personally, I don't need documentation for the foregoing because I experienced it. First I was hit hard by the domestic version of Agent Orange, Ortho "Weed Be Gone" (2,4-D 2,4,5-T). One of the many afflictions which followed was that of continuous sinus leakage. In about 6 months, the mucus turned to water. Obviously I was not making the necessary compounds as fast as I was losing them. I developed arthritis in the right knee. I had it for no more than 2 months when I read about zinc being necessary in at least 27 enzyme systems. I knew that zinc was required in relatively large quantities for that of a trace element. Under normal conditions there is a steady loss of mucus from the body. It seemed an obvious relationship, so I obtained some zinc sulfate pills from the health food store and took 6 or 8 pills a day for a week. At the end of that time, the mucus was more viscous than it had ever been. In 30 days the painful arthritis was gone. Within 6 weeks the shoulder muscle that simply would not heal was repaired and the various hyper-sensitive areas in the sinuses and respiratory tract were de-sensitized by the protective mucus.

It is the function of the mucus to lubricate and protect virtually every part of the body. Therefore, when it loses its ability to function, there is a great variety of physical as well as probable nerve and brain problems which result. The American people are forced to suffer this pain and handicap because the USDA and the land-grant colleges have for decades been controlled by the agricultural chemical companies who insist on selling chemicals even if it kills us all.

Zinc is not a cure-all. It takes a lot more than that to produce high-quality mucus. In excess, it can inhibit the beneficial effects of other elements. It is known that copper is suppressed by excess zinc, and copper is required for heart function. Therefore, those who take zinc should take it only when the mucus loses its viscosity and lubricity or when pain indicates a need.

Obviously, there is no way to maintain good health by taking some of this and a pinch of that. We aren't smart enough. *The only answer is to make sure that the soil contains an abundance of available elements from the total natural mixture, and let the microorganisms pick and choose what they want, so that the natural balance of nutrients comes up through the plant life to us.* There is no legitimate excuse for continuing to degenerate in mind and body. We can have the best health the world has ever known.

Our Forests Are Dying

In the March 1969 issue of *American Forests*, Hugh Fosburgh has written an eloquent article, "All Is Not Well at Baker." Baker is a tract of forest in the Adirondack Mountains of New York. It seems that within a span of only a few years, the dying of all varieties of trees has taken place, except for two of little value—the hemlock and tamarack. At the same time, the insects which attack the various trees have greatly multiplied.

It is clear enough what happened to the Baker Tract, and it is in process in all of the forests and jungles. For instance, "The rate of forest growth in the White Mountains of New Hampshire has declined 18 percent between 1956 and 1965..." ["Acid Rain", *The Amicus Journal*, Winter 1981, National Resources Defense Council (N.R.D.C.)]

The last of the minerals have come up in the forest lands, as in the croplands. Over the last 3 to 6 decades, the finer fraction of unused rock has been turned into subsoil with a consequent great reduction in surface area and hence protoplasm production. Since these are the compounds which impart health, and resistance to disease and insects, the trees have become easy prey to the parasites. Acid rain, so heavy in the northeastern states, has wiped out the last of the carbonates, resulting in excessive acidification of the soil, as it has done to the lakes of that region. When the acidity of water and soil drops below about pH 5.5, it begins to kill off various kinds of microorganisms. Only a few acid-tolerant organisms can survive, and only a few acid-tolerant trees and plants can survive on the poor quality and quantity of protoplasm which the soil provides. No amount of pesticides can arrest the dying in the Baker Tract; only an immediate aerial remineralization program can save what is left of it.

In September, 1961 W. Schwenke presented a paper on "Forest Fertilization and Insect Buildup." The paper described work done in the previous nine years at the Institute of Applied Zoology at the Forest Research Center, Munich, Germany.

The work was based on the observation that forest parasites had greater population density on poor forest soil than on more fertile forest soil, and on the observation that forest soils can be improved by fertilization.

The fertilization consisted of ½ to 1½ tons per acre of limestone plus a light application of NPK. This minimal soil remineralization cut parasite populations on the order of 30 percent to 50 percent. On some of the soils the effect was still observable nine years after the application. They also found that the increase in growth rate produced a value which far exceeded the cost of fertilizing the soil.

Limestone probably has a broader range of elements than any other single type of rock. That is because it is formed from the shells, bones, and organic matter which falls to the ocean floor. It is not, however, a complete balance of elements to support living organisms. This is shown by the observed fact that the lasting effect of the fertilization depended on the minerals that were in the soil before fertilization.

This minimal experiment can be compared with a real mineralization project which has been going on for about 3,000,000 years; that is, all during the present glacial epoch. Two dozen glaciers can be counted in the Himalayan Mountains at the headwaters of the Mekong and Red Rivers of Vietnam. Every year the rivers flood the two river deltas. Every year a rice crop is grown. For as long as anyone remembers, the two deltas have served as the "rice bowl of the Orient." They will continue to be productive soils as long as the glaciers continue to grind the mixed layers of rock in the mountains—unless some educated idiot decides to install flood control projects on the two rivers.

The deltas are nature's demonstration of how to feed the soil organisms which in turn feed the plants. No chemist can ever improve on the natural system for creating life. It is too complicated. *One would be very dull-witted to fail to learn from this demonstration what we must do to reinvigorate our crops, forests and jungles so that civilization can survive.*

In recent years, there has been developed much excellent scientific equipment applicable to the study of biological compounds. There has been a resulting boom in knowledge gained about the compounds that enter the body by way of the food supply. A listing of just a few of the many articles now appearing in the science journals is pertinent to this question of minerals in the food supply:

"Chemical Clue to Obesity Found" (*Science News*, 11/8/80) states that a high-energy enzymatic process for controlling sodium and potassium within the cell is functioning at a low level in fat people. Carbon compounds are stored as fat instead of being used for energy. An enzyme containing sodium, potassium and phosphorous is in short supply. [Author's note: a shortage of one or all elements in the food could cause a shortage of the enzyme. The shortage in the body starts as a shortage in the soil.]

"Mental Disorders: A New Approach to Treatment," (*Science*, 1/5/79) says that choline (found in lecithin) cures a mental disorder called tardive dyskinesia.

"Vitamin D Deficiency Inhibits Pancreatic Secretion of Insulin," (*Science*, 8/15/80).

"Mind-Body Confusion," (*Science News*, 10/11/80). Of 100 people about to be legally confined to a mental institution, about half were found to have physical causes, basically of a dietary nature, which were responsible for their behavior.

"Protein Celebrities Meet in the Brain," (*Science News*, 11/29/80). Interferon, an anti-viral compound, is thought to belong with the pituitary gland hormones and endorphins in affecting human thoughts, emotions, and behavior.

"Vitamin A as a Cancer Shield," (*Science News*, 11/15/80).

"Prostaglandins Thwart Viruses," (*Science News*, 9/6/80).

For a more comprehensive view of the relation of health and nutrition, one might read the 1,129 pages of Vol. I and II of *The Influence of Nutritional Status on Pollutant Toxicity and Carcinogenicity* by Edward J. Calabrese, Univeristy of Massachusetts.

The above references are just a small sampling of the research now going on in the field of biological chemicals. The chemical and pharmaceutical companies are turning these compounds into profit-making products. Nutrition will now come by way of a doctor's prescription. Peculiarly, I have yet to see in a science journal the obvious conclusion that we must remineralize the soil (and stop poisoning and demineralizing the food in growing and processing), so that we will all have an abundance of the natural compounds required to build healthy bodies and functioning brains. It is unfortunate for us that the chemical companies, the government agencies, and the researchers have a vested interest in the 200-billion dollar annual medical bill.

The crop soils are badly demineralized. The minerals that are left have been selectively leached by acidic "fertilizers" so that the minerals in the food supply are not only in short supply, but some elements are virtually missing. This can only result in enzyme shortages. *Enzyme shortages sooner or later result in the physical, mental and spiritual degeneration of nations.*

Alexander Schauss, author of *Diet, Crime, and Delinquency* and *Orthomolecular Treatment of Criminal Behavior,* and other research works, was interviewed in the August, 1980 issue of the farm journal, *Acres, USA.* He puts the cost of crime at $200 billion annually, the same as our national medical bill and about $60 billion more than the defense budget. *Schauss has shown convincingly that diet and crime are directly related.* Several of our more progressive cities now have a system whereby juvenile first offenders are paroled to people capable of supervising their diet. Remarkable records are being made in preventing the first-offense juveniles from becoming repeaters—habitual criminals who would otherwise overflow the prisons.

In Michigan, we always go the stupid route. Our answer to the crime problem is longer sentences. Some prisons and jails have 2 or 3 times the occupants they were built to house. A federal judge has issued orders, so we are going to build more prisons. With what, I don't know. The taxpayers are in revolt. We have 14 percent unemployment. The state can't meet the budget, so we are cutting down on "unnecessary" things like education, welfare, care of the aged, etc.

Along with the rest of the country, Michigan's scholastic achievement scores have been dropping steadily for two decades. We send our malnourished, chemically-toxified, hyperactive, misbehaving, dull-witted kids to school and then scream at the teachers for not turning them into geniuses.

The whole sorry picture could have been changed by now if the state's politicians had jumped on soil remineralization and biomass solar energy 10 years ago. We would now have major and growing machinery and equipment industries related to food and fuel, and a food supply which would have given our people the vitality of mind and body the state so desperately needs. But what can you expect from an elective system which permits the Farm Bureau and the corporate structure generally to buy candidates at election time? The result is that the legislature and the executive branch are putty to be molded in the corporate interests.

The situation is the same at the federal level. The Congress will dispense (out of your pocket) palliatives by the hundreds. But suggest a problem solution which conflicts with corporate interests, and these stout defenders of the common man start squeaking like mice. As Ralph Nader says, "80 percent of the time Congress comes down on the corporate side of an issue." It is my observation that the Congress does something for the people either when there is a massive public demand, or when the corporate structure thinks it would be wise to throw the peons a bone to keep them from rioting in the streets.

In the Congress, the corporations enjoy a "heads I win, tails you lose" situation. They control both major parties. The people, in disgust, have turned to revulsion voting. Every four years of failure to solve problems, by weak and corrupt politicians, elicits a "throw the bums out" election response and we get a new set of bums. Failure doesn't satisfy anybody, so we see third party efforts. Unfortunately, third parties tend to advocate socialism and such anti-human practices as unlimited abortions.

Our people, or their immediate ancestors, came to this country because they did not want to be governed by the arbitrary decisions of other people. Our people are independent and they are smart enough to know that if the doctrine of personal responsibility for the results of one's behavior is abandoned, then we must lose our independence to those who of necessity must control our actions for us. A successful third party must be based on a restructuring of the laws to insure a degree of justice which will enable us to function as a free and peaceful nation.

Meanwhile, the power of centralized wealth holds us to a system of soil destruction which, before the decade of the 80's is over, will destroy our agricultural and technical civilization. In so doing, centralized wealth will also destroy itself, just as certainly as it is now destroying the dollar.

We are losing the soil's underground drainage system. We are losing the last of the soil's life-supporting minerals. It is time for human civilization to die out and relinquish the world to the small number of tribal bands which, as in the past glacial periods, will manage to survive. Most of this process will have taken place by 1990. Why? Simply because a rule of greed has been allowed to perpetuate itself for century after century. "All experience hath shown that mankind are more disposed to suffer while evils are sufferable, than to right themselves by abolishing the forms to which they are accustomed." The evils are no longer sufferable.

5

Perspective

Providing a concise review of further evidence on life's supporting chain of soil fertility-quality nutrition-human health, and a sense of the immeasurably great consequences of allowing any links to weaken, will be the first purpose here. Then a closer look should be taken at how forest disease and insects, plus acidic rains, are indeed "ably assisting" wildfires, weather stresses, and man to bring quickly a "world without trees."

The Soil and Health

Vast quantities of research have been done this century on the infinite manifestations of ill-health in human beings, and on how to alter these states with man-made chemical compounds. A comparatively miniscule amount of thought and research has gone toward understanding and utilizing a balance of the the elementary factors, including soil fertility, which together build and sustain the *normal* state of positive well-being. Simply stated, these health factors (such as pure whole food from fertile soil, pure air and water, exercise, rest, sleep, and sunshine) have not been given prominence in human educational systems, and the degree to which these factors have been ignored or abused is closely reflected in individual and societal health.

So as not to insult the reader's intelligence and good sense by examining *all* the works at hand which are "shouting" evidence of the decisive nature of the soil-health relationship, a representative few examples may be cited to inspire a recognition of the obvious.

Firman Bear of Rutgers University did a study on the trace element contents of vegetables which was published in the 1948 *Soil Science Society of America Proceedings.* This study deserves mention because it clearly shows the very significant fact that foods *which may look the same,* actually may have huge variations in mineral content and thus their health-promoting value. A chart summarizing his findings appeared in the March, 1977 issue of *Acres, USA,* and is reproduced below.

Variations in Mineral Content in Vegetables (Firman E. Bear report. Rutgers U.)

	Percentage of dry weight		Millequivalents per 100 grams dry weight				Trace Elements parts per million dry matter				
	Total Ash or Mineral Matter	Phosphorus	Calcium	Magnesium	Potassium	Sodium	Boron	Manganese	Iron	Copper	Cobalt
SNAP BEANS											
Highest	10.45	0.36	40.5	60.0	99.7	8.6	73	60	227	69	0.26
Lowest	4.04	0.22	15.5	14.8	29.1	0.0	10	2	10	3	0.00
CABBAGE											
Highest	10.38	0.38	60.0	43.6	148.3	20.4	42	13	94	48	0.15
Lowest	6.12	0.18	17.5	15.6	53.7	0.8	7	2	20	0.4	0.00
LETTUCE											
Highest	24.48	0.43	71.0	49.3	176.5	12.2	37	169	516	60	0.19
Lowest	7.01	0.22	6.0	13.1	53.7	0.0	6	1	9	3	0.00
TOMATOES											
Highest	14.20	0.35	23.0	59.2	148.3	6.5	36	68	1938	53	0.63
Lowest	6.07	0.16	4.5	4.5	58.8	0.0	5	1	1	0	0.00
SPINACH											
Highest	28.56	0.52	96.0	203.9	257.0	69.5	88	117	1584	32	0.25
Lowest	12.38	0.27	47.5	46.9	84.6	0.8	12	1	19	0.5	0.20

In a 1977 paper, John Hamaker made detailed comparison of Bear's data with that of USDA's 1975 reprint of the 1963 *Composition of Foods Handbook.* Among other things, he notes the fact that the Handbook only gives data for a single trace element, iron. To quote Hamaker:

> ...but it is a very significant element. A comparison on a part-per-million basis with Bear's highest and lowest, followed by the Handbook average is as follows: snap beans 227, 10, and 8; cabbage 94, 20, and 4; lettuce 516, 9, and 14; tomatoes 1938, 1, and 5; spinach 1584, 19, and 31. In the Bear study, if one trace element is low in all the vegetables, then all the other trace minerals are low. Therefore, the average of these vegetables in 1963 were no better supplied with trace minerals than the lowest in 1948. It has been fourteen years since the 1963 studies. USDA ought to have upgraded

its information and included much more trace element information. Instead, they copied the old 1963 Handbook tables and put them out in a fancy new cover in 1975. An honest set of figures on trace elements would show a lot of zeroes on a part-per-million basis and damn chemical agriculture for the monstrous fraud it is.

All of our food should be as good or better than the best found by Firman Bear. Such standards can be and must be obtained very quickly if we are to survive.

Now, *18* years (of soil demineralization) after 1963, the Handbook is still being distributed by USDA as a valid resource. A letter to them requesting updated information brought a reply from Frank Hepburn, Leader, Nutrient Data Research Group (Federal Bldg., Hyattsville, MD 20782, 301-436-8491) on September 16, 1980. It said, in part: "Revised sections of Agriculture Handbook No. 8 covering cereal grains and grain products, fruits, vegetables, legumes, nuts and seeds are all underway, but with publication dates scheduled for 1981 through 1982. Some of the data will be coming from analytical studies which are just starting. I am sorry that we are not far enough along with any of these sections to provide summary values at this time."

A full Congressional investigation and public disclosure of the methods and results of this research, as a highest form of public service and as a survival necessity, would appear essential at the earliest possible date.

The United Nations Food and Agriculture Organization (FAO) Soils Bulletin No. 17 is entitled *Trace Elements in Soils and Agriculture*, published in 1979. The Bulletin gives data similar to Bear's in showing the wide variations in extent of soil mineral depletion. It notes the *biologically essential* nature of the minerals for health of soil-building microorganisms, plants and humans, and it states that widespread deficiencies now exist; e.g., soil zinc deficiency is documented for 12 European countries, as is boron for nearly every European country. Also noted is the danger of trying to correct deficiencies by adding purified single elements due to their toxicity (for example, boron has been used as a weedkiller).

Nowhere is soil remineralization considered, due to lack of knowledge or concern; yet on page 1 it is stated that in spite of the "favorable development" in fertilizer use, that generally from 2 to 6 times more of the main nutrients are being annually taken from the soil than are added by mineral fertilizers. Crop and manure residues are returning some of these, but a negative balance of these nutrients likely remains.

And what of the trace elements? Again on page 1, this FAO soils bulletin states that trace element deficiencies were first reported in the late 1800's, and that extensive areas of Earth's soils are no longer able to supply adequate amounts to plant life. Furthermore, several factors are together causing an *accelerating* exhaustion of the available soil supply, including these four:

- weathering and leaching
- stimulation of increased yields by one-sided NPK fertilizing
- decreasing use of natural fertilizer materials in comparison with chemicals
- increasing purity of these chemicals used to stimulate growth

Although this bulletin does not provide any solutions, at least it states well the problems that demand solutions, e.g. when it says: "Trace elements are not regularly applied to the soil by the use of the common fertilizers. Their removal from the soil has been going on for centuries without any systematic replacement." (p. 1)

The stimulation of increased yields with the imbalanced chemicals mentioned above can, of course, continue only as long as sufficient soil minerals and soil organic matter remain to be dissolved out and recombined into new plant food (as described in Ch. 2). The well-known "geometric increase" in the use of these chemical concentrates to continue forcing crop production is another clear indicator (and accelerator) of soil demineralization.

The following table from U.N. Food and Agriculture Organization statistics gives an interesting picture of the "progress" of this chemical demineralization process, and suggests a corresponding mineral decline in food crops.

Year	N	P_2O_5	K_2O	Total
1950	3,639	5,864	3,994	13,497
1955	6,521	7,553	6,439	20,513
1960	9,626	9,532	8,109	27,267
1965	16,404	13,634	11,031	41,069
1970	28,677	18,802	15,569	63,048
1975	38,859	22,784	19,937	81,580
1980 Low (est.)	53,100	28,300	23,500	104,900
1980 High (est.)	60,800	34,100	27,800	122,700

Fig. 3. World chemical NPK fertilizer use in Gg (1 gigagram equals 1 billion grams), from FAO 1976.

Note the six-fold increase from 1950 to 1975, and the projection indicating an *8- to 9-fold increase* will have occurred in just the 30 years from 1950-80. A related statistic comes from the booklet "World Crisis in Agriculture" (Alexander et al., 1974), which states that in the U.S. from

1950 to 1970, yields per acre were increased 53 percent and chemical fertilizer use increased *700 percent* in the same period. Food quality and edibility declined (p. 19).

Going hand in hand with the imbalanced fertilizers has been the use of almost innumerable pesticides—"toxic rescue chemistry" (Walters and Fenzau, 1979)—in order to temporarily protect weak crops from insects and disease. That this approach has not been greatly effective and beneficial to the biosphere is shown by the USDA's "Report and Recommendations on Organic Farming" (1980). It states (p. 62): "Organic farming strongly encourages that the use of synthetic pesticides be avoided in crop production. Use of pesticides has increased 40-fold in the last three decades." Also, in their article, "The Risks of Pesticides" (1980), Pimentel and Pimentel state that insecticides (one class of pesticides) have seen a 10-fold increase over the last three decades. No one knows the *total effects* of this increase on human health and that of the soil, etc., but crop losses to insects have nearly doubled (p. 24).

Apparently few people have heard or comprehended the warnings of Dr. Albrecht (and many others) who often said that "insects and disease are the symptoms of a failing crop, not the cause of it." (Albrecht, 1958;1975)

Trace Elements in Agriculture

Prof. B. Nemec (forest remineralization researcher mentioned in Ch. 3 of "Supplementary Perspectives") says nearly *all* elements are found in the ashes of plants (*Trace Elements in Plant Physiology,* 1950). Robinson and Edgington of USDA (1945) give the figure of "approximately 60 elements" as being positively identified in plants.

N.F. Ermolenko (*Trace Elements and Colloids in Soils,* 1972) states that close analyses show that both plant and animal organisms contain almost all the elements of the Periodic System (92 plus), and he stresses the *primary need of the soil organisms* for these elements so they may build up soil fertility via protoplasm, humus and atmospheric nitrogen accumulation.

These articles and books illustrate a story of Earth's living organisms demanding a wide variety of rock-born soil elements in order to fully express that life, and it may now be clearly seen against the background of 100 centuries of interglacial soil "weathering" and depletion.

The following considerations point to some implications of soil depletion, malnutrition—and soil remineralization—for the whole of humanity.

The remarkably healthy people of the Hunza Valley are already the subjects of a number of books and articles.

Sir Robert McCarrison (1936) appointed Director of Nutrition Research in India in 1929, did extensive studies on nutrition, health and deficiency diseases. After he observed the Hunzacuts' magnificent bodies, sound teeth, strength, longevity, intelligence and happy dispositions—human health almost to perfection—McCarrison gave colonies of Albino rats the diet of the Hunzas. He gave other colonies the diets of disease-ridden cultures on the Indian Sub-Continent. He discovered that the rats would invariably duplicate the states of health seen in the various peoples: perfect health and contentment on the foods of Hunza, the diseases of the Madrasi on the Madrasi food, and so on.

In his seven years of work among the Hunzas and Sikhs, both of whom are superb gardeners and farmers, McCarrison never found a case of stomach ulcer, appendicitis or cancer. A group of doctors founded the McCarrison Society in Britain in 1966 to revive his crucial message for humanity. McCarrison summed up that message in one of his published lectures (1936) when he said, ". . . it seems clear that the habitual use of a diet made up of natural foodstuffs, in proper proportion one to another, and produced on soils that are not impoverished, is an essential condition for the efficient exercise of the function of nutrition on which the maintenance of health depends," and combined with healthy bodily activity, "is mankind's main defence against degenerative diseases; a bulwark, too, against those of infectious origin." (p. 306)

John Tobe (1965) reports that there is one ten-bed hospital for the 40,000 people of the Hunza Valley, and it is practically empty all the time.

William Albrecht (former Chairman of Soils, University of Missouri, now deceased) wrote an article published in "The Journal of Applied Nutrition" (1962) and later in The Albrecht Papers (1975), entitled "The Healthy Hunzas, A Climax Human Crop." In it he praises these people highly as an example for the world, of a people thriving in adherence to the natural laws of biology, being supported on soils fertilized by pulverized rock and organic materials grown in place (as opposed to imported). Dr. Albrecht states that the emphasis on incomplete chemical fertilizers has distracted us from seeing the basic nutritional role of powdered rock which, when combined ("chelated") with organic matter via microorganism activity, is then assimilated by the plant "in the form of organic complexities." ("Protoplasm"—Hamaker). Albrecht concludes by saying that the people must be educated to the Hunza example of soil management and consequent outstanding health; especially now (1962) when the word "degeneration" is beginning to be substituted for "disease".

We may note in passing that Dr. G.T. Wrench said essentially the same things as did Albrecht and McCarrison in his brilliant books, The Wheel of Health (1938) and Reconstruction By Way of the Soil (1946). So did Dr. Lionel Picton in his Nutrition and the Soil (1949). Other examples at hand are Mount's The Food and Health of Western Man (1975), in which he reveals how serious and widespread is dietary mineral deficiency, e.g., 66 percent of college women in America possess low-to-absent iron stores; while at the 2nd World Symposium on Magnesium held in Montreal in 1976, the alarm was sounded that "a grave danger of a magnesium deficiency in foods consumed in the developed countries" now exists. Cancer, arteriosclerosis, and heart and bone diseases are implicated as resulting from such deficiencies. (*The Ecologist*, 12/79, p. 317). The same obvious message can be read from *Trace Elements in Soil-Plant-Animal Systems* (Nicholas, 1975), which reveals the continuing findings by researchers of "new" essential elements for human health and that deficiencies can be expected to result in *breakdown of the physiological functions where the element is involved*. They say there are now 14 *known* trace elements *essential* for animal life, and most or all of them are essential for soil microorganisms as well. These are (in order of their discovery as essential): iron, iodine, copper, manganese, zinc, cobalt, molybdenum, selenium, chromium, tin, fluorine, silicon, nickel and vanadium; also boron for "higher plants."

Weston Price wrote an epochal 526-page book entitled *Nutrition and Physical Degeneration* (1945, 1975), which reported his findings from many years of studying people of cultures and lands worldwide. He proved how *rapidly* individuals and entire peoples degenerate physically, mentally, and morally when the diet changes from natural whole foods from fertile soils to the refined and nutrient-poor foods of modern societies. Price, a dentist by training, found (among many other things) that people suffering from tooth decay were ingesting deficient amounts of vitamins and less than half the minimum requirements of calcium, phosphorous, magnesium, iron and other elements. His case showing that severe malnutrition is the *primary* cause of juvenile delinquency and violent criminal tendencies is a powerful if not indisputable one.

In his chapter "Soil Depletion and Animal Deterioration," Price says this in summary:

> In my studies on the relation of the physiognomy of the people of various districts to the soil, I have found a difference in the facial type of the last generation of young adults when compared with that of their parents. The new generation has inherited depleted soil...The most serious problem confronting the coming generations is this nearly unsurmountable handicap of depletion of the quality of the foods because of the depletion of the minerals of the soil. (p. 392)

One chapter of the book is by Dr. Albrecht, entitled "Food is Fabricated Soil Fertility," in which Albrecht again closely correlates the level of nutrition with fertility of soil, and he concludes that, "...it is to be hoped that a national consciousness of declining soil can enlist our sciences and industry into rebuilding and conserving our soils as the surest guarantee of the future health and strength of the nation." (p. 469) This was the need Albrecht saw when these words were written over 35 years ago.

Metabolic Aspects of Health: Nutritional Elements in Health and Disease by John Myers, M.D. and Karl Schutte, Ph.D. (1979), is another major work documenting the elementary facts of the soil-food-health chain, and the disasterous consequences resulting from "ignore-ance" and abuse of the natural human and soil ecology. They stress the following: the very widespread incidence of soil mineral deficiency; the innumerable *forms* of diseases brought on by these deficiencies, including *psychobiological imbalances*; that dozens of known human enzyme systems are absolutely proven to be keyed to soil elements, including zinc, boron, cobalt, manganese, barium, nickel, copper, magnesium and more; and the great need for the natural balance of these elements via the food supply. Schutte, the botanist, demonstrates that the same principles apply for healthy, disease/insect resistant plant growth.

The known evidence on cancer and trace element links is given, such as the study in South Africa showing 89 percent of the cancerous regions as having poor soils, whereas nearly 66 percent of cancer-free regions are on comparatively "rich" soils (p. 121).

The exact relations between the many soil elements and the many forms of cancer have yet to be defined, they say, but it is now clear that they are associated with imbalances in the trace element supply, which key the *normal enzymatic activity of the cell*. The same association has been implicated for atherosclerosis and hypertension. (p. 193)

In light of the Hunzacuts' total freedom from cancer, and the fact that in the U.S. 1 of 4 people are conservatively estimated as due to develop cancer in their lifetimes (Eckholm and Record, 1976), the need for very fundamental re-orientation could hardly be more clear. Gus Speth, Chairman of the Council on Environmental Quality, stressed this point when he recently announced (July, 1980) that the incidence of cancer rate jumped by *10 percent* from 1970 to 1976. Contrast this figure with the 3 percent increase from 1960 to 1970 (*CEQ*, 1980). *Science News* (Vol. 110, p. 310) contains an article summarizing previous articles on the effect of diet as follows: "Diet can have a dramatic influence on the prevention and treatment of cancer. Spontaneous regression of cancer, for instance, appears to have resulted from a change in the balance of trace elements."

The relation of cancer to soil depletion and imbalance is also examined in Voisin's work, *Soil, Grass and Cancer: Health of Animals and Man Is Linked to the Mineral Balance of the Soil* (1959). Voisin's evidence confirms his statements that: "The dust of our cells is the dust of the soil," and "animals and men are the biochemical photograph of the soil." Hur (1975) and *The Soil Association* (1979) offer further reviews of available soil-cancer (etc.) documentation. This relation may be readily understood by a look at the four types of cell processes known to be subject to the balance of trace elements, as summarized in *Trace Elements in Plant Physiology* (Wallace, 1950):

1) synthesis and breakdown of tissue structures
2) energetic processes ("oxido-reductions")
3) regulation of nervous stimuli
4) detoxification of cellular poisons

These processes refer to the actions of about 5000 soil-dependent enzyme systems, all of which can be disrupted or prevented by element deficiency, imbalance, or drugs, pesticides, radiation, etc.(Knight, 1975).

As a single example of the great importance of these enzyme systems, which John Hamaker and many biologists are stressing, consider "superoxide dismutase" (SOD), which has recently come into prominence through the discoveries of Irwin Fridovich, Duke University Biochemistry Professor (*Science*, 9/8/78; Donald, 1980). SOD is found in all cells and functions as a defender of cellular integrity by rendering harmless numerous forms of "superoxide radicals" which continually threaten the cell. Four types of SOD are now known; each is identified simply by the trace element used to bind with the protein that makes up the enzyme. One type requires both copper and zinc, two others require manganese, while the fourth (found in microorganisms) uses iron.

The most significant fact revealed in this research is that SOD activity *is distinctly altered in cancerous cells.* In fact, as Donald reveals, lowered amounts of the manganese-dependent SOD have been found in all tumors examined by cancer researchers Deamer and Yamanaka, and sub-normal amounts of the copper-zinc SOD in many, though not all, the tumors. None of this research mentions the soil as the source of these elements, although it is mentioned that SOD is now being sold in pill form. A check at a local "health food" store turned up the small bottles selling for $11.50 each. (Note: This writer has been purchasing river gravel screenings from California gravel pits for under *$6.00 per ton.*)

Another related article comes from the *Lansing State Journal* (7/30/80) which reports on research proceedings at the Stanford University Medical School. Dr. H. Kaplan states that there are 200 to 300 different types of cancer, and that the "antibody" that will prevent one type will not work for another type. In other words, it is necessary to have all the elements available for the cells' 5000 enzyme systems all the time, if the body's natural immunity system is to function normally. Again, we hear no word on the soil or food quality; the doctors are busy trying to grow hybrid cells in the laboratory which they hope can produce some of the antibodies. How long before "practical applications" become widespread?

Dr. Kaplan says: "It will be necessary to generate literally hundreds of specific antibodies. It's going to take a long time."

$30 billion per year is being spent on such efforts to find "cures" for cancer (Samuel Epstein, 1979), which happens to be about $30 billion more than is going towards soil remineralization. It is interesting, if not mind-boggling, to consider how many doctors could travel to observe the cancer-free Hunzacuts were that $30 billion used for the doctors' tickets at, for example, $2000 per round-trip ticket. No doubt even the remarkable good-naturedness and superior health of the Hunzacuts could be strained by a party of 15,000,000 curious doctors.

How many doctors ("teachers") actually want to learn why there is just one ten-bed hospital for the 40,000 people of the Hunza Valley, and why it is practically empty all the time? (Tobe, 1965)

Prior to a further look at the *behavioral* implications of soil depletion and malnutrition, let's cite a few statistics provided by the article, "The Myth of Health in America" (Fry, 1976), on the general state of ill-health in the U.S., as of 1974:

1) The U.S. Public Health Service reports only 3,000,000 people out of the entire population can be considered healthy—about 1½ percent.

2) The U.S. ranks 89th among nations in death rate.

3) About 1 billion visits to physicians are made annually.

4) 30 million citizens will spend time in a hospital annually.

5) About 9 of 10 (190,000,000) suffer from constipation.

6) Over 21,000,000 suffer from "mental illness."

7) 98.5 percent have defective teeth (31,000,000 have *no teeth*).

8) 60 percent have defective vision.

9) About 77 percent of adults are affected by forms of arthritis and rheumatism.

10) Over 13,000,000 of the 100,000,000 alcohol drinkers are considered "alcoholics."

11) 58.6 percent of children cannot pass a minimum physical fitness test.

12) The average child has eight colds per year.

13) Every child over the age of four has incipient or severe heart problems.

14) Over 50 million suffer from heart diseases.

15) Over 7 million children are "mentally retarded."

16) *Cancer is the number one cause of disease-related death of children.*

17) Total annual disease cost: $104 billion, or roughly $500 per U.S. citizen.

Although updates on all these figures are not at hand, Fry again provides the disease bill projected for 1981: $250 billion, about 4 times the 1950 figures in non-inflated dollars (*Better Life Journal*, 1/81). Since the Dept. of Health, Education and Welfare (1978) gives the figure of $238 billion for 1975, Fry's figure may be too low.

Psychobiological Connections

In his article, "Is America Going Crazy: A nutritional approach to mental health" (*East-West*, 9/80), Tom Monte shows us a curve for outpatients being "treated" for mental illness which looks much like the curves on this book's cover. He gives some more educational facts and figures on the U.S.:

• 15 percent of the population, over 32 million people, are "officially" suffering from mental disorders, although the Department of Health and Human Services (formerly HEW) officials suggest 20 percent is more realistic.
• Whereas in 1950 there were 12,000 psychologists and psychiatrists, there are now over 50,000. In 1955, 380,000 people were in psychoanalysis; by 1977, there were 4.6 million.
• $40 billion is spent yearly by people seeking to maintain or regain their mental health; two million people entered "mental institutions."
• Divorce rates have tripled since 1970.
• Since 1967, Scholastic Aptitude Test (SAT) scores have been sinking fast; combined math and verbal scores have on average dropped almost 100 points.
• Since 1956, arrests of *children* suspected of committing murder, rape, and other violent crimes have increased six-fold.
• Nearly 30,000 men and women took their own lives in 1978, part of a steady climb over many years. Among 20-to 24-year olds, the rate tripled between 1955 and 1975. [Columnist Sydney J. Harris quotes a 900 percent rise in suicides by 15- to 24-year olds in the last decade; there were 5,000 in 1979. (Harris, 1980)]
• Monte also reports on the findings of scientists Fernstrom, Wurtman, and others at the Massachusetts Institute of Technology which show how close is the relationship between dietary nutrients and normal brain function. Dr. Fernstrom is quoted: "It is becoming increasingly clear that brain chemistry and function can be influenced by a single meal. That is, in well-nourished individuals consuming normal amounts of food, short-term changes can rapidly affect brain function." Dr. Michael Lesser, who has been working to improve the diets of schizophrenic and depressed patients in Massachusetts and California, shares his observations: "I can almost say

as a truism that the better the diet, the better the person's mental health. Everything you put into your mouth is going to affect your mind and body...A good diet helps preserve sanity; a poor diet helps lose sanity.''

These same sorts of observations were made by all those who studied the "Healthy Hunzas"; they could not help but note the unusually clear and balanced mental and emotional natures they expressed. Now in *Science News* (5/30/81), we see an article, "Psychiatry for the 80's," which reports on an American Psychiatric Association meeting in New Orleans attended by over 8,000 psychiatrists. The article relates that the meeting was not upon theories of Oedipal complexes or psychodynamic theory but about *recognizing the links of biology and behavior*—specifically, the roles of brain chemicals. As is usual, no direct consideration of the quality of nutrition or soil fertility was reported. Most of the enthusiasm at the meeting was over the possibilities for psychiatrists to acquire their own "armamentarium," i.e., a mixed arsenal of "psychoactive agents" (drugs) aimed at establishing chemical balance in the brain, and presumably, mental health. It is stated that the single trace element lithium, being given to "manic-depressives," has helped 70 percent of those receiving it.

Perhaps most significant in this article are the two Positron Emission Tomography (PET) scanner pictures comparing a "normal" brain to a "schizophrenic" brain. Great differences are quite obvious, and the owner of the chemically abnormal brain is said to be experiencing visual and auditory hallucinations. Since the question of whether to drug, or to abundantly nourish, such a brain is still hardly being asked, the following work of Alex Schauss may be valuable in resolving this "controversy."

The following is a summary from the interview mentioned earlier. Schauss, an experienced criminologist, counselor, and Director of the Institute for Biosocial Research, makes these points:

• The crime rates continue to climb quickly; violent crime went up 11 percent from 1978 to 1979. (It went up another 13 percent in 1980—*Associated Press* Washington, 3/31/81) Over 800,000 people are in prisons and jails.
• 12 million arrests of juvenile offenders were made in 1979.
• 10 million teenage children are alcoholics.
• 30 million Americans take drugs to escape from stress.
• Malnutrition is the prime cause of criminal behavior.
• *All* the essential food nutrients *in balance* are needed by the brain for positive behavioral performance and ability to handle stress.

Of the many amazing cases Schauss has worked with, here are several examples:

• Eskimos and Native Americans living in very remote territories on indigenous food supplies in the Stewart Islands of Alaska, who had been physically and psychologically healthy for centuries, experience the degenerative diseases and moral decay so prevalent in western culture when the foods (not specified) from that culture are allowed in. Crimes are subsequently committed for which these "primitive" cultures didn't even have words in their language to describe; the words had to be invented.

• In Germany, an extremely hyperactive child would react violently, to the point of throwing siblings out of closed windows, within 3 to 5 minutes of receiving small but brain-imbalancing amounts of phosphate additives from processed foods. His parents, and many others experiencing similar problems, noted dramatic behavioral improvements when the diets were better balanced. (A double-blind study of children reported in *Science, 3/20/80,* further proved the dietary links to "hyperactivity" first warned of by Dr. Benjamin Feingold.)

• After Schauss spoke for over three hours on the importance of good nutrition to a group of prisoners, these men decided to try to obtain some nutritional supplements to their prison food. After fighting hard for two years to make these available, even petitioning the Human Rights Commission of the United Nations, these inmates had all their requests denied and were transferred throughout the prison system. This resulted in the transferred men inspiring many other prisoners to seek better nutrition, and finally the facility in Lompoc, California, allowed inmates to choose three supplements which they could purchase with their prison wages. They chose brewer's yeast, wheat germ and dessicated liver. One of the men wrote back to Schauss and said, in part:

> I noticed that supplements motivate a feeling of health and hope in me, also in others around me, many of whom have shown little or no sign of hope before. In fact I saw guys smile today—and this was only a week after they got the supplements—that I had never seen smile before and that is ten years. That is really encouraging.

The Forest Die-Out Continues

The almost unbelievable rate at which the Earth's remaining forest cover is being destroyed by human exploitation (20 to 30 million hectares per year—*Global 2000 Report*; 50 acres per minute—Myers, *The Sinking Ark*), are finally being widely *acknowledged*, and their additional consumption by wildfire is, we have seen, increasingly been made evident. What has, of course, not been widely recognized or acknowledged is the recent evidence disclosing the cyclical nature and accurate timing of the glacial-interglacial-glacial sequence; nor has the last 10,000 years of soil demineralization and retrogressive vegetational succession been brought to present focus within the multitude of human plans, schemes and struggles for prosperity and survival.

If these realities had been clear, perhaps the many environmental modification projects to date would have had their basis in a wholly different appreciation of natural systems: the beauty of their design, the inherent provisions for human prosperity within the natural design, and *the requirements* of natural systems to maintain a perpetual symbiotic relationship with mankind.

Consider again all the factors of forest assault in their simultaneous operation: human deforestation, soil degeneration, insects/diseases, fire, worsening climate, air pollution, acid rains...Then consider John Hamaker's estimation that human actions have accelerated the glacial onset by 500 years, and the "20-year transition period" by some unknown amount.

A discussion of forest die-out would by no means be complete without looking at a picture of how another "team" is moving quickly to help annihilate the forests: insects and disease, of course. This important section has also been placed in the "Perspectives Supplement to Chapters Three, Four and Five." For a more in-depth look at the forest predators aside from man, and their crucial relationship to soil fertility, plus a look at the so-called "acid from heaven" crisis, write to Hamaker-Weaver Publishers, P.O. Box 1961, Burlingame, California, 94010, or Hamaker-Weaver Publishers, Route 1 Box 158, Seymour, Missouri 65746.

6

Introduction

John Hamaker completed this article in May, 1981, and it is likely one of the most important articles that can be found in terms of understanding how our living Earth works, and consequently how a living humanity can and must work *en rapport* with this established planetary ecology. This paramount need is again made self-evident herein, because, as Hamaker describes it, "The climate cycle is a byproduct of the entire life system, all of which rests on the expenditure of atomic energy in the tectonic system."

This forms the central underlying theme of "The Glacial Process and the End of the Food Supply." Once again the *overlying* theme is the fact of human responsibility to uplift and restore that entire life system, and John Hamaker makes the urgency of this great task crystal clear, "We have no time to spare in gaining control of the glacial process—it has already started."

Hamaker appropriately concludes the article with a list of minimal objectives to be met if such a worldwide effort to stabilize and replenish the Earth's biosphere is to succeed. Following the article is a look at how such documents as the U.S. Government's *Global 2000 Report* and the International Union for the Conservation of Nature's *World Conservation Strategy* relate, or do not relate, to the principles and themes of this book's first six chapters. May the reader proceed with understanding.

It is one of the moral functions of science to change this attitude of men to the soil which has borne them; to bring men to a clear recognition of the marvel and beauty of the mechanism on which the existence of all the living beings on the earth intimately depends. This end it attains through the clear views which it opens into the structure and history of the earth by removing the dull conception of mere chance which we almost instinctively apply to the phenomena of nature, and in its place giving an understanding of those processes which lead to the order and harmony of the universe.

Nathaniel Southgate Shaler
The Origin and Nature of Soils, 1891

6

The Glacial Process and the End of the Food Supply

The information about past glacial periods is now sufficient so that there is general agreement on what has happened in the past. There is no agreement on why it happened.

We can say with assurance that the climate cycle requires very close to 100,000 years to be completed. We can say that during that time there are only 10,000 years in which there is a temperate zone capable of supporting an agricultural and technological civilization. We are at the end of the 10,000 year period.

For the purpose of a discussion of the survival of civilization, the climate cycle consists of about 10,000 years of interglacial conditions and 90,000 years of glacial conditions. *If we are to have any chance of survival, we must understand the glacial process so we can take the necessary steps to eliminate glaciation.*

There are two energy systems which are so powerful by comparison to any other factors (such as sun spots, the Milankovitch effects, or the alignment of planets in space) that these latter factors can be dismissed except to note that whatever effect they have, it is superimposed on the glacial process without substantially altering it. Both of the primary energy systems use the energy in the atom. One is the sun and the other is the tectonic system.

The Sun

There is not much to say about this practically constant source of energy. The earth intercepts this supply of energy constantly.

However, if the energy incident to the earth at the higher latitudes is deflected into space instead of being absorbed at ground level, the total amount of energy available to warm the earth is decreased by that amount. During the glacial period the total amount of sun energy reaching the earth is decreased because the CO_2 (from the tectonic system) directs a heavy cloud cover to the polar latitudes. The clouds have a very high albedo, i.e., ability to reflect the sun's rays into space.

The Tectonic System

Everything on this earth, especially the maintenance of a viable environment for all living organisms, is totally dependent on the tectonic system. When the tectonic system runs out of fuel and fails, the earth will be a cold dead planet like Mars. Although everything on and in the earth is connected to everything else, only those factors directly related to glaciation are pertinent to this discussion.

The tectonic system is a thermomechanical system. As such, it is designed to work in conformance with all the known laws governing such systems and in conformance with the known physical characteristics of the materials which comprise the system. The system is also capable of performing in a manner which produces the geological structures which have been found on the land and on the ocean floor. The principal operational elements of such a system are shown in Fig. 1 (page 132-133). For pictorial reasons, the sketch is not to scale.

Operational Components of the Tectonic System

If the tectonic system is to work, certain requirements must be met. These will be described in detail later. The requirements are:

1. The crust must be supported by the hydraulic pressure beneath it.

2. The elevation of the crust at any point must depend on the weight of the crust and the pressure beneath it.

3. There must be a massive release of energy at some point in order to build sea floor at the center of the ocean, melt it down, and send it back. The only such energy supply available is atomic. Heat is also needed to maintain the internal heat requirements of the earth.

4. The energy source must be at the edge of the continents where sufficient pressure is demonstrated to build mountains and hydraulically lift sections of the sea floor to plateau elevations. The energy is released in what I call *continental heaters*.

5. The principal source of radioactive fuel is the unmelted portion of the mantle. Everything which has been melted was melted at the expense of its original supply of radioactive materials.

6. The highest temperatures are in the heaters, where gravity separation of the molten components results in accumulation of a critical mass which, in turn, results in release of energy by explosion.

The next highest temperature is in the core which, according to seismic data, is melted to within 800 miles of the center of the earth in spite of the great pressure at that depth. The core gets its heat from the hot magma discharged from the heaters.

The third highest temperature is in the mantle, which gets its heat primarily from contact with the core as the heat from the core moves across the temperature gradient to the cold of outer space.

The fourth highest temperature is in the Mohorovich discontinuity ("gunk").

7. The pressure at a common elevation under the crust is highest in the heater. At all other points there is a lower pressure caused by the friction of flow of superheated magma out of the heater to the common reservoir (the core) and back up to the crust.

8. The contour of the mantle is a true circle at 90 degrees to the earth's axis. The shear line or line of relative motion between the crust and the mantle is a true circle and lies just above the mantle.

9. There are basically three types of rocks produced in the tectonic system. The effect of gravity separation in the heater is shown in the igneous rocks which show up as intrusions and extrusions in the mountains and hills above it.

The lighter-weight materials expelled from the heater to the core float on top of the core, and the heavier components sink into the core material. The lightweight materials are low in melting point and super-heated and hence more fluid than the core material. They would therefore tend to cut channels through the core material to points of more or less regular usage such as the mid-ocean ridge. The material which arrives at the ridge holds the pressure against the gunk and feeds material into the gunk as required to make up for that which is melted down in the heater.

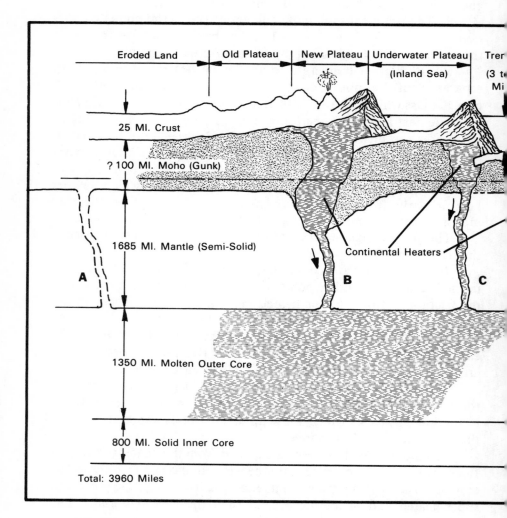

Fig. 1

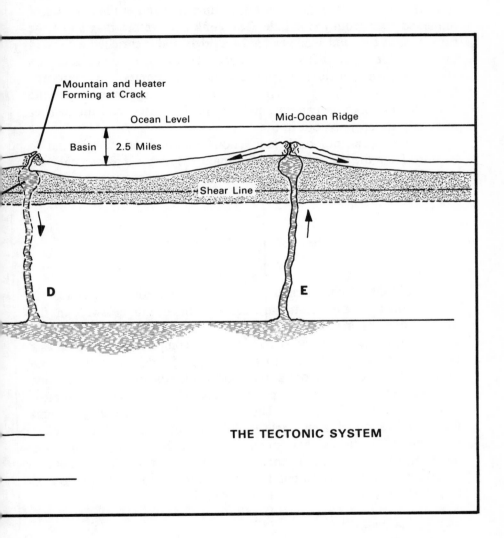

THE TECTONIC SYSTEM

The gunk gets that name for lack of a better one. It has peculiar properties. It is thought that there are several times as much gunk as ocean floor. If so it must move into the heater at a fraction of the velocity of the crust. As the gunk travels, it must tear and erode particles of unmelted rock from the mantle. The gunk is therefore magma of the same type as that which comes out of a ridge, and is enriched with solid bits of mantle which stiffen it like flour added to bread dough. It carries all the elements, including unused radioactive compounds, into the heater where the lighter materials are separated out and moved up to the crust, the radioactive materials are used in the heater, and the heavier materials are dropped out in the core.

The gunk can support heater action wherever used material can be expelled from the heater and gunk or mantle is supplied as the make-up material. The action will not occur if there is enough motion in the gunk to prevent gravity separation.

Description of Components

The mantle

The mantle is the original space debris which formed the earth. It has low-melting-point aluminum silicate above and below it in the molten form. Therefore, the low-melting-point compounds in the mantle must be melted. The higher-melting-point compounds must exist as a porous sintered mass in order to give seismic reflections in at least some respect similar to those from a solid mass. Since the molten compounds exist throughout the mantle, a positive pressure in a heater can initiate a flow in a downward direction. The flow from the heater is very hot and it can erode and melt a channel through the mantle as the heater builds up strength. The heaters have operated all over the mantle. By this time there must be numerous old channels, such as point A, Fig. 1, that are no doubt partially blocked but operable as needed, to conduct a flow of magma to any part of the crust that needs it.

The Ocean Floor

The floor is built by something which I call a ridge toggle because it functions much like a toggle press. The toggle is fifty to several hundred miles wide, as measured along the ridge, and it extends several hundred miles at 90 degrees to the ridge.

Probably no more than fifty miles either side of the ridge is involved in the production of the force which pushes the sea floor toward the land and into the continental heaters.

When there is increased flow at E, Fig. 1, both sides of the toggle lift up until the magma can leak through and fill the crack (Fig. 2, page 136). As the magma escapes from the magma chamber, the toggle drops down. The ocean water and the walls of the rift freeze the magma to some depth. Below that it varies from plastic to molten at the bottom. Since new magma has entered the rift, the two opposing halves of the toggle must move farther apart. The force generated by two members operating at an angle approaching 180 degrees is so great that the ocean floor must move or the material in the rift must fail. The amount of force exerted is testified to by the fact that only a few hundred yards below the surface, the magnetic orientation lines in the rock become completely jumbled together, showing that the pressure forges the hot, somewhat plastic, rock into a cohesive mass.

There is a similar force exerted in the lower portion of the rift when the bottom edges tend to come together as the plate rises. It is doubtful, however, that much pressure is exerted on the ocean floor because the more plastic magma in the lower portion will yield too easily. The act of yielding, however, may force material upward and cut channels through which the magma can enter as it opens above. Such a crack is shown in Fig. 3, p. 137. It is much wider than most such fissures because at the latitude of Iceland the toggle is working against great pressure, there being no heaters to receive the sea floor. The toggle is therefore on the high side of the approximately 3-to-6 mile thickness range of ridge toggles. The ocean floor thickens by cooling on the bottom side with time. A 6-mile thick toggle does not have to rise very much to open a 200-foot wide fissure.

Numerous cracks have been detected parallel to the rift and extending for some distance away from the rift. It seems probable that these are caused by bending. The magma chamber is not very wide, and pressure and volume changes in the rest of the system are reflected immediately in the chamber. The toggle plates are too heavy and long to react quickly to such changes; therefore, one would expect the ends of the toggle plates to receive a cantilevered load at the rift. If the pressure and volume in the chamber increase, the bottom of the plates are put in tension. The top of the plates are in compression. When the chamber pressure and volume decrease, the top of the plates are in tension and the bottom in compression. Since the top is

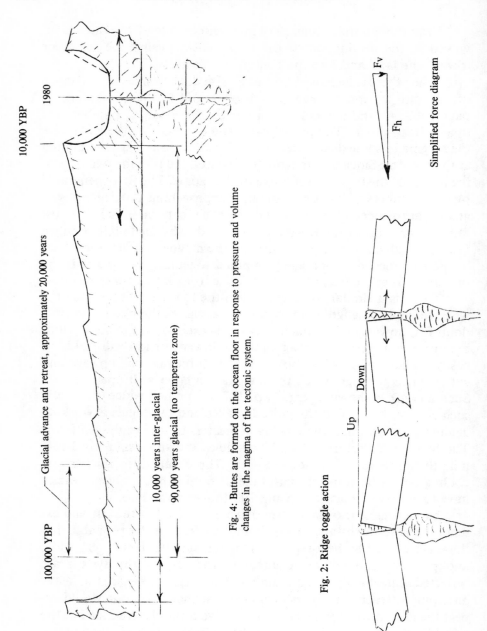

Fig. 4: Buttes are formed on the ocean floor in response to pressure and volume changes in the magma of the tectonic system.

Glacial advance and retreat, approximately 20,000 years

10,000 years inter-glacial

90,000 years glacial (no temperate zone)

100,000 YBP

10,000 YBP

1980

Fig. 2: Ridge toggle action

Up

Down

Simplified force diagram

F_v

F_h

Fig. 3 Tension* rift on the spreading crest of the Mid-Atlantic Ridge, as exposed in southwest Iceland. The faults and fissures break a plain of Basalt lava flows that are a few thousand years old. The foreground fissure has a maximum width of about 60 meters (200 feet) and a maximum depth of about 45 meters (150 feet) below the rim on the near side and twice that below the rim on the far side. View is northeastward along the Almannagia (Great Fissure). Photograph by Bruce Heezen, Lamont-Doherty Geological Observatory of Columbia University.
*See text for explanation.

cold, and cold rock has almost no tensile strength, the tension cracks occur on the top side.

Thus there is probably a bending action in the toggles adjacent to the rift in addition to the up-and-down movements of Fig. 2, which open and close the rift. The force required to keep the ocean floor under pressure and feeding into the heaters (F_h, Fig. 2) is developed in the same manner as the force in a toggle press. The toggle can not buckle because it is uniformly supported by the weight of water and plate on the top side and the hydraulic pressure of the magma on the bottom side.

Butte Formation and Glaciation

The record of pressure and volume of flow at the ridge during the climate cycle is clearly recorded in the butte formed at the ridge. The buttes are visible in Nevada, California, and on the ocean floor. One is formed on either side of the rift every 100,000 years.

The butte shown in Fig. 4 was proportioned on the basis of those in Nevada which were estimated to originally be 20 miles long by 2 miles high. The number of glacial advances and retreats during the last glaciation is an estimate based on some agreement among those who have studied the glacial deposits in depth. An accurate count could be made on the ocean floor.

The two primary users of the magma are the ocean ridges and the inland sea floors being pumped up to plateau status. However, if the weight of the land mass increases by the addition of an ice field, the more fluid portion of the gunk will be squeezed out from under the depressed portion of the continent and into the inner core. The only place it can go from the inner core is out the ridges. Thus during glaciation, as one ice field after another is established, the flow at the ridge increases. As the flow at the ridge increases, the rate of ocean floor movement into the heater increases, and the heaters produce more melt and more pressure. When the glaciation collapses, the situation is reversed. There is a huge demand for magma under the formerly glaciated parts of the land mass, and the pressure and volume available at the ridges decreases accordingly. Over a period of a thousand years, more or less, the material in the center of the ridge collapses, leaving the two buttes facing each other. The material under the dashed lines (Fig. 4) feeds back into the rift to keep the ocean floor feeding into the heaters until the situation stabilizes.

"Flow" of the Ocean Floor

The only large stress possible in the ocean floor is compression. The tensile strength of cold rock is only about 4 percent of compressive strength, and shear strength is between 10 percent and 20 percent of compressive strength. The compressive stress for the floor thickness is probably no more than 10,000 psi. The shear stress is probably no more than 1000 psi. When a toggle is ready to move, it must shear the fracture zone on each side of the toggle. Since the toggles are from fifty to several hundred miles wide along the rift, a force of 100 psi acting on an effective one-mile thickness in the rift would be much more than enough to initiate shear in the fracture zone. The shear crack originates at the toggle and runs as far along the fracture zones as it can before elasticity in the rock absorbs the motion of the toggle. So the toggle has to go through a number of cycles to crack the fracture zones all the way to the shore. Toggles move independently and they will move in the direction that offers the least resistance.

But they do not go very far before they meet too much resistance and have to wait for adjacent toggles to move and help take up the strain in the ocean floor. For this reason they all stay close to the average ridge line (Fig. 5, p. 140). When the stress in the ocean floor is enough to overcome the frictional resistance of driving the ocean floor into the heaters, there is a general feeding into all of the heaters impelled by the elastic stress built up in the sea floor.

A direct shearing stress, such as that in the fracture zones, induces an equal shear stress at 90 degrees. Therefore, the toggle would just as soon shear across its width as down the fracture zones. It will readily do so in response to a higher pressure from one side of the toggle than the other side. The gunk is always ready to heal the fracture zones. It is heavier than ocean floor, so it stops rising about a mile below the sea bottom. Major fracture zones make huge canyons. The ocean floor is not a single plate but a mosaic of a great many pieces always subject to change and motion (Fig. 5).

The floor thickens by freezing on the bottom side and adding sedimentary deposits on the top side as it moves away from the ridge. The total thickness of the ocean floor at the edge of the continent might be 15 or 20 miles. Largely due to the weight of sedimentary deposits, the ocean floor sinks lower as it moves and the deep ocean basins are thus formed.

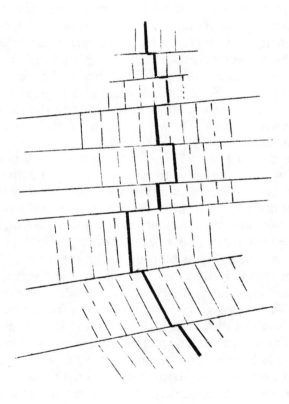

Fig. 5. 8 toggles in the South Atlantic mid-ocean ridge

The rate at which the ocean floor travels varies widely. The variation which is probably common to all sea floors is that they move faster during glaciation than during the interglacial period. The Nevada buttes (Fig. 4) tell us that the floor traveled 20 miles in 100,000 years or 12.6 inches per year, which is well above the 2 inches to 4 inches per year that it has been moving in recent years. Part of that speed of movement is due to the fact that the mid-ocean ridge which built the Great Basin plateau, was close to shore. The ridge itself may have been moving eastward because there was too much resistance to movement on the west side of the ridge. The basin was built so fast and raised out of the water so quickly that the ridges did not have time to be covered with much sedimentary rock. Ocean floor studies of buttes could probably give us a more accurate idea of the increase in speed of floor formation during glaciation relative to the interglacial rate.

In recent centuries ocean floor feeding into the heaters has occurred on about a 100-year cycle. Following a series of heavy earthquakes around the Pacific "ring of fire" which herald the feeding, we have had 50 years of colder-than-average weather. The cold weather is accompanied by more volcanic action and the warm weather by less.

During the hundred-year period, ocean water penetrates deep into the joint between the incoming ocean floor and the mountain above it. It comes back out as superheated steam which cuts the sedimentary rock away. The deep trenches in front of the heaters are formed in this way. The mineralized hot water rises to the surface, causing the upwelling currents so widely observed. The minerals support an abundant sea life and excellent fish yields. But when the ocean floor moves into the heater, all the leaks are sealed and the fishermen must go elsewhere. When the ocean floor feeds, a large amount of heat and liquified gases, mostly carbon and sulfur oxides, are released. The ocean warms up a degree or two, and the gases either dissolve into the water or go up into the atmosphere.

Ocean floor volcanoes form in large numbers at the ridges. The flexing of the toggles causes many leaks, particularly in the fracture zones between adjacent toggles where the rock is subject to both horizontal and vertical shearing forces. These volcanoes evidently result from the fact that there is highly fluid magma at the ridges which, during times when the pressure in the magma chamber is high, is able to blow out. One would expect an accumulation of gases at the ridge peak also, and the two together are probably all that is involved in these volcanoes. As they leave the ridge, they invariably freeze up and are covered with sediment.

There is another type of ocean volcano. Hawaii is the outstanding example. It is standing still while the ocean floor is moving past it to the northwest. When one volcano moves away from it, another forms behind the first. That would only be possible if there were a heater operating in the mantle. How it got started is anybody's guess. Once started there is little likelihood that it will stop until it becomes a part of the continental heater system. As fast as the radioactive material is used up in a batch, the gunk cascades into the heater chamber, expels the used material (through the volcano), and fires it up with new radioactive material. Apparently during the time it abandons one volcano and establishes another directly overhead, the very hot column of magma and gases from the heater have disrupted the ocean floor on both sides of the line of volcanoes, because there are undersea mountains all over the place.

Continental Heater Operation

The land masses are made up of many inland seas raised out of the ocean by heater action. The old heater trenches can be traced out by seismographic studies even though the mountains have long since eroded away. The heaters have long since ceased to be active in the interior of the continent, but the newest two or three are in various stages of development and decay. At position D (Fig. 1) a new heater is starting to function. It started because the ocean floor at position C was forced lower and lower as the mountain chain grew above it. There is always one section of the mountain chain which is heavier than any other. The situation is analogous to stepping on the edge of a thin ice sheet on a pond. At the point of pressure, the ice is forced downward, requiring the ice to bend over the buoyant force of the water in a long bend. The maximum tensile stress is in the center of the bend, and that is where the ice cracks. The crack runs in an arc back to the shore line because the bend produced by a local stress at the shore line runs radially over a 180 degree area of the ice. The ocean floor bends over the buoyant force of the gunk and a crack is formed.

Leakage through the crack draws the more fluid portion of the gunk to the crack and gradually an arc-shaped chamber of magma develops. It is only a matter of time until gravity separation produces a critical mass and the heater begins to function.

The pressure in the gunk between D and C is gradually increased by the pressure developed in the two heaters. As the pressure goes up, the crust between D and C must go up. When the lower edge of the inland sea crust bears against the upper edge of the sea floor, the two grind on each other until the ocean floor can begin to move under the inland sea floor. At that time it becomes easier for the toggles to push the ocean floor under at point D than at point C.

When the floor stops feeding at C, it no longer drags gunk into the heater and it begins to die out. At point B is a heater which has raised its plateau about as far as it can go and is now only helping the heater at C to finish raising the plateau between points B and C.

The heater at point A has died out. The heater chamber has been filled with gunk.

The incoming gunk is much colder than the inshore gunk which is at heater temperatures. Therefore, the melting is faster in the inshore gunk. As the floor feeds new relatively-cold gunk (and any of the floor which advances beyond the protection of the underlying gunk) into the heater chamber, it cascades into the chamber, gradually moving the heater to a position more central to the inland sea it is raising.

When the gunk stops feeding into a heater, the heater "drowns" in its own magma. When it has exhausted the radioactive components to the point where it can no longer develop a critical mass, the heater is dead.

It is not practical to think of the entire arc-shaped heater as a single unit. The eruptions of Hawaiian volcanoes indicate that a few years of settlement are required between explosions. If the settling in the entire arc had to occur all at once, there would not be the great number of heavy earthquakes recorded in the inland seas. Therefore the trenches must be viewed as containing a number of short chambers protected on each end by gunk with the lightweight, low-melting-point molten rock floating just under the crust.

When an explosion occurs, a plasma of many compounds develops around the explosion at very high temperature and pressure. The upward blast must shoot particles from every layer above it into the lightweight aluminum silicate and silicate layers, resulting in the complex granite rock which almost, if not always, forms the cores of mountains. The mountains are the first things formed, which means that the blasts are not far below the crust. For this reason, a great variety of elements can be found in the dikes and sills resulting from the explosions that drive the granite cores upward.

As a result of the explosion, the temperature goes up and some components of the melt gasify to hold the pressure between explosions. Materials below the explosion are driven down to the inner core against great flow resistance. Precisely how everything is handled within the heater is never likely to be known, but *the result is that the light elements are driven up into the crust along with enough traces of all the elements so that when the rocks from the heater are mixed by glaciation with the sedimentary rocks of the ocean floor, the mixture contains a well-balanced quantity of the elements necessary to sustain life.*

Sills are formed as the granite core pushes upward through the sea floor. The weak bond between different layers of sedimentary rock breaks. Huge slabs of rock lift up like the pages of a book; the openings are quickly filled with magma; the result is a layer of young rock between two much-older layers of rock.

Dikes are vertical cracks which are filled with magma. They often contain ores, some showing heavy metal such as gold and silver. These things are in the gunk, and their concentration in the ore indicates that they were gravitationally separated at the time of intrusion.

Volcanoes always form behind the high mountains. They act as pressure relief valves. They form domes in the crust, which are caused by upward pressure of the magma from the heater. They may contain gas or lava in the dome. If gas comes out first, the lava usually follows, impelled by the pressure maintained in other gas pockets. When the heaters die out, the volcanoes become inactive.

Some Geological Structures of the Tectonic System

All along the coast of the Americas lie the remains of a mid-ocean ridge that was wrecked as it tried and failed to enter the heaters operating all along the coastline. The ridge was run over by the westward moving Americas pushed by the Atlantic mid-ocean ridge.

Probably about 45,000,000 years ago, the ridge first made contact with South America, possibly on the Chilean coast. At that time the down-going channels from the heaters were only a few hundred miles from the rising channels to the ridge. When they were close enough, it became easier to flow directly through the mantle, or possibly break through above the mantle to the ridge magma chamber, than to continue to make the long trip down to the core and back. The thin ridges just opened up and let the high-pressure, high-temperature magma flow out into the ocean. The result was an explosive event which would make the explosion of Tambora and Krakatoa behind the Java Trench look like firecrackers.

Huge amounts of ash were released as well as huge amounts of carbon and sulfur oxides. The lower and middle latitudes got hot and dry, just as our southern states did in the summer of 1980, only a lot more so. Because of the large temperature difference between the northern latitudes and the lower and middle latitudes, the huge amounts of water that evaporated from the ocean went to the northern latitudes. The same thing happened in the winter of 1980-81 for a period of 4 months ending in mid-January. The clouds went over Alaska, warming it, and then moved on over Canada. The very cold air came back from Canada over the area east of the Mississippi—but not the water. The whole country was dry until the system gradually collapsed as the sun started moving north and the rains came back in late March.

The difference between what is happening now and what happened when the ridge started breaking up is the amount of carbon and sulfur oxides in the air. It was then so hot in the tropical and temperate zones that the amount of heat in the clouds moving to the polar latitudes was so great that the water fell as rain and washed the ice away. That put a lot of the land mass under water. The oceans heated up so they could absorb very little CO_2.

To make matters worse, with only the heaters on the west side of the Pacific still operating, a huge open leak in the tectonic system, and a major ridge destroyed, the feeding of the heaters slowed down. The system was starved for magma to operate it. The short circuit between the eastern pacific heaters and the ridge stopped the flow into the gunk under the North American continent. With the loss of pressure, the continent sank to a lower elevation, forcing gunk to flow from the continent to the heaters, thus keeping the heaters going until the gunk lost its fluidity and the continent could sink no lower. Only then did the heaters finally burn out and allow the ocean water to freeze the leaks in the collapsed ridge.

Apparently the ridge broke up one section at a time as it came close to the shore. Presumably, the ocean water was able to freeze off each affected section at some distance either side of the point at which the short circuit occurred.

The high pressure from below lifted the ridge almost to sea level. Along the coast of South America, the sea floor has now moved under the off-shore part of the ridge and is now building another row of mountains.

The North American part of the ridge was the last to come ashore, probably because the continent was up against the Eurasian land mass at the northern latitudes. South America can and is moving faster to the west than North America. Nevertheless, we can expect new heaters to develop off the coast of the United States and Canada in a few million years.

The only significant part of the ridge which survived relatively intact consists of the parts of the states of California, Oregon and Washington which are west of the Sierras and the Cascades. They survived because there was a strong outflow of magma from the collapsing Great Basin plateau and the mountains. The magma lifted the ridge gently because the high pressure had been lost from the heaters under the mountain. How?

There is a missing range of mountains which once connected the Sierra Nevadas with Mexican mountains at the lower end of the Gulf of California. Those mountains were replaced by the Gulf. In other words, it was not just a matter of high pressure from the heater getting into the ridge, but a matter of the damage to the ridge at the mouth of the Gulf being so extensive that ocean water could flow into the heaters. The explosions that followed may have been the world's greatest. The magma moved out of the heaters and went into the air as ash and dust. With the pressure released, the magma which had been forcing the Great Basin to high plateau status was free to flow back through the heaters to the place of contact with the water. The flow through the heaters prevented gravity separation and so shut down the heaters. The magma was free to flow in any direction it could.

Thus it was relatively cold low-pressure magma which raised California, Oregon and Washington out of the water.

By this time the Great Basin stopped settling down, and the Gulf stood where a mountain range and its heaters had been. Tahoe and Mono Lakes are probably on sink holes directly over the old heaters. In that area the basin dropped 2,000 to 3,000 feet. And to a lesser degree eastward to the Rockies and northward to the Columbia River

Basin. All of the western canyons (Grand, Snake, Yosemite, etc.) are cracks in the crust which occurred when the supporting magma flowed out from under the Great Basin and the mountains.

The coastal ranges of California are the buttes formed on either side of the San Andreas fault or ridge centerline. A ridge (butte) west of Sacramento and north of Berkeley, according to an aerial photo, still shows the minor buttes (Fig. 4) as well as the sheared west wall of the butte.

The Golden Gate is a crustal crack which resulted in an explosive event that left the hole called San Francisco Bay. Lake Nicaragua and Lake Managua in South America were formed in similar manner.

The Cayman Trench in the Caribbean is a crustal crack opening up because South America is moving to the west faster than North America. South America is also moving faster at its southern end than at its northern end where it connects to North America. It is thus rotating to the west around a point in Guatemala. As the crack opens up, it puts the "Bermuda Triangle" in the Atlantic in tension. It is not surprising, therefore, that large cracks open up in the ocean floor releasing large amounts of carbon and sulphur oxides before they are sealed. Clouds of such gases rising through the air would, as reported, cause an airplane to lose altitude until it had passed through the cloud simply because it would change the oxygen-to-fuel ratio of the mix delivered by the carburetor. Magnetic compasses would "go wild" as a result of a sudden flow of magma under the crust. A ship would drop like a rock in an area where the water had a high concentration of gas bubbles coming up through the water simply because a ship's buoyancy is equal to the weight of water (not gas and water) displaced. You venture into the Bermuda Triangle at your own risk.

Many geological phenomena are easy to understand with a basic understanding of how the tectonic system works. Others are more obscure.

Michigan has about 20,000 feet of sedimentary deposits dating back to the Precambrian over 600 million years ago. That simply means that Michigan has spent a lot more time under water than above it. Deposits of approximately the last 100,000,000 years are either ground up in the two hundred feet of glacial drift, or are already spread out over the Mississippi Valley as it grades down from about 650 feet elevation in Michigan to sea level at the Gulf of Mexico.

The land masses largely go under water when great catastrophies exhaust the magma supply. These are also times when climate is tropical. Most of the life on earth is in the sea. As a result of the explosions, there are plenty of minerals in the seas. It is a biological fact that every living organism will multiply to the limit of its food supply—including the "homo sapien" who, if he's so smart, ought to know better. The abundant sea life uses the minerals and carbon, and their mineral components result in the sedimentary deposits. The shell fish flourish in the sunlit shallow waters over the sunken land masses, and leave the extensive limestone deposits in the middle of the United States and Eurasia.

When the explosions end because of magma exhaustion, carbon and sulfur oxides are quickly used up. When the CO_2 drops to levels which do not overpower the natural cooling capacity of the polar regions, glaciation begins. In the past, glaciation has always resulted in producing a catastrophe in a few million years. If humans could learn to control themselves so they could control the high pressures in the tectonic system, there could be an indefinitely long period of peaceful development of human potential.

The Glacial Process

The tectonic system has a hand in everything that happens on the earth. The thing that controls the climate directly is the discharge of carbon and sulphur oxides by the tectonic system. However, if the CO_2 in the atmosphere is known, it alone indicates the kind of climate we can expect. The CO_2 curve (Fig. 6) is such a record to which has been added a projection of estimated future CO_2 levels. The curve was drawn on the basis of figures available up to 1976. The projection has been accurate since then.

French researchers Dalmas, Ascencio, and Legrand (*Nature* 3/13/80; *Science News*, 5/10/80), using what is probably an accurate technique for determining past CO_2 content of the air as trapped in Antarctic ice cores, found that 15,000 to 20,000 years ago the CO_2 in the atmosphere was 160 ppm. One hundred years ago it was around 290 ppm. Now the CO_2 is at about 340 ppm.

As far as the CO_2 is concerned, the warm interglacial period was in progress 15,000 to 20,000 years ago. The precipitation was less than average and ready to fall in the temperate zone, except for the fact that over a substantial part of the land masses there was a sheet

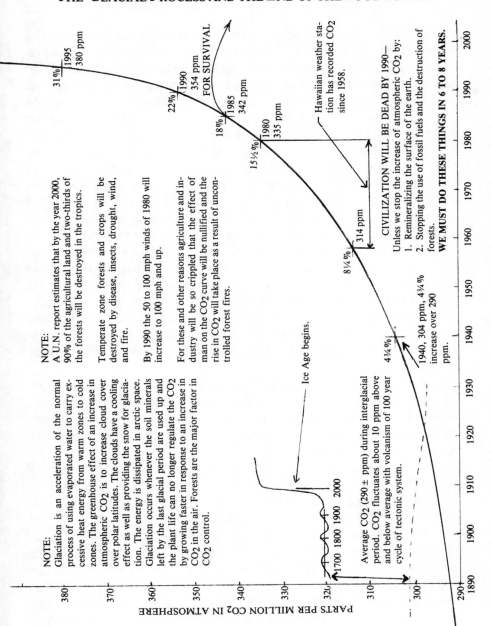

NOTE:

Glaciation is an acceleration of the normal process of using evaporated water to carry excessive heat energy from warm zones to cold zones. The greenhouse effect of an increase in atmospheric CO_2 is to increase cloud cover over polar latitudes. The clouds have a cooling effect as well as providing the snow for glaciation. The energy is dissipated in arctic space. Glaciation occurs whenever the soil minerals left by the last glacial period are used up and the plant life can no longer regulate the CO_2 by growing faster in response to an increase in CO_2 in the air. Forests are the major factor in CO_2 control.

NOTE:

A U.N. report estimates that by the year 2000, 90% of the agricultural land and two-thirds of the forests will be destroyed in the tropics.

Temperate zone forests and crops will be destroyed by disease, insects, drought, wind, and fire.

By 1990 the 50 to 100 mph winds of 1980 will increase to 100 mph and up.

For these and other reasons agriculture and industry will be so crippled that the effect of man on the CO_2 curve will be nullified and the rise in CO_2 will take place as a result of uncontrolled forest fires.

FOR SURVIVAL

CIVILIZATION WILL BE DEAD BY 1990—
Unless we stop the increase of atmospheric CO_2 by:
1. Remineralizing the surface of the earth.
2. Stopping the use of fossil fuels and the destruction of forests.
WE MUST DO THESE THINGS IN 6 TO 8 YEARS.

Hawaiian weather station has recorded CO_2 since 1958.

Ice Age begins.

Average CO_2 (290 ± ppm) during interglacial period. CO_2 fluctuates about 10 ppm above and below average with volcanism of 100 year cycle of tectonic system.

1940, 304 ppm, 4¾% increase over 290 ppm.

31% 1995 380 ppm
22% 1990 354 ppm
18% 1985 342 ppm
15½% 1980 335 ppm
8¼%
314 ppm
4¾%

1700 1800 1900 2000

PARTS PER MILLION CO_2 IN ATMOSPHERE

380 370 360 350 340 330 320 310 300 290

1890 1900 1910 1920 1930 1940 1950 1960 1970 1980 1990 2000

of ice from a few hundred to a few thousand feet thick. Ice has the highest heat of fusion of anything. It takes a great deal of heat to melt it. The ice sheets acted as a giant refrigerator. Therefore, a huge mass of cold air continued to move southward while the ice was melting and forced the warm air to move north over the oceans to replace the air moving south. Glaciation continued even though the CO_2 had dropped to a low level in the air. What did happen is that the annual addition of new ice became less than the annual subtraction of ice due to melting. Thus it was a long time before there was significant loss of ice. When the system did begin to collapse, it started on the windward side of continents. As soon as the weight of ice was removed or reduced over a substantial area, the flow of magma to the ridges was diverted to the depressed land areas, and the ridge buttes were formed by the collapse in pressure in the system. Volcanism was also reduced as ocean floor feeding to the heaters slowed down, which meant a further lowering of the atmospheric CO_2. The temperature of the ocean had dropped very substantially, thus increasing its capacity to store CO_2. With plenty of CO_2 and glacial ground rock to supply the minerals, sea life had to be booming and rapidly returning CO_2 and minerals to the crust as sea floor sediments.

It took about 85,000 years to build up the ice and probably 15,000 years to melt the ice caps back to their interglacial low. However, as one area after another lost its permanent ice field, tundra was replaced by northern latitude trees, and then by temperate zone trees in rapid sequence.

The ocean temperatures cannot begin to rise while the bulk of the glacial water is running into it. So it lags behind the land by perhaps 5,000 years. It may still be warming up and, if so, it may still be giving off more CO_2 than it takes in. At least it has a reduced ability to take in CO_2. This goes along with the fact that sea life required to remove the CO_2 from the water is at low ebb because the depleted soils are no longer giving an abundance of minerals to the ocean. There is a scarcity of minerals on the land and in the sea. This inevitably means a buildup of CO_2 in the atmosphere as more and more CO_2 is supplied by the tectonic system and less and less is put back into the earth's crust by the living organisms.

If the CO_2 in the air was 160 ppm 15,000 to 20,000 years ago, there must have been as little as 100 ppm during the climatic optimum, roughly 4,000 to 8,000 years ago, because the land was covered with a massive growth of temperate zone forests, the sea still held an abundance of sea life, and the tectonic system was under low pressure and volume. If the CO_2 drops that low, then the 290 ppm of 100 years ago is probably too high to provide an adequate margin of safety. This is especially true because the continents are all at about as high an elevation as they go. We can therefore expect more volcanism than during the climatic optimum. The indication is that the CO_2 level has been slowly moving up for 4,000 years toward the level of initiation of glaciation. That level is now — when the curve (Fig. 6) is making a sharp break toward infinity.

Many things are operating to affect the climate. They all have long overlapping time lags so that we can not say that this happens, then this, and then this. *But we can say that the minerals (those available to microorganisms) and the carbon released by the tectonic system can be monitored and can be controlled. We can therefore control climate.* The only thing we might not be able to do is prevent or control catastrophies. However, we may have a few million years in which to learn how to control them. *We have no time to spare in gaining control of the glacial process—it has already started!*

Glaciation is initiated by a change from temperate zone to northern latitude types of trees and by the dying of tropical forests. We are in that stage now. One species of tree after another is dying out. The Forest Service blames insects and foolishly sprays the forests with deadly poisons. Insects always infest trees and other plants (as pathogens invade people) which are weakened by malnutrition and no longer have resistance to their natural enemies. The trees are dying because there are no longer enough available elements in the soil to support them. Drought and high winds join with fire to destroy the dead and dying forests, sending large amounts of CO_2 into the atmosphere. Nitrogen and sulphur oxides from the fires come down as acid rain to acidify the soils and kill more trees. Man is ably assisting in the destruction of the forests. The warm, demineralized ocean can not take up the CO_2 as fast as it is being put into the air. The result is reflected in the CO_2 curve (Fig. 6). The polar ice field is expanding and growing in northeast Canada, and probably across the tops of Scandinavian countries and into Russia. The pressure is rising in the tectonic system as indicated by the accumulation of lava flows along the ridges and by increasing volcanic activity. We are in the high-pressure part of the ocean floor feeding cycle, which at least for a few centuries has occurred about every 100 years. It is a bad time for the

CO_2 to start its telltale climb toward infinity.

Researchers in different fields agree that glaciation starts in a very short time. A pollen study by G. Woillard (Fig. 7) shows that the change of vegetation 100,000 years ago occurred in a 20-year period. Judging from the CO_2 curve, we are at least 5 years into such a period.

Before proceeding with comment on Woillard's study, it should be pointed out that the only thing that might be expected to be constant in the climate system over a short period of geological time, like a million years, is the *average* release of energy from the tectonic system, but energy release is probably not constant for a period as short as 100,000 years. The sun's energy has not been found to vary to a significant degree. Everything else is variable down to the number of heaters and the elevation of their plateaus.

It is not surprising that the last interglacial period ended 115,000 YBP (Years Before Present) instead of taking the average of 100,000 years. On the other hand, the Woillard study was done a bit north of east-central France and may not reflect the timing of an area 1,000 miles east at the same latitude. France was out of the main ice field and may have benefited from warm air off the ocean and warmed up earlier than elsewhere. The fact that there was substantial forest growth spread over about 25,000 years may reflect a warmer location and the benefit of glacial debris carried by rivers and winds from the land north and west of the bog where the core was taken in the Vosges region. There are many variables which affect the details found in localized studies. However, there are solid and important observations to be gained.

Woillard isolated core zones 3, 2 and 1 where a change of vegetation took place in approximately 20 years. The only way that would be possible would be for the temperate-zone trees to die and burn so the colder zone trees could take root in the ashes of the burned forests.

The change in each case was from hazel, oak and alder to pine, birch and spruce. That represents a change from warm-weather to cold-tolerant trees. But even more significant is that this change is from nut-bearing trees to trees which can not yield a proteinaceous crop. That translates to mean a decline in soil minerals to the point where there are insufficient microorganisms in the soil to grow proteinaceous trees (or crops).

Following the last interglacial period (Fig. 7, Zone B, point 3) there were several thousand years of much colder weather than dur-

Nature Vol. 281   18 October 1979

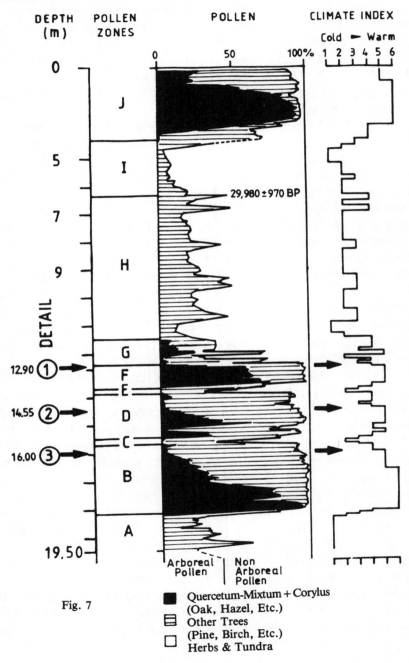

Fig. 7

ing the interglacial period. For a short period of several hundred years (Zone C), it was cold enough to kill almost all the trees, leaving tundra. During this period, erosion of the worn-out soil must have proceded on a massive scale. There were too few microorganisms to prepare the soil to take in water, so the water ran off the surface and gullied the land. The summer rains were torrential because colder air than interglacial air runs into warmer and wetter air than interglacial air, producing very heavy rainfall.

The above description is also valid for what is now happening or about to happen. If it is not too late now to prevent the destruction of the land, it certainly will be sometime before 1985. The present rate of soil erosion is saying loudly and clearly that the United States is going out of the farming business. At the present rate, our 8'' of topsoil will be gone in 100 years. Erosion doesn't work that way, of course. Today's erosion figures are out of date tomorrow because the rate is rapidly accelerating. Furthermore, the erosion starts on the weakest land first, cuts gullies, removes the small amount of organic matter it has left, and the land is of necessity abandoned as useless. Most of the erosion is from the poorest soils and most of it is worn-out subsoil. But when Iowa reports serious erosion (13 to 28 tons per acre per year) on soils which have any slope to them, and California soils have jumped to an *average* 6½ tons per acre per year lost, can a complete failure of agriculture be far behind?

During glaciation all types of vegetation move south. The tropical vegetation largely dies out because of the heat and drought. Minerals are lacking until the glaciers advance far enough to provide wind blown loess (gravel dust) to the tropical zone. However, both tropical- and temperate-zone vegetation survives in protected pockets of land where minerals, water and climate are sufficient for the survival of each type of vegetation.

Glacial deposits older than the last climate cycle are scarce. In Michigan there is a maximum of 220 feet of glacial drift. During glaciation, the weight of ice insures that all of the drift would be churned up. The first thing to come out of the mass would be any worn-out subsoil material because it is so easily entrained in water. Any worn-out subsoil material that does not erode away in the next few thousand years is likely to be removed by glaciation toward the end of the glacial period. South of the glaciated area, the subsoil will generally wash away until it has exposed still useful material at lower levels or until bedrock is reached. What growths are attained in the glacial retreat periods following the interglacial period must be based on the consolidation of unused glacial materials from the past, except in the limited areas glaciated by the limited initial advances following the interglacial period.

When full glaciation sets in (Fig. 7, Zones H and I) there are plenty of minerals for growth, but by that time the total land area covered by ice makes the weather too cold for significant tree growth.

The fluctuations of CO_2 in the air are responsible for the five or more glacial advances and retreats indicated on the ridge butte (Fig. 4) and in the pollen diagram. Initially the re-growths after each glacial advance are effective in lowering the CO_2 level. But in looking at a pollen diagram, we are only seeing a part of the CO_2 picture. To tell it all, we would need a similar diagram of what is happening in the oceans. While the growth on land is dwindling away, the life in the ocean is increasing. With the water getting colder and dissolving more CO_2, and the increasing area of land under glaciation supplying ground rock minerals in increasing amounts, ocean life must increase. Most of that life has only a short life cycle. It can expand quickly to the limit of its food supply. Whereas on land it is the minerals which run out first, in the sea it is more likely to be the CO_2. The shell fish are probably the major element in depleting the CO_2 in the water. Since the CO_2 in the air is in equilibrium with the CO_2 in the water, it also decreases. *Thus it is the living organisms which cause the fluctuations of CO_2 in the air. These fluctuations in turn determine the climate.* By the end of the 90,000 years of glaciation, the pressure in the tectonic system is high, the volcanism is at a maximum, and the CO_2 output from the system is at a maximum. However, the capacity of living organisms to consume the available food supply has no apparent limit. They are obviously capable of completing the carbon cycle by turning it into the carbonaceous sedimentary rocks on the ocean floor.

The time to stop the glaciation is before it starts, because it starts with the destruction of agriculture. Before this decade is over, the evidence shows that our technological capacity to remineralize the soil will have been lost in the chaos of a world of starving and dying nations.

Conclusion

The climate cycle is a byproduct of the entire life system, all of which rests on the expenditure of atomic energy in the tectonic system.

The tectonic system constantly removes materials from the mantle, separates the compounds containing a balance of elements useful to living organisms, and moves them into the mountains or into the atmosphere. Those compounds containing elements not required for life processes are consigned to the core or are recycled to build the basic ocean floor at the ridge.

The tectonic system supplies molten rock to perform three separate jobs. One is to build new ocean floor at the ridges. One is to hydraulically support the crust and to mend rifts and breaks in the crust all over the world. The last job is to build mountains and plateaus so the soil-enriching minerals can move to the lowlands by water and wind erosion. The last job requires the maximum pressure and is done above the continental heater. The distribution of rock between the other two jobs depends on the friction of flow to a particular point as compared with another point. It also depends on changes of weight of crust. Specifically, if glaciers melt from a section of land mass, the hydraulic balance is disturbed and the magma flows easily to that part of the land mass until it is raised up to a state of hydraulic balance with the rest of the crust. Conversely, if the land becomes glaciated, it drops to a state of balance and greatly increases the magma flow to the ridges. Thus, changes in the climate are reflected in change in the direction of flow of the magma, a fact which probably has something to do with changes in polarity of the earth's magnetic field.

The climate changes are recorded in the buttes formed at the ridges, but the reason for the climate changes is basically the fluctuation of the level of CO_2 in the atmosphere. The amount of CO_2 determines whether the pattern of air flow around the hemisphere is a wave of low amplitude or high amplitude. If the CO_2 level is high, the amplitude is high and almost all of the moisture is carried to high latitudes where it produces glaciation.

The microorganisms can increase in quantity or die out in remarkably short periods of time. Their food supply contains the two variables, carbon and minerals. They in turn are the source of the protoplasm compounds of all other life. If either the carbon or the minerals or both are depleted in the land and/or in the sea, the life system collapses.

Glaciation starts because the minerals are used up in the land and in the sea. That ends a glacial cycle of 20,000 to 25,000 years, depending on when the last glacial advance is assumed to have started. Subsequent cycles are shorter as indicated on Woillard's pollen diagram and the climate index drawn from the pollen diagram (Fig. 7). The interglacial cycle is probably the longest because the soil and plant life have a great ability to recycle the minerals, whereas the ocean life uses both the carbon and minerals in the chain of life and dumps them on the ocean floor where there is very little recycling.

Once started, the glaciation can not be stopped because the ice load reverses the flow of magma from the inner core into the gunk under the crust to flow out of the gunk into the inner core. This increases the feed rate into the heaters, which results in a greater release of CO_2 into the atmosphere. The increase in CO_2 requires a greater equilibrium pressure differential between the CO_2 in the atmosphere and that in the ocean in order to increase the rate of absorption of CO_2 into the water. The sea life can expand to use up the CO_2 in the water and thus increase the rate of CO_2 absorption, but then it must die back and allow time for the slow process of CO_2 absorption into the ocean. Because of the requirement of a greater amount of CO_2 in the atmosphere in order to increase the rate of absorption (as opposed to the direct consumption of CO_2 by plant life on the land), the CO_2 never drops to interglacial levels. Therefore the temperature constantly gets colder as indicated by Woillard. The sea life is responsible for the CO_2 fluctuations which result in glacial advance and limited retreat.

From what we are now seeing of the relation between CO_2 and establishment of the glaciation now in progress, it now seems doubtful if the CO_2 in the air ever rises as high as twice the interglacial level. It could happen if we could continue to burn fossil fuels, but it won't happen. The dead have little use for energy and they are poor producers of fossil fuels.

There is no doubt that there is a point of no return at which no matter what we do, the increase in CO_2 from the tectonic system exceeds the capacity of the remaining forests and sea life to remove the CO_2. At that point a remineralization program becomes useless. Given the time such a program will take, we may already have passed the point of no return. Replacing fossil fuels with wood plantations may give us the margin of survival.

The limit of glaciation is reached when it has built up so far south that the annual melting equals the annual ice buildup. At that point volcanism moves quickly to a lower level because magma is no longer forced to flow out from under the glaciated area into the core. The ocean floor slows its feeding of fuel to the heaters and the output of molten rock and the CO_2 dissolved in it is reduced to interglacial levels. As the rains come back to the middle latitudes, the life on the land flourishes on the newly remineralized soils. As the glaciers melt back, the magma once again flows under the depressed areas. In the next 10,000 years the minerals on the land and in the oceans will support sufficient life to keep the CO_2 at the interglacial level. But when the minerals are too few to support enough life to hold down the CO_2 level, it begins to rise and the death of the temperate and tropical zone forests swiftly initiates the air flow pattern which brings glaciation to polar latitudes and extreme, killing heat and drought in between.

The whole world takes part in the making of climate. Every factor is complex and has its own time lags built in. The only sharply identifiable time in the whole climate cycle is the time at which the temperate zone climate is destroyed and we stop eating. We can look at the satellite pictures, see a cloud mass moving toward us, and figure we will soon get rain. It is doubtful if we will ever go very much further in forecasting. But we can easily chart the CO_2 content of the atmosphere and know whether or not we have enough minerals in the soil and in the water. The CO_2 chart is now telling us very clearly that glaciation, the time of no temperate zone, is almost upon us.

The solution to this crisis is obvious from the cause. We must remineralize the world's soils and put carbon into the earth as fast as we can in order to reverse the CO_2 curve and bring it back to a safe level.

The following is a list of minimum objectives which must be met in order to effect our survival:

1. Stop the use of fossil fuels by 1985.

2. Have mature tree plantations to take the place of fossil fuels. This is possible using fast-growing trees on mineralized soils. Soil remineralization has been discussed in previous papers such as "Food, Energy, and Survival."

3. Incorporate ground gravel dust in all sewage waters and make sure there are enough excess minerals in the discharge to remineralize the rivers and estuaries. Remineralize all other coastal waters where shellfish growth is possible.

4. Remineralize all forests and jungles sufficiently to stop the dying and increase the rate of growth.

5. Remineralize all crop lands to increase food quality and yield to compensate for the increasing loss of crops to drought and cold growing seasons.

These five minimal objectives must be met by 1985. They can only be met by a colossal effort on an international scale. To attempt any less is to resign ourselves to death by malnutrition and starvation.

6

Perspective

Global 2000

The Global 2000 Report to the President was commissioned in 1977 by President Carter and finally released in July, 1980 as a 3-volume work of over 1,000 pages. Mr. Carter explained its purpose in his Environmental Message to the Congress (May 23, 1977):

Environmental problems do not stop at national boundaries. In the past decade, we and other nations have come to recognize the urgency of international efforts to protect our common environment.

As part of this process, I am directing the Council on Environmental Quality, working in cooperation with the Environmental Protection Agency, the National Science Foundation, the National Oceanic and Atmospheric Administration, and other appropriate agencies, to make a one-year study of the probable changes in the world's population, natural resources and environment through the end of the century. This study will serve as the foundation of our longer-term planning.

Before quoting a few of the report's findings, it is well to note, on these U.S. government projections, this word from Vol. 1, the summary ("Entering the Twenty-First Century"): "They do not predict what will occur. Rather, they depict conditions that are likely to develop if there are no changes in public policies. A keener awareness of the nature of current trends, however, may induce changes that will alter these trends and the projected outcome."

Here then are a few of *Global 2000*'s "Principal Findings."

• Rapid growth in world population will hardly have altered by 2000...population will grow from 4 billion in 1975 to 6.35 billion in 2000...In terms of sheer numbers, population will be growing faster in 2000 than it is today, with 100 million people added each year compared with 75 million in 1975.

• The large existing gap between the rich and the poor nations widens.

• Significant losses of world forests will continue over the next 20 years as demand for forest products and fuelwood increases...The world's forests are now disappearing at the rate of 18 to 20 million hectares a year (an area half the size of California), with most of the loss occurring in the humid tropical forests of Africa, Asia, and South America.

• Atmospheric concentrations of carbon dioxide and ozone-depleting chemicals are expected to increase at rates that could alter the world's climate and upper atmosphere significantly by 2050. Acid rain threatens damage to lakes, soils, and crops.

• Extinctions of plant and animal species will increase dramatically. Hundreds of thousands of species—perhaps as many as 20 percent of all species on earth—will be irretrievably lost as their habitats vanish.

• Regional water shortages will become more severe.

What are *Global 2000*'s projections on climate change to the year 2000? It says this:

Because climate has a profound effect on our lives and economies and has possible consequences for the future, we cannot ignore it, yet there are unresolved problems which make statements about future climate very uncertain. This is to say, not enough is known about climate to provide us with a reliable predictive capability...Before the future climate can be reliably estimated, science must understand it well enough to build realistic quantitative models that relate cause and effect...Such models are yet primitive and incomplete.

And on the carbon dioxide crisis:

Carbon dioxide increase is thought to produce a warming of the earth by the so-called greenhouse effect. (p. 51, Vol. II)

As discussed in Chapter 4 and in the climate section of this chapter, the experts are more or less evenly divided over the prospects for warming or cooling, and most felt the highest probability was for no change. (p. 337, Vol II)

Therefore, in Table 13-46, "Summary of Impacts on the Environment" projections, the global, regional, and local climate effects are in every case given as "No impact projected." (p. 392)

This same table projects many forms of severe environmental devastation from expanding consumption of fossil fuel and nuclear energy technologies. It says this about carbon dioxide:

- CO_2 emissions will increase from 26 to 34 billion short tons per year, roughly double the CO_2 emissions of the mid-1970s.
- 446 million hectares of CO_2-absorbing forests will be lost.
- Burning of much of the wood on 446 million hectares will produce more CO_2. (446 million hectares equals 1,070,400,000 acres)
- Decomposition of soil humus will release more CO_2.
- A doubling of the CO_2 concentration by 2050 could increase the average temperature of the earth by about 3 degrees C, melting much of the polar ice...

And about Agriculture and Food:

> Land productivity is declining in many industrialized countries as well as LDCs (Less Developed Countries). Losses of range and farmland to desertification by 2000 could total 2,800 million hectares...One half the total irrigated land is already damaged by waterlogging, salinization and alkalinization.

If it is not obvious at this point, it is important to realize that the projections given by this report, and those offered by John Hamaker, while similar in some ways, are fundamentally different in a number of ways, including these three:

1. Hamaker's whole thesis emphasizes ecological problem solutions beginning now on a worldwide scale. *Global 2000* admittedly suggests no solutions, but concurs with Hamaker in asserting, "Prompt and vigorous changes in public policy around the world are needed to avoid or minimize these problems before they become unmanageable. Long lead times are required for effective action. If decisions are delayed until the problems become worse, options for effective action will be severely reduced." (p. 5, Vol. I)

2. Hamaker, to a great degree, performs the absolutely essential task of recognizing and understanding the many interactions and "feedbacks" within the whole man-environment ecology, and he realizes where we are in the long-term soil-climate cycle. In contrast, *Global 2000*, "the foundation of our longer-term planning," took this approach:

> The elements of the Government's global model were not, of course, designed to be used together as an integrated whole. The constituent models were developed separately and at different times to serve the various projection needs of individual agencies (Vol. II, p. viii).

Exercises cutting feedback within integrated world models reveal that the omission of system linkages greatly influences the results of forecasts, which suggests that the Government's Global Model...is presenting a distorted picture of the probable future. The predictive error incurred by omissions of feedback is cumulative over time: in most cases it is not highly significant over a 5-year period, but becomes important in a 20-year period and may become paramount over a 50-year span." (Vol. II, p. 681)

John Hamaker has already made it abundantly clear that the errors of such a fragmented approach can bcome quite "paramount" in only a 5-year period at this point. The Report concludes Vol. I with the admission: "The inescapable conclusion is that the omission of linkages imparts an optimistic bias to the *Global 2000* study's (and the U.S. Government's) quantitative projections." (p. 45)

3. Hamaker's fundamental assumptions and perceptions of the present state of the biosphere—and of humanity's capacity to build up its health and fertility, should also be seen in sharp contrast to the assumptions and projections of the *Global 2000* authors. No better nor more important example of this could be presented than their views of the soil and future productivity therefrom.

This book's first six chapters have presumably made clear Hamaker's findings, findings that are based on the documented natural cycles and observable, easily-proven processes of fertility creation. The following section on the *Global 2000* views of soil, food and agriculture is needed to make unmistakably evident the distinctions between the two views on the most basic factor of health and survival. Certainly the truth in either or both views must be recognized and applied on an unprecedented scale if humanity is to prevent *either* the rapid and quickly irreversible socio-ecological decline and glaciation projected by Hamaker, *or* the relatively slower, eventually irreversible decline into misery conservatively projected by the U.S. Government—were those government projections valid.

Global 2000 On The Soil Support System

As noted, *Global 2000* does not acknowledge the prior 10,000 years of interglacial soil demineralization; in fact, loss of soil minerals is not recognized specifically at all in its listing of "the five major agents of soil loss." (Vol. II, p. 277). These are given as a classification for "what is now known of world land degradations" as follows:

1. Desertification;
2. Waterlogging, salinization, and alkalinization;
3. Soil degradation that follows deforestation;
4. General erosion and humus loss from "routine agricultural practices";

5. Loss of lands to urbanization and related developments.

Before quoting the report's somewhat fantastic food production increase projections, a few of its views on the deterioration of soils are important to note:

> Soil is a basic agricultural resource, but it is a depleting, salifying, and
> eroding resource. Lost soil fertility can be restored, but only after long
> periods of time and at great cost. (Vol. II, p. 297)
>
> Restoration of mildly damaged soils could be accomplished over a
> decade with fallowing and green manuring...but restoration of severely
> damaged land would require much longer... (Vol. II, p. 416)
>
> Accelerated erosion, loss of natural fertility and other deteriora-
> tion...may have more effect in the coming years than is indicated in the
> *Global 2000* food projections. (Vol. I, p. 20)
>
> To what extent does soil deterioration on existing croplands affect the
> world's agricultural potential? The limited data available suggest the
> outlines of an answer...showing scattered but alarming examples of soil
> deterioration. The primary problems include: (1) loss of topsoil to erosion,
> (2) loss of organic matter, (3) loss of porous soil structure, (4) build-up of
> toxic salts and chemicals. (Vol. II, p. 276)

Apparently, the most basic underlying cause of all these problems—worldwide soil demineralization—is outside the awareness of the
authors. This statement is made regarding the present state of deterioration:

> Changes in soil quality cannot be directly and accurately measured
> over large geographic areas, and too few sample measurements have been
> made to obtain a detailed statistical picture at the global (or even, with a
> few exceptions, at the national) level...The study of world soil conditions
> is further complicated in many regions by the use of synthetic fertilizers and
> high-yield varieties, which may maintain or even increase production for a
> time, temporarily masking losses of soil and deteriorating soil structure.
> (Vol. II, p. 276)

Concluding the section, "Deterioration of Soils," the authors state a
message as significant and clear as any in the report:

> ...Whether the soils of the world will deteriorate further or be
> reclaimed will depend in large part on the ability and willingness of govern-
> ments to make politically difficult policy changes. . .Assuming no policy
> change—the standard assumption underlying all of the *Global 2000* study
> projections—*significant deteriorations in soils can be anticipated virtually
> everywhere including in the U.S.* Assuming that energy, water, and capital
> are available, it will be possible for a time to compensate for some of the
> deterioration by increasing...inputs...(fertilizers, pesticides, herbicides,

etc.), but the projected increases in energy (and chemical fertilizer) costs will make this approach to offsetting soil losses ever more expensive. Without major policy changes, soil deterioration could significantly interfere with achieving the production levels projected in this Study. (p. 283)

Global 2000 food projections, and the means to achieve them, "...Assuming no deterioration in climate or weather" (Vol. II, p. 13) are based upon.... "The food and agriculture projections developed by the U.S. Department of Agriculture which foresee a *90 to 100 percent increase* in total world production over the 1970-2000 period...The projection increases are based in part on a projected *4 percent increase* in arable area." (Vol. II, p. 272—emphasis added)

Such tremendous gains in global food production could, without a doubt, occur if generous soil remineralization programs are instituted (and, of course, greater gains could come from replacing certain unnecessary non-food crops with essential food crops). How do the USDA authors involved in the study believe the gains will occur? Such gains obviously require greater soil fertility and thus "fertilizer"—presumably the balance of elements and materials which are responsible for producing fertility and life. However, for this most crucial study, the authors have decided to impose on it the narrow, commercially-institutionalized definition of "fertilizer": packaged concentrates of acidic "nitrogenous fertilizer, phosphates (P_2O_5) and potash (K_2O)." (Vol. II, p. 100) More of these authors' views are best related, if not fully comprehended, by further direct quotes from the study:

> Because of this tightening land constraint, food production is not likely to increase fast enough to meet rising demands unless world agriculture becomes significantly more dependent on petroleum and petroleum-related inputs. Increased petroleum dependence also has implications for the cost of food production. ,.the real price of food is projected to increase 95 percent over the 1970-2000 period... (Vol. I, p. 16-17)
>
> ...A world transition away from petroleum dependence must take place, but there is still much uncertainty as to how this transition will occur. (Vol. I, p. 27)
>
> Farmer's costs of raising, and (costs of) even maintaining yields have increased rapidly...Costs of...fertilizers, pesticides, and fuels have risen very rapidly throughout the world, and where these inputs are heavily used, increased applications are bringing diminishing returns. (Vol. I, p. 18)
>
> While there have been significant improvements recently in the yields of selected crops, the diminishing returns and rapidly rising costs of yield-enhancing inputs suggest that yields will increase more slowly than projected. (Vol. I, p. 19)
>
> The 90 to 100 percent increase in food production projected through 2000 under Alternative I suggests roughly a 180 percent increase in fertilizer

use, from 80 million metric tons in 1973-75 to 225 million in 2000...Measures of fertilizer per arable hectare...point up the increasingly input-intensive nature of food production through the end of the century. (Vol. II, p. 99)

Note: "...the 'fertilizer' projections are intended to apply to a full package of yield-enhancing inputs," including "pesticides, herbicides, irrigation, etc." (Vol. II, p. 283)

Chapter 6 projects that by 2000 global use per hectare of "fertilizer" (as defined in that chapter) will be 2.6 times that of the record levels reported in the early 1970s. Usage in LDCs is projected to quadruple... "The per-hectare usage of fertilizers in all regions can be expected to increase at essentially the same rates as total applications." (Vol. II, p. 283)

While U.S. Department of Agriculture officials regard the global levels of fertilizer use projected for 2000 to be safe when applied carefully by trained personnel, they are aware that improper use leads to increased dangers. Improper use can aggravate rather than alleviate problems of soil deterioration and declining fertility. (Vol. II, p. 284)

...Nitrous oxide from fertilizer usage...depletes the ozone layer. If this phenomenon turns out to be serious, the world could find itself in the tragic situation of having to support the human population at the cost of subjecting the world's biota to damaging doses of cosmic and ultra-violet radiation, at least one effect of which would be increased incidence of skin cancer in human beings. (Vol. II, p.284)

From the perspective of ecology, the known terrestrial effects of increased fertilizer usage are surprisingly benign. The addition of large amounts of three critical nutrients (phosphorous, potassium and fixed nitrogen) might be expected to produce many changes in soils. The most apparent effect is simply the intended increase in plant growth...("...the number of malnourished people in LDCs could rise from 400 to 600 million in the mid-1970s to 1.3 billion in 2000."—Vol. I, p.17)...Increased nitrogen usage contributes to reduction of soil organic matter, thus degrading soils and contributing carbon dioxide to the atmosphere...Generally soil organic matter declines to...40 to 60 percent of the original content. Soil quality deteriorates as well. While in most cases crop yields can be maintained through the continual applications of chemical fertilizers, through plowing with large tractors, and through irrigation, the modern methods of farming tend to lock agriculture into a particular mode of cultivation and resource allocation if high yields in degraded soils are to be maintained. (Vol. II, p. 284)

While mortality from methemoglobinemia is now extremely rare, the presence of high levels of nitrate in drinking water supplies poses a health hazard that is already a valid concern in the United States, and the projected doubling-to-quadrupling of fertilizer applications by 2000 could make this disease more serious and more widespread. (Vol. II, p. 285)

The reader has perhaps already posed the question: What can the short and long-term value be of such fertility-depleting "fertilizers" and overall increasing fossil fuel dependence be? And how can anything but overall degradation of soil, humanity, and the "globe" result from pursuing these "traditional" but ecologically out-of-date technologies? The *Global 2000* authors, being oblivious to soil remineralization and recycling potentials, believe that ecological destruction must result from human food production methods, as shown by this conclusion to Chapter 6, "Food and Agriculture Projections":

> Fertilizer and pesticide pollution problems can also result from misuse. Even relatively small quantities...can generate major environmental problems...The fast growth in the use of fertilizers and pesticides implied by the projections for most LDCs over the next three decades point up the need for expanding and upgrading farm education programs and monitoring input use to insure the optimum trade-off between food production increases and environmental quality.
>
> In summary, while solutions to foreseeable environmental problems in expanding food production are theoretically available, their application—particularly in those parts of developing countries experiencing the greatest environmental stress—is in question. Ultimately, the environmentally positive or negative nature of increases in food production is likely to depend on short-term versus long-term costs. The real food price increases projected for the decades ahead could well make the short-term costs of environmentally positive agriculture seem high and the long-run costs of an environmentally negative agriculture seem small. In the industrialized countries, internalizing the costs of pollution...could narrow the margin between short-term and long-term costs and accelerate the move to an environmentally positive agriculture. In most developing countries, however, questions of grain gaps and calorie gaps are likely to outweigh problems of environment well beyond the year 2000. (Vol II, p. 104)

Presumably no commentary is needed on those statements. A section on "Feedback to the Food and Agriculture Projections" (p. 414) reveals another interesting assumption, namely: "Yields are assumed to continue increasing at essentially the same rates as in the past two decades," despite the fact that former USDA researcher Lester Brown, now Worldwatch Institute president, has documented that chemically-induced yields have been falling or leveling off in the U.S., China, France, and elsewhere (*The Worldwide Loss of Cropland*, 1978, Worldwatch paper No. 24).

Also:

> Pollution by pesticides and fertilizers is assumed not to constrain the use of pesticides and fertilizers (p. 414)...over the period of the projections there will be no major improvement in the food supply for the world's poorest

populations, and what improvements do occur will require an increase of 95 percent in the real price of food...(p. 415)

For the LDCs, the food projections assume that land deterioration will not be more serious than in past decades, because farmers will be aware of the problems, will institute practices preventing more extensive deterioration, and will charge more for their crops to cover increased costs. There is a significant discrepancy between these assumptions and the environment projections...(they) anticipate significant increases in the intensity of use of agriculture lands in the LDCs and very few preventative or remedial measures. The primary LDC remedial measures implied by the food projections are a fourfold increase in the use of fertilizers, herbicides, and pesticides and a large increase in irrigation...Futhermore...deforestation will increase the degradation of the LDC agricultural lands...increased erosion and...a fuelwood shortage...will result in an increase in the burning of dung [150 to 400 million tons/year—ed. note] that would have otherwise been returned to the soil as nutrients.

The food projections assume that agricultural pests and diseases will not present more difficult problems in the future than they have in the past. The projections indicate that these problems will be managed through a global doubling in the use of pesticides. A still larger increase is anticipated for the LDCs.

By contrast, the environmental projections suggest that pest and disease problems will increase, especially if reliance continues to be placed primarily on pesticides. (p. 415-17)

These excerpts should more than suffice to make plain the contrast between the approach designed to restore the entire ecology from the soil up, and that approach found effective, in years past, for extracting soil fertility reserves via fossil fuel-based chemical technologies. The crucial choice to move ahead swiftly and intelligently with the one, or to attempt an intensification of the other (as *Global 2000* "projects"), should be seen in its total ramifications for human life on Earth, now and in the potential future. If this can be done, the sensible human mind may well perceive that there isn't actually any choice.

In this connection may be considered these words from *Global 2000*'s "Conclusions" of Vol. I:

Vigorous, determined new initiatives are needed if worsening poverty and human suffering, environmental degradation, and international tensions and conflicts are to be prevented...New and imaginative ideas—and a willingness to act on them—are essential.

Global Future: Time To Act

This is the title of the 200-page follow-up (released in January, 1981) to the *Global 2000 Report*, intended to begin developing solutions, says the preface, for the "problem areas needing priority attention...The report presents a collection of considered assessments and new ideas for actions the United States could take, in concert with other nations, for a vigorous response to urgent global problems."

This report may be summarized briefly by noting that nothing is yet forthcoming on the requirement to remineralize the soils and stabilize or restore degenerating ecosystems, although its recommendations to begin immediate worldwide communication and cooperation are a beginning.

One of the authors, Gus Speth, Chairman of the Council on Environmental Quality, has been informed by a number of people of John Hamaker's breakthroughs in understanding. Speth writes:

"What the recent reports do emphasize in a new way are the accelerating pace and scale of the problems and their interrelationships—the web of causes and effects that bind them together." Yet he does not offer a single word on remineralization potential, just a vague statement that "soil enrichment techniques" should be encouraged. Here is the brief paragraph, under "Techniques for sustainable agriculture," where this possibility is mentioned:

> The *Global Report* projections assume that global use of agricultural chemicals will accelerate. However, continued rapid increases in their use may not be feasible. The manufacture of nitrogen fertilizers and...pesticides, is based on fossil fuels and will be subjected to steeply rising costs. In addition, many of these chemicals produce a wide range of serious environmental consequences, some of which adversely affect agricultural production. Alternatives that can contribute to raising agricultural yields on a long-term sustainable basis are available and should be encouraged. Among them are integrated pest management and soil enrichment techniques. (p. 34-5)

Finding ways to assist soil microorganisms in assimilating atmospheric nitrogen is also highly recommended (p. 38), but no connection between this and the aforementioned soil enrichment techniques is made.

Recommendations on reforestation, renewable energy, and CO_2 are also given—in isolation from their relations to the soil system—as follows:

> U.S. support for a global fuelwood program that would double the rate of tree planting in developing countries over a 5-year period is highly desirable. U.S. efforts should take at least three forms: support for the large expansion of World Bank fuelwood-forestry lending recently pro-

posed by the bank, a major expansion of AID and Peace Corps fuelwood assistance, and support for adoption of a global fuelwood program at the 1981 UN Conference on New and Renewable Sources of Energy.

The World Bank has concluded that massive reforestation is essential and recommends raising the global rate of tree planting five-fold, from 1.25 million acres a year to 6.25 million acres. (About 50 million acres of forest are being "consumed" yearly—*Global 2000,* Vol. II, p. 126)

An interagency task force should be established to chart a realistic path for achieving the goal of getting 20 percent of our energy from renewable energy by the year 2000.

The United States should ensure that full consideration of the CO_2 problem is given in the development of energy policy. Efforts should be begun immediately to develop and examine alternative global energy futures, with special emphasis on regional analyses and the implications for CO_2 buildup. Special attention should also be devoted to determining what would be a prudent upper bound on global CO_2 concentrations. (Vol. II, p. 125-130)

The World Conservation Strategy

This strategy, published by the International Union for the Conservation of Nature, is the result of three years of research and discussion involving more than 450 government agencies and over 100 countries. It was "launched" on March 5, 1980 in London and 32 other capital cities across the world. A summary of the WCS appears in the April, 1980 *Not Man Apart.* It is difficult to criticize a document and worldwide educational effort that represents a giant leap forward from no strategy or concern at all, but as well-meaning as it may be, it too fails to recognize the naturally-retrogressed *and* humanly over-exploited state of the present late-interglacial soil and biosphere. Instead, according to "How To Save The World: A Bold New Campaign" (*Not Man Apart*), it suggests that: "The biosphere is like a self-regenerating cake, and conservation is the conduct of our affairs so that we can have our cake and eat it too. As long as certain bits of the cake are not consumed and consumption of the rest of it is kept within certain limits, the cake will renew itself and provide for continuing consumption."

It also says that most countries are poorly organized to conserve, that severe soil degradation is already a critical problem, that deserts may soon adversely affect 630 million people, that tropical forests are quickly becoming extinct, and that time is running out. In spite of these realizations, the strategy gives no emphasis to remineralizing or otherwise "enriching" soils, reforesting large areas or establishing biomass energy plantations, nor to restoring—implying *giving to or nourishing*—Earth's poverty-stricken ecosystems in any sufficient way.

Apparently, its authors have accepted the common belief that policies of "conservation," even on a worldwide scale, will function to prevent collapse of Earth's (late-interglacial) life support systems, and human civilization. (*The Survival of Civilization* will of course be sent to the *Global Future* and *World Conservation Strategy* authors as soon as possible.)

In concluding, the growing perspective of the reader may well consider these wise words of this "How To Save The World..." article:

> The devastation of the biosphere is the ultimate threat to the survival and well-being of human beings. It is seldom perceived as such, because for many peoples and their governments it is overshadowed by apparently more pressing concerns: war, poverty, epidemics, the energy crisis, inflation, unemployment. Nevertheless, failure to conserve living resources is closely linked to the worsening of the other problems.

John Hamaker offered a similar message in an open letter to the readers of *Acres, USA* (April, 1980), and part of it is of value to consider in this connection. John wrote—

> A letter from Bruce Walker of Saskatoon in the Dec. '79 issue was recently brought to my attention. I would like to correct a couple of misstatements.
>
> Bruce spoke of John Hamaker's 'theory on gravel dusts.' Surely he is not referring to the use of ground glacial gravel dust on the soil as being theoretical. It is exactly the same stuff that nature left on the whole earth during the last glacial period so that life could once again flourish. The fact that nature knows what to use to furnish the mineral base for all life on earth is hardly theoretical. The facts and laws of nature comprise all the science there is.
>
> Unfortunately, virtually all of the smaller particles of glacial till from very fine sand (.004 inch) and smaller on the soils of most of the earth have been stripped of useful elements during the 10,000 years since the last glaciation. Those particle sizes must be replaced or we must die.
>
> We can commit mass suicide in a number of ways. We can continue to pollute the biosphere with nuclear contaminants. We can do the same thing with non-biodegradable organic compounds. We can push the button on nuclear war. But the quickest and surest way is to fail to remineralize the soil.
>
> In my opinion, this inter-glacial civilization will be dying out by 1990 and totally destroyed by 1995. If it occurs, it will be because too few people are able to examine the evidence, perceive the inevitable consequences, and take corrective action.
>
> John D. Hamaker

7

Introduction

John Hamaker's *Taxes, Freedom, and the Constitution* was first written in October, 1972, and is a condensation of thought from forty years' study of economic and ecological principles, and from an earlier manuscript entitled *Total Freedom*.

Taxes, Freedom, and the Constitution explains the significance of the compound interest curve on the cover of the book. The article must stand alone on its own merits in truth, and no "Perspective" section will follow it.

The newly-written preface explains the relation of this chapter to the rest of this book.

Leading into that preface, a powerful statement from the opening address to the 10th anniversary meeting of the Club of Rome (7/13/78) is worthy of consideration. It was spoken by Aurelio Peccei, internationally respected economist, and founder-president of the Club of Rome. Peccei said, in part:

> Whatever evaluation or forecasts we undertake, they are just sectoral, fragmented, or short-term. Never is our vast assortment of resources mobilized across disciplines and boundaries with a view to pursuing common, global goals.
>
> As a consequence, we are all pitifully unprepared to cope with the formidable challenges and threats looming ahead. Although such a bitter reality is seldom recognized, it is high time to understand at least two essential things.
>
> One is that mankind as a whole is striding rapidly towards a momentous crossroads where there can be no place for mistakes; yet, its values, institutions and bearing are still a reflection of the past and certainly cannot carry it safely into the future. That something fundamental is wrong with its

entire system is quite evident—for even now it is unable to assure the minima of life to all its members, to be at peace with itself, or to be at peace with Nature.

The second is mankind's desperate need to break this vicious circle, while it can still get free and mold its future.''

Many more of Peccei's words are valuable to consider. In direct relation to the messages of this book, however, these few stand out:

...There is much charitable talk about basic human needs but no earnest drive at the very roots of this knot of problems, no concrete commitment to eradicate hunger, deprivation and ignorance from the world, once and for all...Neither are there reliable plans or even ideas on how to find work for the 300 million able-bodied men and women currently unemployed, or how to create the 1,000 million more jobs which will be needed during the 1980s and the 1990s...

Almost half the world's scientists are engaged in "defense" projects, and the annual military expenditure is approaching 400 billion dollars—which breaks down to more than one billion dollars a day. "The world," said President Carter at the United Nations, "spent last year (1976) 60 times as much equipping each soldier as we spent educating each child."

The great step is then for all of us, and especially for those who command knowledge and power, to realize that—if we will it—ahead lies not catastrophe but the best part of the human venture. The keystone is the full development of the human being—the human revolution which can guide and crown all other revolutions of our time.

7

Preface

In the past, some nations have failed because their agriculture systems removed minerals from the topsoil faster than minerals could come up from the subsoil. The people of such nations migrated to new lands and lost their identity as a nation. They left behind deserts.

More often, nations have failed because their economic systems permitted the wealth to become centralized in the hands of a few people. The impoverishment of the rest of the people inevitably resulted in revolution of one sort or another.

In the world today, almost every nation is in the process of failing for both reasons. We not only have to remineralize the earth, but we must design a society which meets everyone's need for survival.

Our present economy is completely autocratic. The wealth has become so highly centralized that a very few men now control the whole nation. If they say we will use fossil fuels for energy, we use fossil fuels. If they say we will use chemical "fertilizers" and poisons on the land, we use chemical "fertilizers" and poisons. If they say we will continue to manufacture billions of pounds annually of non-biodegradable organic compounds, we will continue to manufacture the non-biodegradable organic chemicals even though the waste dumps have already doomed the underground water supply and we have endured untold genetic damage and sickness. If they say to build nuclear power plants, H-bombs, and war materiel, we build them.

Clearly, the rule of wealth is diametrically opposed to the survival of humanity. Clearly, we must break the power of wealth or resign ourselves to death centered about the year 1990.

If we had the time, we could start by reforming elections to remove all the influence of wealth. Presently, the electoral system attracts the sort of people who will take the corporate money and do the corporate bidding, which results in the absurd national decisions above described. Unfortunately, there is no time left for election reform which would improve the quality of people in government. Therefore we must work with what we have. The only things that can possibly have any effect on most of the members of Congress is the fear of death and the fear of not getting re-elected. It is up to the people to impress one or both of these fears on those who are supposed to represent us. There is no other chance for survival. What must be done, must be done now.

At one time this nation belonged largely to its people, but as the wealth became more and more centralized, the ownership shifted to the centralized pools of wealth whose only purpose is reinvestment of earnings in order to acquire more ownership. At this time it is probably true that three-fourths of the nation's value is owned by less than 4 percent of the population and the investment funds they control. A few hundred people actually make the decisions for all of us. The control is exercised in many different ways, from advertising propaganda to hired legislators and corporate penetration into the administrative branches of government under the heading of political patronage. The rest of us "go along to git along" because the guy above us controls our jobs.

I don't know how many trillions of dollars there are in the investment funds, but I do know that the doubling time is now something like 5 or 6 years. Reagan's 1967 dollar, now worth about 35 cents, will be worth 17 cents about 1985. The real value of the nation will probably be less in 1985 than it is now, but the ownership will be represented by twice as many dollars. That is the cause of inflation—other factors in the economy simply play catch-up as a matter of necessity. The Carter administration refused to come to grips with the cause of inflation, and the Reagan administration is doing an even worse job. With such leadership, the dollar will be worthless by the end of the decade and the nation will be in financial crisis. Actually, it will happen before that because of the food supply crisis.

Assuming that we are unwilling to accept the disasters which are set to destroy us, the first step to getting a stable monetary unit is to exchange the dollar at 1000 to 1, if need be, for a new monetary unit with real purchasing power. The next step is to change all of the laws to insure that money is constantly recycled into the economy instead of accumulating for unlimited periods of time. According to the mathematics of exponential equations, we must abandon the idea that anything will work forever. Right now the CO_2 curve, the population curve, and the curve for compound interest (or profits), are all out of control because they are all attempting to climb toward infinity. They have reached irrational end points and they must be dealt with. To fail to do so means anarchy and death on a broad scale from many causes in this decade.

The U.S. led the world to political freedom. Now that freedom is being abandoned everywhere in favor of some type of socialism. That means committee control of everything. Nobody has liked what they get from committees because committees aren't smart enough to do everybody's thinking for them. Now is the time to show the world that Total Freedom, the union of political and economic freedom—a rule of law rather than people—is the one system that can bring a peaceful and constructive future to the world.

The paper, *Taxes, Freedom, and the Constitution*, is a brief statement of the changes in law which will recycle the wealth and make the economy and the government work for all the people. It is a time for doing what must be done if civilization is to continue.

The changes which must be made in the way we treat the environment in order to survive imply massive changes in the present economic establishment. Huge investments in plants and equipment must be scrapped. That is not going to happen unless the people who want to survive put up one hell of a fight in the same kind of a hurry. We must gain control of legislative bodies so we can move rapidly to effect the massive changes required. The situation calls for generous use of the recall option. It calls for massive demonstrations. The Polish "Solidarity" movement in an excellent example of how a people can impress their demands on government. The Poles do so at great risk. In this country there is no power which can stand against an aroused populace.

If anyone thinks there is an easy route to the other side of Armageddon, he is just kidding himself. Paraphrasing Jesus (Matthew 5:18), "None of the law shall be changed unless it all be changed." Nobody said it would be easy.

                                                        J.D.H.

7

Taxes, Freedom and the Constitution

Fundamental change is required to save this nation from becoming a totalitarian state. Decay is evident in every facet of our society, but few understand the cause. The Rightists simply blame it all on "communism," which is an effect rather than the cause. The Liberals frantically search their first aid kits for palliatives to treat the most painful effects of the underlying cause. This essay tells why "the rich get richer and the poor get poorer." It tells why centralization of wealth occurs, and it prescribes the only solution possible within the framework of a representative democracy.

In the rush toward industrialization, it became expedient for people to turn toward specialization. They forgot that this is an orderly universe and an orderly world which works according to scientific, i.e., natural laws which are inviolable. Now the extent of environmental destruction has forced us to recognize that everything in the environment has an effect on everything else. With that recognition, the first feeble efforts at a multidisciplinary approach to problems has begun. We have yet to recognize that the design of a viable social order can not be accomplished by sociologists who know nothing of economics, economists who know nothing of sociology, and lawyers who know only their allegiance to the laws of the status quo. Few of them recognize that the social order and the environment are completely dependent on each other.

There is a relationship between mathematics, overpopulation, and poverty which is simple enough and startling enough to draw the attention from the trees long enough to see the forest. The population problem has forced us to recognize that numbers which increase according to an exponential equation become totally incompatible with the finite limits of the world. We must, therefore, change our breeding habits to stop the increase and, preferably, decrease our numbers. It is not optional. It is mandatory. Those nations which fail to comply are doomed to poverty, pollution, starvation, and death. This fact will dominate both domestic and foreign policy in the years ahead.

In the matter of economics, a similar exponential equation is destroying our economy and our democracy. It is the rot that runs through the forest. Benjamin Franklin willed $100 to the city of Philadelphia. It was to be kept at compound interest until it reached $1,000,000. The inheritance paid off in a little less than 200 years. If the million were kept at 6 percent compounded annually for 20 years, it would reach 3.2 million; in 40 years, 10.3 million; and in 60 years it would reach 33 million. At 3 percent it would be only 5.9 million in 60 years; but at 7 percent it would be 57.9 million. Long before Franklin's time many people made business investments of much more than $100 and realized more than 6 percent. Those investments which were invested in the steady money-making businesses, and passed on through inheritance, now are valued in the hundreds of millions. Today these fortunes control capital now measured in hundreds of billions. Applying the 20-, 40-, or 60-year factors shows by inspection that the rate of increase of such vast sums has far exceeded the potential rate of growth of the economy. The growth rate of the centralized pools of wealth has exceeded the finite limits of the capacity of the economy to support it. This is particularly so now, because the growth of population is the primary basis for the growth of the economy. The population growth must be stopped.

One dollar can be plotted as a series of curves (Fig. 1) using a different rate of interest compounded annually for each curve and plotting time on the abscissa against fund increase on the ordinate. The result is the accumulation of a single dollar—the factor to be multiplied by the amount of the initial fund to find its present value. It will be noted that the curves bend gently upward until half to one million dollars is reached. Then in a 50- to 100-year period, the curve breaks upward toward infinitely large numbers. The number of years it takes to reach the break-point depends on the rate of interest (or profit). At 3 percent it takes about 450 years, at 6 percent about 220

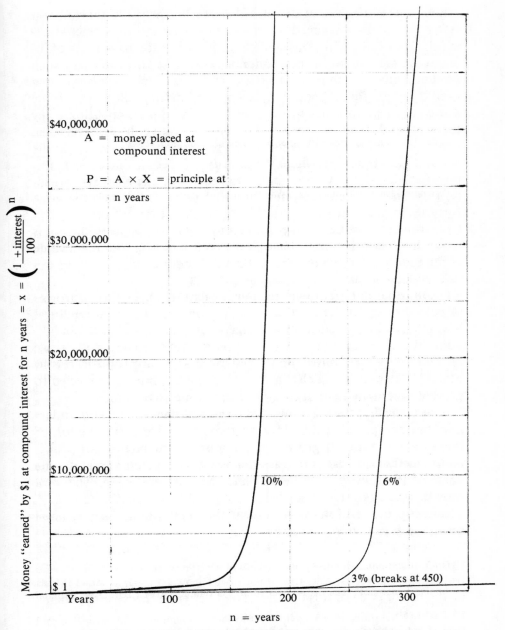

Fig. 1   The Irrational Behavior of Funds at Compound Interest

years, and at 10 percent about 125 years to reach the break-point. After that point is reached, the rate of increase in funds reaches absurdly large rates of increase which have no relation to the rate of increase of *real values* in the economy. Therefore, the only way such fortunes can continue to increase is to expand ownership over everything in the economy which makes money. Because of the power of large fortunes to buy out or freeze out competition, they take control of the most stable and lucrative businesses. The theoretical end result is one fortune in possession of everything in the country. In practice, when a majority of people have been impoverished, there is a revolt and a wiping out of all debts. Historically, this has occurred every few hundred years, i.e., when the large fortunes in a country have reached the break-point in the curve and have transferred much of the ownership from the people to the pools of wealth. They then have the power to reach out for every real value in the economy. The more they take, the faster the process works until they have it all.

One does not argue with the laws of nature. One either conforms or pays the penalty. The mathematics of compound interest is natural law. We are in the self-destruct stage. Our economy is at the break-point in the curve. If we continue to permit funds to accumulate, we are certain to have our economy destroyed and our people in revolt. Money, like everything else in the environment, must be recycled to prevent destructive pollution of the economic environment.

Specifically, there is now about one and one-half trillion dollars in public and private debts. Most of these debts are owed to pools of money which annually grow by the amount of the interest (or profit) added to them. In 60 years, at an average of 7 percent interest, the value of the funds would be 58 times their present value. The total growth rate has far exceeded the real growth rate of the economy. The best-protected funds have passed the break-point. They are well on the way to owning the entire country.

Senator Phillip Hart has said, "...200 decision makers control two-thirds of all production." Senator Fred Harris has said that centralization of wealth and the question of how to re-distribute it will be the major issue of this decade. It had better be, because the claims to ownership by those funds are going to try to double in ten years time. An awful lot of people and small businesses are going bankrupt. Inflation and government and personal debt will continue at high rates of increase. Super-wealth has a counterfeiting machine and a government to legalize its product. It can buy us all.

The excessive rate of growth of large sums of money according to an exponential equation is responsible for virtually all the deficiencies of the present capitalistic system as follows:

1. The constant growth of large pools of money in excess of real growth in the economy is highly *inflationary*. The avidity with which the holders of great wealth seek to multiply it leads to *over-expansion of industrial capacity, over-extension of credit to consumers, and viscious competition for ownership of all income-producing values.*

2. The inflationary "boom" is turned into a "bust" when a significant number of people have used up their credit, and when competition caused by over-production has closed out the least competitive companies, further depleting the consumer demand. Small savings are robbed by inflation. So great is the ever-ready inflationary capacity of large pools of wealth, that the *cycle of boom and bust* has occurred roughly every ten years since 1840. In each one there is a transfer of ownership from those who fail to those who have larger funds subsidizing them at the exponential rate. Example: In 1935 there were 750 breweries. In 1970 only 140. The rate of *bankruptcy* and *conglomeration* insure that there will be a lot fewer breweries after this "bust" period. The power of the major funds now dominates the economy. Production has become centralized, leaving behind centers of poverty.

3. *Charity and the government pick up the bill* to feed the people left destitute. If all present government and private debts were collected from the people tomorrow, most of us would be penniless or in debt. Almost everything in the country would be owned by about one-half of one percent of the people or the businesses in which they hold a controlling interest. *Most of the people are broke.* The wealth has become highly centralized. Inflation eats up the savings of older people, and they are forced on welfare or social security. They have relied on fund growth for security. Insurance and private pension funds pay off about 40 percent and 10 percent respectively, and they pay off in inflated dollars. Social security is not an insurance fund. It is a tax on present producers to feed older, less productive workers forced off the job by the *fixed wage, fixed 8-hour day, maximum profits concept*. If social security tax payments had been funded at compound interest, inflation of the dollar would be far worse than it is, and the government would be well on the way

toward ownership of the entire country. The 153 billion dollars in private pension plans doesn't help the 90 percent of contributors who get nothing back, but it sure helps the big corporations with their conglomeration plans.

4. Because the people of this country have been largely separated from ownership of the real wealth, the pressure of the rapidly multiplying huge pools of wealth has moved toward *exploitation of the people and their resources in less developed countries.* To insure those investments, large sums have been spent since WW II to insure "friendly" national legislators and administrators. The result has been the *absurdly hopeless policy of "Containment of Communism."* Meanwhile, revolt grows within our nation.

5. The forced flow of wealth from the people to the funds (directly and indirectly through taxation) reduces large numbers of people to *poverty* and the majority of the working force to the *insecurity* of having only the job between themselves and poverty. These demoralizing stresses induce *crime, alcoholism, dope addiction, prostitution* — all escape mechanisms to alleviate the pains, needs, and wants that attend poverty.

Poverty provides little market demand. *The total national product must therefore shrink relative to actual need.* This contraction means that more people enter the ranks of poverty. *As the funds increase, poverty increases*—"the rich get richer and the poor get poorer." Those who still work are heavily taxed to sustain the poor. Ultimately *it is the taxpayers who revolt.* Presently this "Silent American" has refused to raise property taxes and he has heard and approved of what George Wallace has been saying. The sleeping giant has awakened. The establishment has kept him ignorant of the cause of his dilemma. If he runs true to form, he will wind up with a *dictatorship* on his back.

We are ruled by an exponential equation. Either we control it or we will join the two-thirds of the world's population which have yielded to dictatorship for survival. Sooner or later, those who fail to control their breeding will have to be restrained by legal means in order that the nation can survive as a human society. Right now is the time to protect ourselves from the rule of centralized pools of wealth if we are to save our political freedom.

This brief, broad view of the economic (and resultant social) problems has served to show that the rich get richer and the poor get poorer because of the fact that money "earns" money at an exponential rate, whereas the economy expands directly with population and the technical ingenuity of the people. The difference between the two rates is the margin of power by which the owners of wealth impose poverty on everyone else.

In a barter economy, the rate of increase of the economy is directly related to the needs of the people. The amount of labor and skill in a bartered item is known to all, and the exchange proceeds on an equal basis so that the balance of the economy is never upset. The invention of money obscured the equality of labor exchange. Starting with the concept that an economy is simply a system for exchanging equal units of labor value, we can discover why the imbalance in our economy occurs. By considering taxes in the general sense of any burden placed on producers, the elements of unequal exchange can be isolated. What are the burdens placed on workers? Do they receive equal labor value in return?

Taxes, in the broad sense, are government-enforced demands for a share of the consumer goods. Nothing has monetary value until human labor is applied to it. Thus a tax is forced human labor. Whether or not equal goods and services are given in exchange for the tax determines whether it is a service institution or a means of enslaving the people.

We can further simplify taxes if we note that all taxes collected ahead of the consumer goods sales tax are added to the cost of goods sold and are therefore sales taxes, i.e., claims for a share of consumer goods. The burden of taxation cannot be shifted from consumer goods. The graduated income tax passed in 1913 to effect a more equitable distribution of income has failed to do so primarily because it can be shifted to the cost of consumer goods. Recognition of this fact by outlawing all taxes ahead of the sales tax will return to all the people very important increments of freedom.

Deferment of taxation to the point of consumption of goods makes it much more feasible for a frugal person to accumulate funds to start a business. Only when this freedom to use our national fund of ingenuity and initiative is established can we expect to eliminate the welfare rolls and withdraw workers from government into the productive economy. Then our tax burden will be lowered accordingly and this, too, is an increment of freedom.

A further increment of freedom to be gained by elimination of taxes at the production level is that politicians could no longer sell loopholes in exchange for campaign support. This practice has resulted in establishing economic advantages for the highest bidders with the result that farmers, for instance, can not compete with agribusiness which can lose money on farming and make it up elsewhere in the conglomerate where tax loopholes support it. Thus the big corporations would be less powerful and the government less corrupt. These are important increments of freedom for the people.

Within the broad definition of taxes, there are three taxes which are included in the cost of consumer goods which government says are lawful but which are collected by individuals.

When the *inheritor* of wealth goes to the market place for a yacht or a mansion, he brings no products or labor to exchange. The same thing is true of a *land speculator* who does nothing to increase the value of land but whom the government allows to collect the increased value. The same is true of the stockholder, who by the grace of government and a *stock split*, finds himself in possession of a share of several years of company surplus earned by the ingenuity and effort of a good working force. He brings to the consumer market place no value which he has earned if it is profit above the true market value (rightful interest) of his original investment. These government-sanctioned private taxes have the same effect as government taxes. They increase demand without increasing supply and therefore inflate the price. They take units of labor without giving units of labor, which is slavery.

This element of slavery is what makes possible the rapid conglomeration of companies and ultimately the centralization of the nation's wealth. Man-hours of labor can be legally expropriated from each person's paycheck to obtain a pool of wealth with which to buy a new plant from which to hire people from whom man-hours of labor can be expropriated to obtain a new pool of wealth, etc. When slavery is legalized, the anti-trust laws have all the effect of a pea shooter against an elephant.

It is these three something-for-nothing deals which, by means of the exponential equation, generate sufficient funds to transfer all ownership from the people to the funds. They are taxes collected directly by the property class and enforced by the government it controls. In Russia, the dictatorship serves the Communist Party which controls all the property. In this country it is the Demopublican party that serves the property class.

Recently one other private tax system has been invented. It is the 2 percent "savings stamps" tax on consumer goods. Since private taxes have been given the cloak of legality throughout recorded history, there is little basis for objecting to one more such tax on the grounds that only government can collect taxes. To argue the point would open up the whole can of worms.

Another general class of taxation consists of taxes on savings, such as property taxes. The Demopublican property party has seen fit to levy savings taxes almost exclusively on property. The effect has been to drive the older workers with little income (they are thrown out of industry when deemed unprofitable) out of their homes. The homes then become the property of the mortgage holders. The people are trapped in apartments and in boxes called mobile homes. The property tax is an excellent device for transferring ownership from the people to the centralized pools of wealth.

Savings are stored labor. If the individual is to be able to take care of himself, he must be permitted to accumulate the results of labor and use it to support himself over unproductive periods. The government that collects property or other taxes on stored labor is patently an institution of slavery.

Another class of taxes are those used to control imports and exports. *When we have obtained economic freedom, we are going to be able to work a four-hour day and have a standard of living and a quality of living which is beyond most people's imagination.* Other nations can and will obtain the same results. But it can not be done if we attempt to compete with technically advanced nations overpopulated with wage slaves. We must therefore control our foreign trade to protect our own progress. As other nations turn toward freedom, we can establish free trade with them and operate as a single economy with a common standard of living. Maybe some day it will be one world. Meanwhile, we have yet to establish one peaceful nation.

Finally, there are special-use taxes based on the principle that if government performs a service for a particular group, they should pay for it. Gasoline taxes pay for roads. Unfortunately, the pressure group that results from the pooling of such funds has not led to intelligent environmental planning. Special use taxes are no longer practical.

One wonders why the people have tolerated these burdens for countless centuries. The answer is two-fold. Those who hold power have always been those who have access to the unearned values. They have written the laws to suit themselves. Until very recent times they have kept the people illiterate. Even to this day, all preachers and most school teachers fear to discuss the three something-for-nothing deals. It is only because these three causes of the centralization of wealth have brought us to the brink of crisis that the great power of wealth to perpetuate itself is slowly yielding to the force of necessity. For two-thirds of the world's people, these ancient prerogatives of rulers have yielded to the force of bloody revolutions led by ostensibly altruistic dictatorships. Hopefully, an enlightened electorate will bring these institutions down in this country without the loss of political freedom won with so much blood through the centuries.

What should be done to return these values to those who produced them?

Inheritance and land rent value must be collected by the government. This will decrease the sales tax required.

The privately collected tax on the earnings of a working force in excess of interest is composed of increased technical efficiency, human effort, and product demand. Heretofore, this has always accrued to ownership simply because they have hire, fire, and bribe control over the management. The unions now contend for this value, while the white collar workers who had a good deal to do with the increased earnings sit on the side lines and take whatever is handed out.

Instead of the single inflationary force of profit-taking, we now also have an inflationary force from union wage demands. In monopolistic or near-monopolistic necessity industries, the reaching for profit and wages is passed on to consumers as inflated price. Of necessity, less favored industries and unorganized workers follow along behind. This built-in inflation can be slowed by recession. It might be stopped by depression. But after recovering, it would start up again. The dollar is depreciating at a chaotic rate because we no longer have any semblance of a free market product evaluation.

In order to solve this problem, we are going to have to redefine the "commodity called labor" as human beings and redefine the investor as one enjoying the privilege of investing his savings at whatever interest rate the market will currently support. We must transfer the management of each company from the ownership board of directors to the working force. This will result in companies whose size rests solely on economic factors. No group of workers will remain in a conglomerate if it costs them money to do so. The better producers will pull out, and the massive pools of wealth that now dictate to government will be dispersed among small companies. We will have, for the first time since man left the barter economy, free market conditions. Of greatest value is the right of a working force to earn all it can earn. Under this incentive, there will soon be an abundance of goods in the market place. Since the working force will no longer be bound by the rigid (most profitable) 8-hour day, they will work when there is work to do and cut hours back when the demand declines. Technical improvements will be used to shorten hours instead of eliminating people from the payroll. The security (now based on the total payroll) of the individual and the company will both be vastly increased. Interest rates will decline to true market values. Since supply and demand are both relatively constant factors and the rigid artificial factors will be gone from the economy, the economic cycles will cease.

Small businesses initiated and managed by one or two persons must be permitted to operate as they have been. These are some of the creative geese who lay the golden eggs. They probe all the diverse avenues for economic development. They develop products, services, and jobs. Of necessity, they must have full control over their initiative.

Our economic troubles are man-made. They persist to this late day in the history of civilization because greed has maintained institutions of enslavement. Even our Constitution contained a provision for the return of run-away slaves. In the intervening 200 years, human populations have covered and been compressed into the habitable lands. The means of destruction of human life have been perfected. We are at Armageddon. Either "good" will triumph over "evil" or all or most of humanity will be destroyed.

Every conceivable economic system except economic freedom has been tried without bringing internal peace to any nation, let alone between nations. It is time to test whether or not man, freed of his shackles, can find peace. In the United States, the first step toward that end is the establishment of Constitutional basis for constructing a free society.

Proposed
General Revision of the
Constitution of the United States of America

Preamble:

We the people of the United States, in order to form a more perfect union, establish justice, insure domestic tranquility, provide for the common defense, promote the general welfare, *establish and preserve the integrity of the laws of creation, provide for equality of education, establish a just distribution of earnings, eliminate the perpetual growth of accumulations of wealth, insure freedom from taxes on earnings and savings,* and secure the blessings of liberty to ourselves and our posterity, do ordain, *establish,* and *amend* this Constitution for the United States of America.

Article I

Section 1

All Legislative Powers herein granted shall be vested in a Congress of the United States which shall consist of a Senate and a House of Representatives, and *in a one-house Educational Congress, and a one-house Environmental Congress.*

The Congress of the United States shall retain legislative power in all matters not delegated to the Environmental Congress and to the Educational Congress. In the event of conflict over legislative authority between any two of the Congresses, a nine-person board appointed by the third Congress which is not involved in the conflict shall arbitrate the matter. If no agreement is reached, the matter shall be decided by the Supreme Court.

Section 11

An Educational Congress shall be established to provide equality of educational opportunity for all and to maintain educational standards and facilities which will most enhance the quality of life for the nation's citizens. In the performance of its purpose, it shall establish school zoning laws based solely on proximity to the school, and in all other matters every child shall be treated as such without regard to race, creed, or color.

The Educational Congress shall be composed of one member from each state. The term of office shall be four years, with a limit of two consecutive terms.

All school funds shall be budgeted and submitted to the Congress for approval and inclusion in the national budget. No public school shall receive tax funds from any other source.

Section 12

The Environmental Congress shall be composed of one elected environmentalist from each state. The term of office shall be eight years with a limit of two consecutive terms.

It shall be the duty of the Environmental Congress to identify and to establish and maintain the integrity of the laws of creation with the object of attaining a perfect environment for human habitation. The perfection of the food supply shall be the first responsibility.

The Environmental Congress shall have the power to pass all general laws and specific regulations as it deems necessary to perform its duty. Where the interest of other units of government conflict with the environmental needs, the laws and regulations of the Environmental Congress shall be held by the courts to have preference.

All measures required to implement the planning, research, inspection, standardization, etc., necessary to the purpose of reaching for the perfect human habitat are within the powers of the Environmental Congress. All Executive Branch agencies may be overruled by and must make information available to the Environmental Congress on matters germane to the environment.

The Environmental Congress shall have the authority to establish its own budget which will be submitted to Congress for inclusion in the national budget.

Amendments to the Constitution of the United States

Article XXVII

The purpose of this amendment is to provide freedom from oppressive taxation and the oppression of unearned wealth.

No taxes shall be laid on earnings or savings or on any other wealth except as follows:

1. Inheritance taxes (including gift taxes) shall be collected in an amount and in a way which assures that no able-bodied inheritor except a spouse can live for more than four years of adult life at average cost on the savings (or funds earned by them) of the deceased.

2. All foundation, charitable and religious organizations, any other non-business organizations, and all public monopolies shall divest themselves of all income-earning property and income-earning money, and in the future operate on the gifts or payments from those who support them.

All businesses which loan other people's money shall make service charges only. All interest shall be apportioned among those whose money is used.

No income-earning funds shall be established by any unit of government. All units of government shall retire all debts in not more than 20 years from date of ratification and thereafter operate on current taxes.

3. Land taxes shall be collected by a Federal tax agency to the full rent value. All land titles shall be exchanged for land-holding grants which are valid only as long as the holder pays the current land tax and uses the land for its agreed purpose. Present land owners may have the option of selling to the government or receiving the current tax minus the tax paid at the effective date for the life of the last surviving present owner or owners. The right of eminent domain shall be reserved to the Environmental Congress.

4. Sales taxes uniformly applied to all retail sales of consumer goods may be applied by any governing unit.

5. Tariffs shall be used as required to establish and maintain a maximum diversity of skills and jobs within the nation. All direct subsidies to industry shall be illegal. An individual balance of trade shall be maintained with all nations with whom we do not establish free trade. Free trade may be established by Congress with those nations which also establish economic and political freedom.

The Congress shall write enabling laws as required to effect the provisions of this amendment.

Article XXVIII

The purpose of this amendment is to establish merit as the sole basis for the distribution of earnings.

1. The only lawful income from capital goods investments shall be interest as established competitively and currently, with the exception of economic units employing less than ten persons.

2. All capital goods must be financed by invested funds.

3. The only lawful return for human effort shall be the rated fair share of value of the product of the working force, less expenses, with the exception of economic units with less than ten persons under the active direction of an initiator of an enterprise and units not operating in a competitive market.

4. Companies which operate under this amendment shall be operated by the working force according to democratic practices. Investors shall have no vote in decision-making but shall have the right to a hearing at their request. No worker may be laid off except by a two-thirds majority of those who know his work record.

5. All domestic companies shall divest themselves of ownership in all foreign countries. All foreign companies shall divest themselves of all ownership in domestic companies.

6. The Congress shall write enabling laws to effect the provisions of this amendment. All provisions shall be met within a period of ten years of ratification.

The proposed Constitutional amendment provides the increments of freedom previously described. In addition, it provides for division of the legislative branch into three units according to function.

Education is a national responsibility. It can be neither adequate nor equal until it is funded from a single source. Neither can it enjoy the freedom to teach truth unless it is protected by Constitutional law. By separating education from the political pressures of the existing Congress and local dominance, perhaps our educators can center education more on fact and less on beliefs and propaganda for the status quo.

The environmental problem centers about the fact that every living thing has both its metabolism and function controlled by coded instructions in its nucleic acids. There are no instructions for handling biologically active particles never before experienced in the natural environment, nor for handling those natural biologically-active particles in concentrations not heretofore found in the natural environment. In short, the integrity of the natural environment for all living things must be re-established. Just stating the problem defines the enormous industrial changes that must take place. It can only occur if it is guided by professionally competent environmentalists. The present politically strangled legislatures composed mostly of lawyers, insurance salesmen, and rich men are technically and politically incapable of passing the laws and devising the alternate production methods. They can pass the buck to the agencies, but these are so corrupted by industrial influence that they are impotent to accomplish their purpose. Witness the scandal of malnutrition and protein shortage caused by pollution of the soil and the destruction and pollution of nutrients in food processing. The fact that we are said to be within 10 or 12 years of exhaustion of the known available and irreplacable oil and gas supplies and have not yet developed free steam supplies, available almost anywhere on the continent below one mile depth, is an arrogant insult to the people by a government enslaved by economic powers. We must have a separate environmental authority, environmentally oriented, and independent from political influence.

In summary:

The capital goods and personal property must be dispersed among all the people if they are to attain financial security and the independence of action required to initiate an economy of abundance to replace the present hand-to-mouth rat-race economy of scarcity. To accomplish this, 100 percent of both earnings and savings must be protected by law against the greed of those who hold power. The autocracy of ownership in the corporation must be broken to enable the people who work there to become a flexible economic unit of production responsive to supply and demand.

The educational process must be free of all duress. It must be adequately and equally funded for all people.

The physical environment must be decontaminated. It must be planned for the future—in some matters, thousands of years into the future.

The objectives cannot be obtained without fundamental change in the Constitution.

If wind could solve our problems, the Demopublican politicians would have done it long ago.

The politicians talk of tax reform as a matter of closing loopholes and/or confiscatory taxes at high levels of income. It is nonsense. If they taxed 100 percent over $50,000 and closed all the loopholes, it would only accelerate the process of conglomeration of companies. Instead of taking profit, owners would leave it in the corporation where it can be used to buy more companies. The power of wealth, not spending money, is the prize sought. Railroad cars, yachts, airplanes, expense accounts, pseudo-retirement plans—all have been used by corporate ownership as private property exempt from personal income tax. The bill must be paid in the price of goods in the consumer market place. A feudal prerogative can not be effectively restrained by the cynical manipulation of a tax which is itself an enslaving institution.

The politicians talk about inflation as a political argument at election time. Not one of them proposes measures which will get at the cause by stopping the flow of wealth from the people, and the welfare government that sustains them, to the centralized pools of wealth which now own most of us. In between elections they openly acknowledge that the only way the inflation rate of the exploitative economy can be slowed is to arbitrarily raise interest rates, thus decreasing credit transactions and throwing marginal producers out of work. So great is the inflationary pressure from government debt, national corporations, and national unions that only a serious depression can significantly slow the rate of destruction of the dollar.

The politicians talk about unemployment at election time. Between elections they talk about welfare and make-work. Meanwhile, small businesses fall like dominoes at the rate of 10,000 a year. The economists in the ivory towers have told politicians that free trade is the ideal international trade system. So the politicians have authorized free trade because this is what their masters (the owners of the centralized pools of wealth) want. The expropriated earned surplus of numerous corporations has been used to ship whole plants, machinery, technique, and management personnel to countries where labor is cheap. The low-cost goods shipped back to this country have eliminated numerous industries. Even the steel and auto industries are finding they are not competitive. There has been a large shift from production to service industries. In the process of going out of production, our real unemployment and under-employment has soared. The phony government statistic does not give the true figure. The true figure includes the forced retirees over 50, and the 40 million under the poverty level. The government picks up the check for everything, including the price of wars to keep the "free world's" people and resources safe for exploitation by the controllers of our centralized pools of wealth. The government, of course, passes the bill to the people who do the work. This "free trade" has become one more tool by which the rich get richer and the rest of us get poorer. The Communists fan the flames and watch us destroy ourselves.

The politicians say we can't have a depression again. Establishment economists have told them so. The fact is that the only thing which has held a depression in check since WW II was an expanding economic system based primarily on electronics, constant war production, and an expanding federal and personal debt load. Environmental costs here, and cheap labor abroad, move industry and capital to foreign lands where the costs can be evaded. We are fed up with the cost of war. Government and personal credit have about run out. So have "good times" run out.

The politicians have no answers because the exploitative economy does not work. As long as history has been recorded, nations have failed every few hundred years. Before the industrial revolution, inheritance and land speculation were the primary factors in bringing all the land into the hands of a few people. Those who owned the land had the power to run the government. To protect their ownership, they raised the land rent to raise armies and build castles. When the rent rose above 50 percent of the crop value, revolt and redistribution of the land always occurred. As trade developed, the profit system was developed and again a share of the labor was confiscated by ownership.

As governments became more complex they, too, learned to take a share of the labor. Thus the total tax at the point of revolt is made up of the personal levies by ownership plus the taxes levied by the government which serves the ownership class.

If we add up the total taxes in this country, we have approximately 35 percent taken by government plus an inexact amount represented by the burden of inheritors, land speculators, and profit in excess of a theoretical free market interest on money. The total tax is probably in excess of 50 percent. The Wallace movement is a gut reaction to the fact that most of the farmers have been run off the land and the majority of city workers are on a treadmill which barely allows them to run in place let alone show progress in savings to secure their old age. Which direction will that gut reaction be turned—toward fascism—toward socialism—or toward freedom?

Elsewhere in the world, the trend is toward some form of socialism. In this country, the greatest experiment in political democracy ever undertaken was launched with the Declaration of Independence. In the following two centuries, we have been sorely corrupted by a capitalistic system which included the three something-for-nothing deals, which in concert with an irrational exponential equation causes the centralization of wealth and power. By the simple expedient of making our capitalistic system honest, we can gradually disperse the wealth among the people. In the hands of the people, it will support an excellent standard and quality of living. It will never accumulate to sums whose rate of increase reaches toward infinite quantity and infinite power—and arrives at infinite weakness in that the whole system can be destroyed by a single dollar accumulating its interest for a long period of time.

All of the industrialized "free nations" which now contain large fortunes and funds operating at high rates of interest have the same problem. The bonanza of productivity resulting from widespread public education has peaked. The ever-present ability of the pools of wealth to accumulate ownership is now the dominant force. Within 10 to 20 years the industrialized "free nations" will all either establish economic freedom under law or they will be under dictatorship.

The something-for-nothing deals have brought the funds of wealth in this country to the point where they have caused a 60 percent inflation in the last 15 years. If given our economic freedom, we can work our way out of this mess. Without economic freedom, we are going to lose our political freedom to some form of dictatorship because this economy does not work.

It is pure fantasy to believe that this economy can last for more than a few years without redistribution of wealth. Rep. Wright Patman of the House Banking Committee says, "About 15 U.S. manufacturers receive a total of 88 percent of all business profits..." About the only money-making property left to take is the land, and they are gobbling it up. We mere mortals can not compete with fortunes which enjoy the luxury of perpetual life. Nor can the monetary system withstand the inflation of funds increasing exponentially to become so powerful that they can fix profits and prices of necessities. Taxes must inevitably keep rising to pay for the palliatives used to soften the impact of the ever-more-numerous problems which arise as our nation and its environment degenerate. The working taxpayers, who inevitably pay for everything, will almost certainly be forced to demand radical change before 1980. Whatever they demand they will get.

The working taxpayer has always been deceived. His churches, his schools, his government, and the publishers have all played the part of the scribes and pharisees who paid their tithe but ignored the weightier matters of law and justice. History (especially recent history) has shown that the alternative to justice under law is dictatorship. That is too high a price to pay for the job security enjoyed by the hypocrite.

It is time to continue the American Dream with a declaration of freedom from enslaving institutions. That can only be done by a Constitutional revision. We will probably need a new political party to get it.

Postscript

The four and a third acres of mineralized soil was planted in the fall of 1980 with a low-protein, white wheat developed for pastries. It was the 5th crop grown since the soil was mineralized. There was an abundance of soil moisture in the spring, and growth was excellent until the heads started forming. During this period the soil cracked open twice for lack of rain. I was therefore surprised to find that the yield was 60¼ bushels per acre. The county extension agent estimated that the average yield in the county was 45 to 50 bushels per acre. Because of the cost of testing, I have no comparative data on the elements in the wheat. However, I did get a protein analysis of 9 percent. In the case of the comparative test between mineralized and chemically grown corn (Chapter 2), the indicated protein (not a trace reading for the chemically grown corn) was about the same, but the element analysis was far superior in the mineralized corn. The results would no doubt be the same with the wheat. In any event, the wheat makes a loaf of whole wheat bread with the good flavor possessed by all foods having high mineral content in natural balance.

Another five and two-thirds acres, which had not been used in the last 13 years, was planted to corn in 1981. The farmer who planted the corn used commercial NPK fertilizer. As it grew, I came to the conclusion that it was going to be the best corn crop in the area. How could this be? I had secured a spectrographic analysis and thoroughly studied that soil myself. It was incapable of growing a crop. Thinking is, of course, an agonizing experience for all of us. However, I decided some thinking was required.

I got a handful of the NPK fertilizer used on the corn. By repeatedly stirring up the fertilizer in water, allowing it to settle, and then pouring off the solution, the water-soluble NPK and the adhesive used to keep the fertilizer granulated were removed. What was left was ground glacial gravel dust. I obtained another brand and checked, with the same result.

The residue from 13 poor-weed crops was mostly on top of the soil, with some penetration into the top inch of soil. At that elevation it was of little use to the soil life because it was dried out for most of the growing season. Nevertheless, there was a slow change taking place from plant residue to skins (cell walls) of microorganisms, which represented a storage of carbon and nitrogen. When this material (sometimes called leaf mold) was disked into the topsoil and mixed with the very finely ground gravel dust in the fertilizer, a substantial microorganism population was inevitable. The result was a respectable yield of corn on a soil which is basically worthless.

One question which has been bothering me for some time is why people in the same area were getting any crops at all, if my 10 acres was of such poor quality. The answer, of course, is that the filler in the chemical fertilizer is supplying enough minerals to prevent a collapse in the yield.

The large difference in the yield of various farms varies with the color of the soil. Those farmers who have returned the crop stalks to the soil have the highest yields. In so doing they have maintained a better reservoir of carbon and nitrogen in the soil to supply the crop. Unfortunately, the acid in NPK is constantly dissolving organic matter and inorganic material from the soil. With an estimated 30 to 50 percent of the acidic component of NPK winding up in the rivers, it is obvious that a lot of the fertility elements are going the same way.

In the 50's and 60's, the agricultural experts were helping the fertilizer industry by recommending to the farmer that dumping the barnyard waste into a pond was more economical than spreading it back on the land, because the same amount of fertility elements could be obtained more economically from NPK fertilizer. They learned the hard way that crops won't grow without organic matter. So now they say the organic matter is required to "buffer" the soil. Technically, a buffering agent is one that tends to neutralize an acid or a base. Crop residue won't do that, but if it is put into the soil and there are any minerals at all present, microorganisms will multiply. Obviously, the basic elements in the protoplasm are the most available elements in the soil for buffering the acidity in NPK. If the rains are gentle, the dissolved protoplasm may be reconstituted into new organisms before it is leached or eroded into the river. And that can take place only if there are enough basic elements in the soil so the microorganisms can find what it takes to bring order out of chaos. The natural mixture of elements is geared to natural conditions—not to the absurd practice of deliberately acidifying the soil. Basic elements would have to be added to the natural mix to compensate for the man-made acid.

Nitrogen is the most acidic component. If I can get 60 bushels per acre of wheat without nitrogen fertilizer, why should the farmer buy it from the chemical companies?

Phosphorous should be left where found because those deposits contain large amounts of fluorides. The agricultural soils are now badly contaminated with fluorides. Fluoride levels in food are increasing. Cattle concentrate the fluorine in their bones. When the bonemeal is used in pet foods, fluorosis results. Do we wait until the overt symptoms of fluorosis show up in half the population before we stop this nonsense?

There is plenty of phosphorous and potassium in the natural rock mixture and at a much lower price.

If a farmer uses 200 pounds of a 15-15-15 NPK fertilizer, he gets about 100 pounds of gravel dust per acre. That costs no more than 75 cents. The fertilizer costs $25 to $30. What the farmer pays for is five paper sacks and some chemicals, neither of which he needs. Sooner or later the chemicals will destroy the land. Some bargain!

The USDA's Conservation Service has finally come to the conclusion that we are not going to continue the habit of eating much longer. They base their conclusion on the following: We had 18 inches of topsoil a couple of hundred years ago; now we have an 8" topsoil. The United States is losing 6.4 billion tons to erosion every year. All of the soils are eroding, and a fourth of them are eroding at a destructive rate.

How widespread is the practice of using gravel dust as the filler in a sack of NPK, I do not know. In those areas where gravel screenings or sand has been the most economical filler available, the dust has probably been used for years. I suspect that it is now a general practice because all soils have been largely stripped of some elements, and there is no cheaper way to add them.

Generally speaking, the biological fertilizers, as exemplified by "Eco-Agriculture," use a mixture of minerals in combination with a compost or compost-like material which is high in nitrogen and carbon.

Organic farming, as advocated by the Rodale organization, concentrates on organic matter plus specific minerals such as greensand and granite dust.

The chemical NPK will accelerate erosion. Eco-Ag and organic methods will slow the rate of erosion and maintain a better balance of elements in the soil. None of them are applied in amounts sufficient to build up the mineral supply in the soil. All of them are partially dependent on the dwindling availability of the small amount of gravel and sand remaining in the soils. They work best on the strongest soils.

All three fertilizing methods are dependent on annual applications. If anything were to interrupt the production and distribution for one crop year, we would starve to death in large numbers.

None of these will sustain our food supply indefinitely. They will not do the all-important job of removing the excess CO_2 from the atmosphere. They are all too expensive. We must have a bulk production and distribution of gravel dust. Without it there is no future for civilization.

* * *

"Hazardous Substances and Sterile Men" is the title of a powerful condemnation of the organic chemicals industry in the September, 1981 issue of *Acres, U.S.A.* Ida Honorof has summarized research on this subject. From 10 to 23 percent of American males are sterile (very unlikely to father a child). In 1938 only ½ of 1 percent of males were sterile. In 30 years half of the males will be sterile. From 67 to 83 percent of all birth defects are caused by men. The chances of causing a deformed child to be born increase with the quantity of chemicals in the sperm. Twenty chlorinated chemicals alone have been found in the sperm. Birth defect rates in the United States are believed to be about 6 percent—it seems only a few years since that estimate was 3 percent. Many of the chemicals contaminate our food supply.

So there you have it—a nice painless way to put humanity out of its misery: just keep on eating the poisoned foods of chemical agriculture. Quite painless except for the cancers, the deformities, the stillbirths, and as many different ailments as there are parts in the body. Either we stop the manufacture of organic chemicals which are not readily biodegradable or we destroy ourselves.

"The balance of nature," in part, means that for every living organism there is a predator, so that no organism can populate the earth to the exclusion of all others. Our asinine, conceited view of ourselves as masters of nature has led us to make a wreck of the balance of nature. We are paying a high price and we will continue to pay for a long time, even though we turn quickly to a rational conception of our role in the natural order. I have seen radical improvements in the ecology on two small plots of land when the poisoning was stopped and minerals applied to the land. Perhaps nature can rather quickly reestablish the animated part of the balance of nature.

*   *   *

In the pages of this book have been listed many crises, all of which have the potential of bringing death to humanity on a massive scale. It has also been shown that there are solutions to all of the problems.

It is obvious that those who make the decisions for all of us have done a rotten job. The world needs to come under new management. A change of management is what the various forms of socialism are all about—"us instead of them." On the whole, I think it's fair to say that management by "us" is no better than management by "them," and generally worse. So let's face it: those who have been making the decisions are no better and no worse than you and I. We have all acquiesced in and taken advantage of the rotten laws by which we have lived. The new management must live by a new code.

A people prosper or decline according to the code and the supporting law by which they live. The Constitution is our code. Laws without end have not been able to prevent this nation from arriving at the brink of self-destruction. The authors of the Constitution had a right to expect succeeding generations to improve on the code. It is incredible and disgusting that 200,000,000 of us have sat on our backsides for decades and watched crisis after crisis developing with no effort made to improve the code. It must be that there's enough larceny in each of us to make us like the system.

Historians have recorded 6,000 to 8,000 years of riches and poverty, wars and famine, side-by-side with spurts of technical progress. Now we have arrived at a point where technical progress is destroying us. The social order is unable to control it. So the question each of us must answer is quite simple, "Shall we change the social order to make it work for all of us, or do we simply await our extinction?"

I have long felt that the majority of people would do the right thing if given a choice. Had I not felt so, this book would not have been written. Assuming that my intuition is correct, what must we do to effect the radical changes required?

The crux of the problem is the Congress. How do we get control of it? How do we do it within the time frame demanded by the CO_2 crisis? We have dozens of organizations in the nation all devoted to worthwhile objectives. Take it from Julius Caesar: as long as the people remain divided, they will never beat the establishment. There must be an overall objective of basic reform to which all subscribe, or the establishment will defeat us one by one in the Congressional committees which write the laws. What it boils down to is voting power.

What I am suggesting is a "Survival Movement" on the order and scale of the Polish Solidarity Movement. Those organization leaders who favor survival should call a meeting of organization heads for planning and action.

The first requirement would be to analyze the members of Congress with a view towards the 1982 elections to insure complete control by that time. With sufficient voting strength, a strong majority can be established in the House. Numerous recall actions would probably be required to gain control of the Senate.

The other prime requirement is to get TV time to explain our predicament to a maximum number of citizens. It is the only media which can reach the people quickly. The FCC "equal time" provision may be one possibility. However, I suspect that, as in the case of the Solidarity Movement, massive street demonstrations will be required to get publicity and political support. To succeed, the "Survival Movement" must have the same spontaneity as the Poles have shown. It has got to be everybody's "do it yourself" project. Anything less will be too little and too late.

"People power" is the strongest force on earth when used. It has torn down dictatorships by the dozens. It can tear the rot out of this nation, and that in all nations, and it may yet insure our survival.

What matters is unity of action in support of a comprehensive program which has the potential of insuring the survival of civilization.

John D. Hamaker

Bibliography

Adam, D.P. 1975. Ice Ages and the Thermal Equilibrium of the Earth, II. Quaternary Research 5, 161-171.

Adam, D.P. 1976. Reply to Comment by William L. Donn. Quat. Res. 6, p. 317.

Adam, D.P. 1976. Reply to Comments by J.G. Lockwood. Quat. Res. 6, 451-53.

Albrecht, W.A. 1952. Soil Fertility — A Weapon Against Weeds. The Organic Farmer, June.

Albrecht, W.A. 1958. *Soil Fertility and Animal Health*. Fred Hahne Co., Webster City, IA.

Albrecht, W.A. 1975. The Healthy Hunzas, A Climax Human Crop. In *The Albrecht Papers*. Acres, U.S.A., Raytown, MO.

Albrecht, W.A. 1975. *The Albrecht Papers*. Acres, U.S.A.

Alexander, G. and the Ambassador College Ag. Res. Dept. 1974. World Crisis in Agriculture. Ambassador College Press, Pasadena.

Allaby, M. 1971. Living Soil. The Ecologist 1:17, Nov.

Ambler Pennant 1950. Editorial. Vol. 2: 2.

Andersen, G.W. and Andersen, R.L. 1963. The Rate of Spread of Oak Wilt in the Lake States. Journal of Forestry, Nov.

Andersen, N.A. et al 1967. The Stalactiform Rust on Jack Pine. J. For., June.

Andersen, S.T. 1961. Interglacial Plant Successions in the Light of Environmental Changes. In INQUA Report of the VI International Congress on Quaternry, Vol. II, Warsaw (Lodz 1964).

Andersen, S.T. 1966. Interglacial Vegetational Succession and Lake Development in Denmark. The Palaeobotanist 15: 1, 2.

Andersen, S.T. 1969. Interglacial Vegetation and Soil Development. Medd. Dansk Geol. Foren. Kobenhavn, Bind 19.

Andersen, S.T. 1979. Brown earth and podzol: soil genesis illuminated by microfossil analysis. Boreas 8, 69-72.

Anderson, John F. and Kaya, Harry K. (eds.) 1976. *Perspectives in Forest Entomology*. Academic Press, New York.

Anderson, R.F. 1960. *Forest and Shade Tree Entomology*. John Wiley & Sons.

Andrews, J.T. et al 1972. Past and Present Glaciological Responses to Climate in Eastern Baffin Island. Quat. Res. 2, 303-14.

Anonymous 1948. New Disease Threatens Western White Pine Stands. J. For., April, p. 294.

Anon. 1981. Building stronger bones for old age. Science News 201, Sept. 8.

Anon. 1981. Reagan budget slashes environmental programs. International Wildlife, May/June.

Aucoin, J. 1979. The Irrigation Revolution and its Environmental Consequences. Environment 21: 8, Oct.

Baker, B.H. and Kemperman, J.A. 1974. Spruce Beetle Effects On a White Spruce Stand in Alaska. J. For., July.

Bakshi, Bimal 1976. *Forest Pathology*. Delhi: Controller of Publications.

Banik, Allan and Taylor, Renee 1960. *Hunza Land*. Whitehorn Pub. Co., Long Beach, CA.

Barry, R.G. et al 1973. Synoptic Climatological Studies of the Baffin Island Area. In *Climate of the Arctic*, eds. Weller, G. and Bowling, S.A., Univ. of Alaska.

Baule, Hubert and Fricker, Claude 1970. *The Fertilizer Treatment of Forest Trees*. BLV Verlagsgesellschaft mbH, Munchen, Germany.

Beal, J.A. et al 1964. Beatle Explosion in Honduras. Amer. For., Nov.

Bear, Firman E. 1962. *Earth, The Stuff of Life*. Univ. of Oklahoma Press.

Bell, Marcus et al 1974. Influences of Fertilization on Forest Production and the Forest Environment. Biocon Research Ltd., Victoria, B.C.

Berg, Norman 1981. Comments: From the SCS Chief. Soil and Water Conservation News, June.

Bernard, Harold 1980. *The Greenhouse Effect*. Ballinger, Cambridge, MA.

Bess, H.A. et al 1947. Forest Site Conditions and the Gypsy Moth. Harvard Forest Bull. No. 22.

Birkeland, P.W. 1974. *Pedology, Weathering, and Geomorphological Research*. Oxford Univ. Press, London/New York.

Bloomfield, H. 1979. Elms For Always. Amer. For., Jan.

Blum, B. 1980 Coal and Ecology. EPA Journal, Sept.

Bohn, H.L. 1976. Estimate of Organic Carbon in World Soils. Soil Sci. Soc. Am. J. 40, 468-9.

Bollen, W.B. 1959. *Microorganisms and Soil Fertility*. Oregon St. College, Corvallis.

Bormann, F.H. and Likens, G.E. 1979. *Pattern and Process in a Forested Ecosystem*. Springer-Verlag, New York.

Bowling, S.A. 1973. Possible Significance of Recent Weather and Circulation Anomalies in Northeastern Canada for the Initiation of Continental Glaciation. In *Climate of the Arctic*, eds. Weller, G. and Bowling, S.A., Univ. of Alaska.

Boyce, J.S. 1948. *Forest Pathology*. McGraw-Hill.

Bridges, E.M. 1978. Interaction of Soil and Mankind in Britain. J. Soil Sci. 29, 125-39.

Bruce, J.G. 1973. A Time-Stratigraphic Sequence of Loess Deposits on Near-Coastal Surfaces in the Balclutha District. N.Z. J. Geol. Geophys. 16, 549-56.

Brown, Lester R. et al 1976. Twenty-two Dimensions of the Population Problem. Worldwatch paper – 5, Worldwatch Institute, Washington.

Brown, L.R. 1978. Vanishing Croplands. Environment 20: 10, Dec.

Brown, L.R. 1978. The Worldwide Loss of Cropland. Worldwatch paper – 24, Worldwatch Institute, Washington.

Buringh, P. 1970. *Introduction To The Study of Soils in Tropical and Subtropical Regions*. Centre for Agriculture Publishing and Documentation, Wageningen.

Calabrese, Edward J. 1980. *The Influence of Nutritional Status on Pollutant Toxicity and Carcinogenicity.* Univ. of Massachusetts.

Calder, Nigel 1975. *The Weather Machine.* The Viking Press.

Caliendo, M.A. 1979. *Nutrition and the World Food Crisis.* MacMillan, New York.

California Dept. of Conservation 1979. *California Soils: An Assessment* (Draft Report).

California Div. of Mines 1957. *Mineral Commodities of California.* Bull. 176, San Francisco.

Carter, L. 1976. Pest Control: NAS Panel Warns of Possible Technological Breakdown. Science 191, Feb. 27.

CEQ (Council on Environmental Quality) 1978, 1979, 1980. *Environmental Quality.* (Annual Report), Washington.

CEQ and Dept. of State et al 1980. *The Global 2000 Report to the President.* Includes Vol. 1, Entering the Twenty-First Century; Vol. 2, The Technical Report; Vol. 3, Documentation on the Government's Global Sectoral Models: The Government's "Global Model", U.S. Government Printing Office, Washington.

CEQ and Dept. of State et al 1981. *Global Future: Time To Act.* U.S. Government Printing Office, Washington.

Charlesworth, J.K. 1957. *The Quaternary Era.* Edward Arnold Ltd., London.

Chaston, P.R. 1980. Snowiest Cities of the Decade. Weatherwise, April.

Cline, A. 1981. Damage From Acid Rain Could Run Into Billions. S.F. Examiner, Jan. 16.

Commonwealth Forestry Review 1979. Serious pine disease (Scleroderris canker) found in Canada. Vol. 58: 3, 177, Sept.

Commonwealth Scientific and Industrial Research Organization (CSIRO) 1976. Carbon Dioxide and Climate Change. Ecos No. 7, Feb.

Connola, D.P. and Wixson, E.C. 1963. Effects of Soil and Other Environmental Conditions on White Pine Weevil Attack in New York. J. For., June.

Co-ordinating Committee on Pesticides 1981. Pesticides in Your Food. Ecology Center Newsletter 11: 2, Feb., Berkeley.

Cornelius, R.O. 1955. How Forest Pests Upset Management Plans in the Douglas-Fir Region. J. For., Oct.

Crutzen, P.J. et al 1979. Biomass burning as a source of atmospheric gases CO, H_2, N_2O, NO, CH_3Cl and COS. Nature 282, Nov. 15.

D'Antonio, M. 1980. The Poisoned Harvest of Acid Rain. San Mateo Times, Sept. 13.

Day, W.R. 1929. Environment and Disease. Forestry 3: 1.

Day, W.R. 1938. Root-Rot of Sweet Chestnut and Beech Caused By Species of Phytophthora — I. Cause and Symptoms of Disease: Its Relation to Soil Conditions. Forestry 12: 2.

Day, W.R. 1939. Root-Rot of Sweet Chestnut and Beech Caused By Species of Phytophthora — II. Innoculation Experiments and Methods of Control. Forestry 13: 1.

Day, W.R. 1949. Forest Pathology in Relation to Land Utilization. Emp. For. Rev. 28: 2.

Day, W.R. 1950. The Soil Conditions Which Determine Wind-Throw in Forests. Forestry 23: 2.

Day, W.R. 1950. Forest Hygiene — II. The Imperfection of the Environment and Its Importance in the Management of Forests. Emp. For. Rev. 29: 4.

DeBell, D.S. and Ralston, C.W. 1970. Release of Nitrogen By Burning Light Forest Fuels. Soil Sci. Soc. Amer. Proc. 34, 936-8.

Delcourt, H.R. 1981. The Virtue of Forests, Virgin and Otherwise. Nat. History, June.

Delmas, R.J. et al 1980. Polar ice evidence that atmospheric carbon dioxide 20,000 years BP was 50% of present. Nature 284. March 13.

De Villiers, O.D. 1961, 1962. Soil Rejuvenation With Crushed Basalt in Mauritius (Part I & II). Int. Sugar J., Dec. & Jan.

Dimbleby, G.W. 1962. *The Development of British Heathlands and Their Soils*. Oxford Forestry Memoirs No. 23, Oxford.

Dimbleby, G.W. 1964. Post-Glacial Changes in Soil Profiles. Proc. Roy. Soc. B, 161, p. 355-62.

Donald, A. 1980. Superoxide Dismutase: A Dramatic New Enzyme Discovery That Protects Against Radiation and Prevents Disease. Bestways, Aug.

Dwinell, L.D. and Phelps, W.R. 1977. Pitch Canker of Slash Pine in Florida. J. For., Aug.

Eckholm, Erik 1976. *Losing Ground*. W.W. Norton.

Eckholm, E. and Record, F. 1976. The Two Faces of Malnutrition. Worldwatch paper No. 9, Worldwatch Institute, Washington.

Eckholm, E. 1979. Planting for the Future: Forestry for Human Needs. Worldwatch paper No. 26, Worldwatch Institute, Washington.

Edell, D.S. 1979. Public letter on the current state of trace mineral knowledge from the Univ. Hospital of San Diego Co.

Ellefson, P.V. 1974. Douglas-Fir Tussock Moth Infestation: A Challenge to Forestry Professionals. J. For., June.

Emiliani, C. 1972. Quaternary Hypsithermals. Quat. Res. 2, 270-73.

Environmental Fund 1981. World Food Crisis in 1981? The Other Side, No. 23, Summer.

Epstein, S. 1979. Cancer and Inflation. The Ecologist 9: 7, Oct/Nov.

Ermolenko, N.F. 1972. *Trace Elements and Colloids in Soils*. Israel Program for Scientific Translations, Jersalem.

Fairbridge, R.W. 1972. Climatology of a Glacial Cycle. Quat. Res. 2, 283-302.

FAO 1976. Annual Fertilizer Review 1975. Food and Agric. Org. of the U.N., Rome.

FAO 1979. Trace Elements in Soils and Agriculture. Soils Bull. - 17, UNFAO, Rome.

FAO/IUFRO 1965. Symposium on Forest Diseases and Insects. Unasylva 19(3): 78.

Farb, P. 1957. Will We Let Our Elms Die? Amer. For., July.

Fedde, G.F. 1964. Elm Spanworm, A Pest of Hardwood Forests in the Southern Appalachians. J. For., Feb.

Ferrari, J.P. and Pichenot, M. 1976. The canker stain disease of plane tree in Marseilles and in the south of France. Eur. J. For. Path. 6, 18-25.

Fink, J. and Kukla, G.J. 1977. Pleistocene Climates in Central Europe: At Least 17 Interglacials After the Olduvai Event. Quat. Res. 7, 363-71.

Flenly, John 1979. *The Equatorial Rain Forest: a geological history*. Butterworths, London/Boston.

Flint, R.F. 1971. *Glacial and Quaternary Geology*. John Wiley & Sons, New York.

Flohn, H. 1979. On Time Scales and Causes of Abrupt Paleoclimatic Events. Quat. Res. 12, 135-49.

Flohn, H. 1979. Quoted in "Can We Control Pollution?" by E. Goldsmith. The Ecologist, Dec.

Forestry Abstracts 1939-40. Vol. 1, p. 17-18. Imperial Forestry Bureau, Oxford.

Fosburg, H. 1969. All Is Not Well At Baker. Amer. For., March.

Fowler, M.E. 1952. Aircraft Scouting for Pole Blight and Oak Wilt. J. For., March.

Frakes, L.A. et al (eds.) 1977. *Climatic Change and Variability*. Cambridge Univ. Press, p. 353.

Fridovich, I. 1978. The Biology of Oxygen Radicals. Science 201, Sept. 8.

Fry, T.C. 1976. The Myth of Health in America. Dr. Shelton's Hygenic Review 37: 7, 150-52.

Fry, T.C. 1981. American Maladies. . . Lack of Fruits and Vegetables. Better Life Jour., Jan.

Furniss, R.L. and Carolin, B.M. 1977. *Western Forest Insects*. USDA Misc. Pub. – 1339.

Godwin, Sir Harry 1973. *The History of the British Flora*. Cambridge Univ. Press.

Goldsmith, E. The Future of Tree Disease. The Ecologist 9: 4/5, Aug.

Goldsmith, E. 1980. Pesticides Create Pests. The Ecologist 10: 3, March.

Goldthwait, R.P. (ed.) 1971. *Till, A Symposium*. Ohio St. Univ. Press.

Gore, R. 1979. An Age-Old Challenge Grows. Nat. Geog., Nov.

Graham, S.A. 1924. Forest Entomological Problems in the Lake States. J. For., Jan.

Graham, S.A. 1952. *Forest Entomology*. McGraw-Hill.

Grainger, A. 1980. The State of the World's Tropical Forests. The Ecologist 10: 1/2.

Green, Fitzhugh 1977. *A Change In The Weather*. W.W. Norton.

Gress, E. 1981. Canada grows increasingly impatient with pollution from U.S.; S.F. Sunday Examiner & Chronicle, Jan. 4, p.15.

Gribbin, John 1977. *Forecasts, Famines and Freezes*. Simon & Schuster, New York.

Gribbin, John (ed.) 1978. *Climatic Change*. Cambridge Univ. Press.

Haasis, F.W. 1923. Root Rot As A Factor In Survival. J. For., May.

Hamaker, J.D. 1976. Life or Death — Yours. Acres, U.S.A., July-Oct.

Harley, J.L. and Russell, R.S. 1979. *The Soil-Root Interface*. Academic Press, New York.

Harley, W.S. 1980. The Significance of Climatic Change in the Northern Hemisphere 1949-1978. Monthly Weather Review 108: 235-48.

Harris, Sydney J. 1980. "Facts" column. S.F. Examiner, date lost.

Hay, E. 1976. America's 8 Biggest Forest Killers. Amer. For., April.

Heinrichs, J. 1981. Tragedy of the City Forest. Amer. For., April.

Heller, R.C. and Bega, R.V. 1973. Detection of Forest Diseases By Remote Sensing. J. For., Jan.

Henderson, Hazel 1978. *Creating Alternative Futures*. G.P. Putnam's Sons, New York.

Henderson, Hazel 1981, *The Politics of the Solar Age: Alternatives to Economics*. Doubleday.

Henderson, M. et al 1963. The Microbiology of Rocks and Weathered Stones. J. Soil Sci. 14:1.

Henderson, M. and Duff, R.B. 1963. The Release of Metallic and Silicate Ions From Minerals, Rocks, and Soils By Fungal Activity. J. Soil Sci. 14: 2.

Hensel, Julius 1894. *Bread From Stones — A New and Rational System of Land Fertilization and Physical Regeneration*. A.J. Tafel, Philadelphia.

Hensel, Julius 1977. Bread From Stones. Health Research (reprint). Mokelumne Hill, CA.

Hepting, G.H. 1970. The Case for Forest Pathology. J. For., Feb.

HEW 1978. *Health United States*. Dept. of Health, Education and Welfare. Hyattsville, MD.

Heybroek, H.M. 1966. Dutch Elm Disease Abroad. Amer. For., June.

Hills, L.D. 1979. The Versatile Tree Killer. The Ecologist 9: 4/5, Aug.

Holdgate, M.W. and Woodman, M.J. (eds.) 1978. *The Breakdown and Restoration of Ecosystems*. Plenum Press, New York.

Hollin, J.T. 1980. Climate and sea level in isotope stage 5: an East Antarctic ice surge at ²95,000 BP? Nature 283, Feb. 14.

Holstein, W.J. 1978. Third World Time Bomb: Trying To Survive While Killing the Earth. S.F. Examiner & Chronicle, Nov. 19.

Howard, Sir Albert 1947. *The Soil and Health*. Devin-Adair. New York.

Huang, T.C. et al 1973. Atmospherically Transported Volcanic Dust in South Pacific Deep Sea Sedimentary Cores at Distances Over 3,000 KM from the Eruptive Source. Earth and Planetary Science Letters 20, 119-124.

Huessy, Peter 1979. The Other Side (publication of The Environmental Fund), No. 16, May, p. 1 says — "Even with its present crowding, the developing world is destined to lose 90 per cent of its agricultural land due to the twin forces of urbanization and desertification within the next two decades, according to a UN figure. Two-thirds of the tropical forests will disappear as well, as demands for firewood and cropland escalate." Estimates based on the report of the Director of the United Nations Environment Programme, Mostafa Tolba, to the governing council in 1978.

Hunt, C.B. 1972. *Geology of Soils*. W.H. Freeman & Co., San Francisco.

Hur, Robin 1975. *Food Reform: Our Desperate Need*. Heidelberg Pub., Austin, TX.

Hutchison, O.K. and Schumann, D.R. 1976. Alaska's Interior Forests. J. For., June.

Imbrie, J. and Imbrie, K.P. 1979. *Ice Ages, Solving the Mystery*. Enslow Pub., Short Hills, NJ.

Iversen, J. 1954. The Late-Glacial Flora of Denmark and its Relation to Climate and Soil. Geol. Survey of Denmark, II Series, No. 80, Kobenhavn.

Iversen, J. 1958. The bearing of glacial and interglacial epochs on the formation and extinction of plant taxa. Uppsala Univ. Arsskr. 6, 210, Uppsala.

Iversen, J. 1960. Problems of the Early Post-Glacial Forest Development in Denmark. Geol. Surv. of Denmark, IV Series, Vol. 4, No. 3, Kobenhavn.

Iversen, J. 1964. Retrogressive Vegetational Succession in the Post-Glacial. Jubilee Symposium Supplement to the Journal of Ecology and the Journal of Animal Ecology. British Ecological Society/Blackwell Scientific Publications.

Iversen, J. 1969. Retrogressive development of a forest ecosystem demonstrated by pollen diagrams from fossil mor. Oikos Suppl. 12, 35-49. Copenhagen.

Iversen, J. 1973. *The Development of Denmark's Nature since the Last Glacial*. Geol. Surv. of Denmark, V. Series, No. 7-C, Copenhagen.

Jackson, M.L. and Truog, E. 1939. Influence of Grinding Soil Minerals To Near Molecular Size On Their Solubility and Base Exchange Properties. Soil Sci. Soc. Am. Proc. 1939, 136-43.

Jackson, M.L. et al 1973. Global Dustfall During the Quaternary as Related to Environments. Soil Sci. 116, 135-45.

Jacobs, J.D. and Newell, J.P. 1979. Recent-Year-to-Year Variations in Seasonal Temperatures and Sea Ice Conditions in the Eastern Canadian Arctic. Arctic 32, 345-54.

Jennings, D.H. 1963. *The Absorption of Solutes By Plant Cells*. Oliver & Boyd, London.

John, Brian 1977. *The Ice Age, Past and Present*. Wm. Collins & Son, Glasgow.

John, Brian (ed.) 1979. *The Winters of the World*. John Wiley & Sons, New York.

Johnson, Hugh 1978. *The International Book of Trees*. Simon & Schuster, New York.

Jones, M.J. 1980. The Spruce-Budworm Disaster: An Integrated Approach. Amer. For., June.

Justus, J.R. 1978. Inadvertent Weather and Climate Modification. 145-91 of *Weather Modification: Programs, Problems, Policy, and Potential*. Committee Print for the 95th Congress, 2nd Session. Reproduced by the Library of Congress, Congressional Res. Serv.

Kellogg, William and Schware, Robert 1981. *Climate Change and Society: Consequences of Increasing Atmospheric Carbon Dioxide*. Westview Press, Boulder, Co.

Kerr, R.A. 1977. Carbon Dioxide and Climate: Carbon Budget Still Unbalanced. Science 197, Sept. 30.

Kessler, Jr., K.J. 1978. Gnomonia Canker, shoot blight, and leaf spot of Yellow Birch. USDA For. Serv. Res. paper NC-152.

Klemesrud, J. 1980. Parents Band Together To Fight Dangers to Unborn. S.F. Chronicle, Oct. 2, p. 22.

Knight, Granville 1975. In *Nutrition and Physical Degeneration* (the Foreward). Price-Pottenger Nutrition Foundation, La Mesa, CA.

Krasil'nikov, N.A. 1958. *Soil Microorganisms and Higher Plants*. Israel Program for Scienteific Translations. U.S. Dept. of Commerce.

Kubiena, W.L. 1953. *The Soils of Europe*. Thomas Murby, London.

Kubiena, W.L. 1970. *Micromorphological Features of Soil Geography*. Rutgers Univ. Press.

Kukla et. al 1972. The End of the Present Interglacial. Quat Res. 2, 261-69.

Kukla, G.J. and Koci, A. 1972. End of the Last Interglacial in the Loess Record. Quat. Res. 2, 374-83.

Kukla, G.J. et al 1977. New data on climatic trends. Nature 270, Dec. 15.

Lamb, F.B. 1973. If Only in Cliches, For Pete's Sake, Tell It Like It Is! Amer. For., May.

Lamb, Hubert H. 1966. *The Changing Climate*. Methuen & Co., London.

Lamb, Hubert H. 1977. *Climate: Present, Past and Future*, Vol. 2, Climatic history and the future. Methuen & Co., London.

Lamb, Robert 1979. *World Without Trees*. Paddington Press, New York.

Leaphart, C.D. 1963. Dwarfmistletoes: A Silvicultural Challenge. J. For., Jan.

Leeper, E.M. 1976. Replace Toxic Pesticides, Says NAS Study. BioScience 26: 3, March.

Legget, R.F. (ed.) 1961. *Soils in Canada*. Univ. of Toronto Press.

Legget, R.F. (ed.) 1975. *Glacial Till*. Royal Society of Canada, Special Publ. 12.

Lewis, W.M. and Grant, M.C. 1980. Acid Precipitation in the Western United States. Science 207, 176-77, Jan. 11.

Liebig, Justus 1852. Organic Chemistry in its Application to Agriculture and Physiology. In *Liebig's Complete Works on Chemistry*. T.B. Peterson, Philadelphia.

Likens, G.E. et al 1979. Acid Rain. Scientific American 241: 4, Oct.

Lovejoy, P.S. 1917. Forest Biology. J. For., Feb.

Lozek, V. 1972. Holocene Interglacial in Central Europe and its Land Snails. Quat. Res. 2, 374-83.

Mahaney, W.C. (ed.) 1978. *Quaternary Soils*. Geo. Abstracts, Norwich, England.

Marbut, C.F. 1928. *Soils: Their Genesis, Classification and Development*. A course of lectures given in the graduate school of the USDA, Washington.

Marbut, C.F. 1935. *Atlas of American Agriculture*, Part III - Soils of the U.S., USDA, Washington.

Marlin, C.B. (ed.) 1965. *Insects in Southern Forests*. Louisiana St. Univ. Press, p.v.

Marks, G.C. and Kozlowski, T.T. 1973. *Ectomycorrhizas*. Academic Press, New York.

Marshall, V.G. 1973. *The Effects of Manures and Fertilizers on Soil Fauna: A Review*. Dept. of the Environment, Canadian For. Serv., Victoria.

Massey, H.F. and Jackson, M.L. 1952. Selective Erosion of Soil Fertility Constituents. Soil Sci. Soc. Amer. Proc., p. 353.

Matthews, S.W. 1976. What's Happening to Our Climate? Nat Geog. 150: 5, Nov.

Maugh, T.H. 1978. The Fatted Calf (II): The Concrete Truth About Beef. Science 199, Jan 27.

McCalla, T.M. 1939. The Adsorbed Ions of Colloidal Clay As A Factor in Nitrogen Fixation By Azotobacter. Soil Sci. 48: 4, 281-86.

McCarrison, Robert 1936. *Nutrition and Health*. Faber & Faber, London.

McClaren, A.D. and Peterson, G.H. (eds.) 1967. *Soil Biochemistry*, Vol. 1, Marcel Dekker, New York.

McClaren, A.D. and Paul, E.A. (eds.) 1975. *Soil Biochemistry*, Vol. 4, Marcel Dekker, New York.

Mertz, W. and Cornatzer, W.E. 1971. *Newer Trace Elements in Nutrition*. Marcel Dekker.

Miller, W.E. et al 1978. Timber Quality of Northern Hardwood Regrowth in the Lake States. For. Sci. 24: 2, 247-59.

Mohr, E.C.J. and Van Baren, F.A. 1954. *Tropical Soils*. N.V. Uitgeverij W. Van Hoeve, The Hague and Bandung.

Monte, Tom 1980. Is America Going Crazy? East-West Journal 10: 9, Sept.

Moore, T.R. 1976. Sesquioxide-cemented soil horizons in northern Quebec: their distribution, properties, and genesis. Can. J. Soil Sci. 56, 333-44.

Mori et al 1977. Utilization of Organic Nitrogen as the Sole Nitrogen Source for Barley. Proc. of International Seminar on Soil Environment and Fertility Management in Intensive Agriculture. Society of the Science of Soil and Manure, Tokyo.

Morison, C.G.T. and Clarke, G.R. 1928. Some Problems of Forest Soils. Forestry 2: 1.

Morris, Richard 1980. The Glaciers Will Come, and Come Quickly. Special to the S.F. Chronicle, Sept. 9.

Morrow, P.A. and LaMarche, Jr., C.C. 1978. Tree Ring Evidence for Chronic Insect Suppression of Productivity in Subalpine Eucalyptus. Science 201, Sept. 29.

Mount, J.L. 1975. *The Food and Health of Western Man*. John Wiley & Sons, New York.

Mueller, O.P. and Cline, M.G. 1959. Effects of Mechanical Soil Barriers and Soil Wetness on Rooting and Trees and Soil-Mixing by Blowdown in Central New York. Soil Sci. 88: 2.

Myers, Norman 1979. *The Sinking Ark*. Pergamon Press, New York.

National Academy of Sciences 1975. *Understanding Climatic Change*. U.S. Committee for the Global Atmospheric Program, Washington.

National Academy of Sciences 1975. *Forest Pest Control*, Vol. IV of An Assessment of Present and Alternataive Technologies, Washington.

Nicholas, D.J.D. and Egan, A.R. 1975. *Trace Elements in Soil-Plant-Animal Systems*. Academic Press, New York.

Nichols, J.O. 1968. Oak Mortality in Pennsylvania — A Ten-Year Study. J. For., Nov.

Neubert, R.W. 1969. Trees With Temperatures. Amer. For., April.

Painter, R.H. 1951. *Insect Resistance in Crop Plants*. McMillan, New York.

Pelisek, I.J. 1977. Changes in the Forest Stands and Soils in Europe. Trees (Journal of the Men of the Trees), Summer.

Perlman, D. 1981. Acid Rain's Worldwide Threat. S.F. Chronicle, Jan. 16, p.6.

Petersen, J. 1980. Battling Bugs From Above. Amer. For., April.

Phillips, David 1977. *From Soil to Psyche*. Woodbridge Press, Santa Barbara, CA.

Picton, Lionel J. 1949. *Nutrition and the Soil*. Devin-Adair, New York.

Pimentel, D. et al 1976. Land Degradation: Effects on Food and Energy Resources. Science 194, Aug. 12 (on erosion in Iowa, etc.).

Pimentel, D. and Pimentel, M. 1979. The Risks of Pesticides. Nat. Hist. 88:3, March.

Ponte, Lowell 1976. *The Cooling*. Prentice-Hall, p. 138-39.

Posner, Barabara 1979. *Nutrition and the Elderly*. D.C. Heath, Lexington, MA.

Powers, H.R. et al 1974. Incidence and Financial Impact of Fusiform Rust in the South. J. For., July.

Price, Weston A. 1945, 1975. *Nutrition and Physical Degeneration*. Price-Pottenger Nutrition Foundation, La Mesa, CA.

Raeside, J.D. 1964. Loess Deposits of the South Island, New Zeland, and Soils Formed on Them. N.Z. J. Geol. Geophys. 7, 811-38.

Raukas, A. et al 1978. Methods of Till Investigation in Europe and North America. J. Sed. Petrol. 48: 1, 285-94.

Rennie, P.J. 1957. The Uptake of Nutrients by Timber Forest and its Importance to Timber Production in Britain, Quart. J. For. 51: 2, April.

Rensberger, B. 1977. 14 Million Acres a Year Vanishing As Deserts Spread Around Globe. N.Y. Times, Aug. 28

Richards, Paul 1973. The Tropical Rain Forest. Scientific American 229: 6, 58-67.

Roberts, W.O. and Lansford, Henry 1979. *The Climate Mandate*. W.H. Freeman.

Robertson, J. 1979. The Mountain Pine Beetle: Friend or Foe? Amer. For., Feb.

Robinson, L.W. 1966. Decline of the Saguaro. Amer. For., May.

Robinson, W.O. and Edgington, G. 1945. Minor Elements in Plants, and Some Accumulator Plants. Soil Sci. 60: 1, 15-28.

Rodale, J.I. 1948. *The Healthy Hunzas*. Rodale Press.

Rode, A.A. 1962. *Soil Science*. Published for the National Science Foundation Washington, by the Israel Program for Scientific Translations, Jerusalem.

Romans, J.C.C. 1962. The Origin of the Indurated B$_3$ Horizon of Podzolic Soils in North-East Scotland. Soil Sci. 13:2.

Roth, E.R. 1954. Spread and Intensification of the Littleleaf Disease of Pine. J. For., Aug.

Roth, L.F. et al 1977. Marking Ponderosa Pine To Combine Commercial Thinning and Control of Armillaria Root Rot. J. For., Oct.

Russell, E.W. 1973. *Soil Conditions and Plant Growth*. Longman, London.

Sanders, F.E. et al (eds.) 1975. *Endomycorrhizas*. Academic Press, New York.

Schauss, Alex 1978. *Orthomolecular Treatment of Criminal Behavior*. Parker House, Berkeley, CA.

Schauss, Alex 1981. *Diet, Crime, and Delinquency*. Parker House.

Schaffner, Jr., J.V. 1943. Sawflies Injurious to Conifers in the Northeastern States. J. For., Aug.

Schell, I.I. et al 1973. Recent Climatic Changes in the Eastern North American Sub-Arctic. In *Climate of the Arctic*, eds. Weller, G. and Bowling, S.A., p. 76-81.

Schoen, R. et al 1974. Argillization by Descending Acid at Steamboat Springs, Nevada. Clays and Clay Minerals 22, 1-20.

Schultz, C.B. and Frye, J.C. 1965. *Loess and Related Eolian Deposits of the World*. Univ. of Nebraska Press.

Schultz, Gwen 1974. *Ice Age Lost*. Anchor Press/Doubleday, Garden City, New York.

Schutte, Karl H. and Myers, John A. 1979. *Metabolic Aspects of Health*. Discovery Press, Kentfield, CA.

Schwenke, W. 1961. Forest Fertilization and Insect Buildup. Paper No. 24-21, Proc. of 13th IUFRO Cong., Pt. 2, Vol. 1, Vienna.

Shaler, Nathaniel S. 1891. *The Origin and Nature of Soils*. U.S.G.S., Washington.

Shigo, A.L. 1972. The Beech Bark Disease Today in the Northeastern U.S. J. For., May.

Shotton, F.W. (ed.) 1977. British Quaternary Studies. Clarendon Press, Oxford.

Simpson, Sir George 1934. World Climate During the Quaternary Period. Quart. J. Roy. Met. Soc. 85, 425-71.

Simpson, Sir George 1957. World Temperature During the Pleistocene. Quart. J. Roy. Met. Soc. 85, 332-49.

Smith, G. 1980. Acid rain killer of forests, too, official warns. Toronto Globe, July 22, p.1.

Soil Association 1979. Nutrition and Organic Farming. Journal of the Soil Association., Dec.

Soil Conservation 1975. Vol. 4l: 3, p. 22 (on Iowa erosion), Washington.

Soles, R.L. et al 1970. Resistance of Western White Pine to White-Pine Weevil. J. For., Dec.

Spaulding, P. 1948. The Role of Nectria in the Beech Bark Disease. J. For., June.

Speers, C.F. 1958. The Balsam Woolly Aphid in the Southeast. J. For., July.

Speth, Gus 1980. Reported in San Mateo Times, July 5.

Stevenson, T. 1976. Plight of the Palms. Amer. For., Oct.

Stotzky, G. et al 1980. Acid Precipitation — Causes and Consequences. Environment 22: 4, May.

Stuiver, M. 1978. Atmospheric Carbon Dioxide and Carbon Reservoir Changes. Science 199, p. 253, Jan. 20.

Syers, J.K. et al 1969. Eolian Sediment Influence on Pedogenesis During the Quaternary. Soil Sci. 107: 6.

Taylor, R. 1969. *Hunza Health Secrets*. Award Books, New York.

Thompson, L.G. 1977. Microparticles, Ice Sheets and Climate. Inst. of Polar Studies Rep. No. 64, Ohio St. Univ.

Thompson, L.G. and Mosley-Thompson, E. 1981. Microparticle Concentration Variations Linked with Climatic Change: Evidence from Polar Ice Cores. Science 212, May 15.

Tobe, John 1965. *Guideposts to Health and Vigorous Long Life*. Modern Publications, St. Catherine, Ontario.

Toops, C. 1981. The Stinking Cedar Is In Big Trouble. Amer. For., July.

Trotter, R.J. 1981. Psychiatry for the 80's. Science News 119, May 30.

Turner, C. and West, R.G. 1968. The subdivision and zonation of interglacial periods. Eiszeit. u. Gegen. 19, 93-101.

USDA 1963, 1975. *Composition of Foods*. Agric. Handbook No. 8, U.S. Government Printing Office, Washington.

USDA 1980. Report and Recommendations on Organic Farming. Washington.

USDA Bureau of Soils 1906. *Soil Survey Field Book*. Washington.

USDA Forest Service 1967. Tioga's Ghosts. What's New In Research. Pac. SW For. Range Exp. Sta., March 13.

USDA Forest Service 1974-78. Forest Insect and Disease Conditions in the United States. Washington.

USDA Forest Service 1976. Proc. of First International Symposium on Acid Precipitation and the Forest Ecosystem. Gen Tech. Rep. NE-23, Northeastern For. Exp. Sta. Upper Darby, PA.

USDA Forest Service 1980. Effects of Air Pollutants on Mediterranean and Temperate Forest Ecosystems, Symposium Proc. Pac. SW For. and Range Exp. Sta., Berkeley.

USDA Soil Conservation Service 1975. *Soil Taxonomy*. Agric. Handbook No. 436, Washington.

van den Bosch, Robert 1978. *The Pesticide Conspiracy*. Doubleday, New York.

Vilenskii, D.G. 1957. *Soil Science*. Israel Program for Scientific Translations, Jerusalem.

Voisin, Andre 1961. *Soil, Grass and Cancer: Health of animals and men linked to the mineral balance of the soil*. Crosby Lockwood & Son., London.

Volobuev, V.R. 1964. *Ecology of Soils*. Daniel Davey & Co., New York.

Wallace, J.N. 1980. Is the Green Revolution Over? S.F. Sunday Examiner & Chronicle, Aug. 17, p. 34.

Wallace, T. 1950. *Trace Elements in Plant Physiology*. Chronica Botanica Co., Waltham, MA.

Walters, Charles and Fenzau, C.J. 1979. *An Acres U.S.A. Primer*. Acres, U.S.A., Raytown, MO.

Watts, W.A. 1980. The Late Quaternary Vegetation History of the Southeastern United States. Ann. Rev. Ecol. Syst. 11, 387-409.

Watts, W.A. 1980. Late Quaternary Vegetation of Central Appalachia and the New Jersey Coastal Plain. Ecological Monographs 49: 4, 427-69.

Weatherwise 1980. Vol. 33: 1, Feb. "The Weather of 1979" issue.

Weatherwise 1981. Vol. 34; 1, Feb. "The Weather of 1980" issue.

Webster, B. 1980. Tropical Forests: Relatively Youthful? N.Y. Times, Jan 8.

Wells, G.S. 1965. The Bark Beetle. Amer. For., June.

West, R.C. and Haag, W.G. (eds.) 1976. *Ecology of the Pleistocene*, Vol. 13 of Geoscience and Man. School of Geoscience, Louisiana St. Univ.

West, S. 1980. Acid From Heaven. Science News 117, Feb. 2.

West, S. 1981. Fertilizing atmospheric ammonia. Science News 117: 25, June 21.

Wexler, H. 1953. Radiation Balance. In *Climatic Change — Evidence, Causes, and Effects*, ed. H. Shapley, Harvard Univ. Press.

White, Deborah (ed.) 1977. *XV International Congress of Entomology*. Entomological Soc. of Amer., College Park, MD.

Whittaker, C.W. et al 1959. Liming Qualities of Three Cement Kiln Flue Dusts and a Limestone in a Greenhouse Comparison. Soil and Water Cons. Res. Div., USDA, Beltsville, MD.

Whittaker, C.W. et al 1963. Cement Kiln Flue Dusts for Soil Liming. U.S. Fertilizer Lab., Soil and Water Cons. Res. Div., USDA, Beltsville, MD.

Whittaker, R.H. et al 1974. The Hubbard Brook Ecosystem Study: Forest Biomass and Production. Ecological Monographs 44, 233-52.

Whittaker, R.H. and Likens, G.E. 1975. In *Primary Productivity of the Biosphere*, eds. H. Lieth and R.H. Whittaker, Springer-Verlag, Berlin, p. 305.

Willett, H.C. 1953. Atmospheric Circulation. In *Climatic Change — Evidence, Causes, and Effects*, ed. H. Shapley, Harvard Univ. Press.

Williams, Jill (ed.) 1978 *Carbon Dioxide, Climate and Society*. Pergamon Press, p. 229.

Williams, L.D. 1978. Ice-Sheet Initiation and Climatic Influences of Expanded Snow Cover in Arctic Canada. Quat. Res. 10, 141-49.

Williams, W.T. 1978. Acid Rain: The California Context. CBE Env. Rev., May.

Woillard, Genevieve 1978. Grand Pile Peat Bog: A Continuous Pollen Record for the Last 140,000 Years. Quat. Res. 9, 1-21.

Woillard, G. 1979. Abrupt end of the last interglacial s.s. in north-east France. Nature 281, Oct. 18.

Wong, C.S. 1978. Atmospheric Input of Carbon Dioxide From Burning Wood. Science 200, April 14.

Woods, F.W. 1953. Disease as a Factor in the Evolution of Forest Composition. J. For., Dec.

Woodwell, G.M. 1978. The Carbon Dioxide Question. Scientific American 238: 1, Jan.

Woodwell, G.M. et al 1979. The Carbon Dioxide Problem: Implications for Policy in the Management of Energy and Other Resources. (A Report to) Council on Environmental Quality, Washington.

Wrench, G.T. 1945. *The Wheel of Health*. Lee Foundation for Nutritional Research, Milwaukee.

Wrench, G.T. 1946. *Reconstruction By Way Of The Soil*. Faber & Faber, London.

Wright, E. and Graham, D.P. 1952. Surveying for Pole Blight. J. For., Sept.

Wright, Jr., H.E. 1972. Interglacial and Postglacial Climates: The Pollen Record. Quat. Res. 2, 274-82.

Yaalon, D.H. (ed.) 1971. *Paleopedology*. International Society of Soil Science, Jerusalem.

Yaalon, D.H. and Ganor, E. 1973. The Influence of Dust on Soils During the Quaternary. Soil Sci. 116, 146-54.

Young, A. 1976. Tropical Soils and Soil Survey. Cambridge Univ. Press.